In *The Restorative Prison*, Byron R. Johnson, Michael Hallett, and Sung Joon Jang show how entrepreneurial, transformative ideas can help to solve one of the most complex problems facing American society today. Masterfully blending behavioral science research and an expert's knowledge of the criminal justice system, this book delivers both solutions and inspiration.

—*Arthur C. Brooks, Professor, Harvard Kennedy School and Harvard Business School, and New York Times bestselling author*

Religion has been entwined with the prison since the birth of the penitentiary two centuries ago, but in this urgent and insurgent new book, Johnson and colleagues argue that faith may now be our only hope for escaping the unholy mess that mass incarceration has become for families and communities in the United States. Although the work is based on sophisticated research, the promised salvation is not to be found in the form of criminological expertise but rather from the lived experience of 'wounded healers' – those who have suffered the darkness but found the light. We can only pray they are right.

Shadd Maruna, Professor, Queen's University Belfast

Under what conditions can religious volunteers be a source of prison reform? What do hope and restoration look like, in a failing, oversized and inhumane prison system? The religious life of prisons is, increasingly, 'where the action is'. This passionately written and meticulously researched book promotes a positive vision of religiosity, meaning, connectedness and well-being, showing how such practices can, or should, be made possible even in the darkest places.

—*Alison Liebling, Professor of Criminology and Criminal Justice, Cambridge, UK*

It is now common to find regular requiems for the role of religion in American life. In the midst of this growing din about the decline of religion as an active social agent in the life of Americans, Byron R. Johnson, Michael Hallett, and Sung Joon Jang present a compelling argument for the robust role of religion in creating prisons that help restore people to a positive, prosocial life trajectory, even, in the most extreme example, for inmates who will never leave prison. Because many of the early concepts of correctional rehabilitation are rooted in Christianity, it might be easy to dismiss this book as reactionary tome, written to harken back to the good old days. However, while the authors acknowledge the comingled history of religion and rehabilitation, the authors make a new argument, based on insights about the process of desistance for individuals involved in crime. Modern criminologists now agree that that true desistance for people involved in crime involves the personal choice to adopt, and live, a new, prosocial identity. The authors astutely point out that religion in general, and Christianity in particular, is involved in the same basic enterprise for everyone, not just prisoners. There is no need to reinvent the wheel – in many cases, religious programs in the prison are in the right place at the right time for the new effort to create prisons that restore rather than destroy life. As a result, this book is a must read for all people interested in the growing push for prison reform, even for those who have no particular interest in religion.

—*Shawn D. Bushway, Senior Policy Research, Behavioral and Policy Sciences Department, RAND Corporation*

The Restorative Prison does an excellent job of highlighting the positive impact of faith-based programming within correctional walls. The perspectives shared by the authors offer a fresh way to think about the effectiveness of rehabilitative programs and the purpose of our prisons.

—*Bryan Collier, Executive Director, Texas Department of Criminal Justice*

THE RESTORATIVE PRISON

Drawing on work from inside some of America's largest and toughest prisons, this book documents an alternative model of "restorative corrections" utilizing the lived experience of successful inmates, fast disrupting traditional models of correctional programming. While research documents a strong desire among those serving time in prison to redeem themselves, inmates often confront a profound lack of opportunity for achieving redemption. In a system that has become increasingly dysfunctional and punitive, often fewer than 10% of prisoners receive any programming. Incarcerated citizens emerge from prisons in the United States to reoffend at profoundly high rates, with the majority of released prisoners ending up back in prison within five years. In this book, the authors describe a transformative agenda for incentivizing and rewarding good behavior inside prisons, rapidly proving to be a disruptive alternative to mainstream corrections and offering hope for a positive future.

The authors' expertise on the impact of faith-based programs on recidivism reduction and prisoner reentry allows them to delve into the principles behind inmate-led religious services and other prosocial programs – to show how those incarcerated may come to consider their existence as meaningful despite their criminal past and current incarceration. Religious practice is shown to facilitate the kind of transformational "identity work" that leads to desistance that involves a change in worldview and self-concept, and which may lead a prisoner to see and interpret reality in a fundamentally different way. With participation in religion protected by the U.S. Constitution, these model programs are helping prison administrators weather financial challenges while also helping make prisons less punitive, more transparent, and emotionally restorative.

This book is essential reading for scholars of corrections, offender reentry, community corrections, and religion and crime, as well as professionals and volunteers involved in correctional counseling and prison ministry.

Byron R. Johnson is Distinguished Professor of the Social Sciences at Baylor University. He is the founding director of the Baylor Institute for Studies of Religion (ISR). He is a leading authority on the scientific study of religion, the efficacy of faith-based organizations, and criminal justice. Recent publications have examined the impact of faith-based programs on recidivism reduction and prisoner reentry. He is the project director of the Global Flourishing Study, a longitudinal study of 300,000 participants from around the world, that seeks to advance human flourishing research and its intersection with society, heath, economics, psychology, religion, and spirituality. Recent books include *The Quest for Purpose: The Collegiate Search for a Meaningful Life*, and *Objective Religion: Volume One – Competition, Tension, Perseverance*.

Michael Hallett is a Professor in the Department of Criminology & Criminal Justice at the University of North Florida. His work has appeared in numerous books and journals, including *Punishment & Society, Journal of Offender Rehabilitation, Contemporary Justice Review, Critical Criminology*, and others. In 2006, Hallett received the Gandhi King Ikeda Award from Morehouse College for his book *Private Prisons in America: A Critical Race Perspective* (University of Illinois Press). Hallett received the Outstanding Graduate Alumnus Award from his doctoral alma mater, Arizona State University, in 2007. He currently also serves as a Senior Research Fellow at Baylor University's Institute for Studies of Religion. Hallett has been principal investigator on grants from the U.S. Department of Justice, Florida Department of Juvenile Justice, Jesse Ball DuPont Foundation, and several other organizations.

Sung Joon Jang is Research Professor of Criminology and co-director of the Program on Pro-social Behavior within Baylor's Institute for Studies of Religion (ISR). Jang is quantitative criminologist and one of the leading researchers of general strain theory. His research focuses on the effects of religion and spirituality as well as family, school, and peers on crime and delinquency. His research has been published in social scientific journals in the fields of sociology, criminology, psychology, and social work. Jang is the founding President of the Korean Society of Criminology in America and has been active in the American Society of Criminology. He is currently conducting a series of studies on the rehabilitative effects of faith-based programs on prisoners in Colombia and South Africa as well as in the United States. Jang is co-principal investigator of the Global Flourishing Study, a five-wave panel study of 300,000 participants from 22 countries, in which he seeks to examine the effects of religion and spirituality on human flourishing in terms of physical and mental health, income, purpose in life, virtues, social relationship, and civic engagement.

THE RESTORATIVE PRISON

Essays on Inmate Peer Ministry
and Prosocial Corrections

Byron R. Johnson,
Michael Hallett,
and Sung Joon Jang

Routledge
Taylor & Francis Group

NEW YORK AND LONDON

First published 2022
by Routledge
605 Third Avenue, New York, NY 10158

and by Routledge
2 Park Square, Milton Park, Abingdon, Oxon, OX14 4RN

Routledge is an imprint of the Taylor & Francis Group, an informa business

Library of Congress Cataloging-in-Publication Data
Names: Johnson, Byron R., author. | Hallett, Michael A., author. | Jang, Sung Joon, author.
Title: The restorative prison : essays on inmate peer ministry and prosocial corrections / Byron R. Johnson, Sung Joon Jang & Michael Hallett.
Description: New York, NY : Routledge, 2022. | Includes bibliographical references and index.
Identifiers: LCCN 2021011050 (print) | LCCN 2021011051 (ebook) |
ISBN 9780367775179 (hardback) | ISBN 9780367766375 (paperback) |
ISBN 9781003171744 (ebook)
Subjects: LCSH: Prisoners—Religious life. | Church work with prisoners. |
Criminals—Rehabilitation.
Classification: LCC HV8865 .J64 2022 (print) | LCC HV8865 (ebook) |
DDC 365/.665—dc23
LC record available at https://lccn.loc.gov/2021011050
LC ebook record available at https://lccn.loc.gov/2021011051

ISBN: 9780367775179 (hbk)
ISBN: 9780367766375 (pbk)
ISBN: 9781003171744 (ebk)

DOI: 10.4324/9781003171744

Typeset in Bembo
by codeMantra

CONTENTS

ACKNOWLEDGMENTS

We are thankful to our colleagues at the Baylor University's Institute for Studies of Religion (ISR), who have offered helpful advice and encouragement for our ongoing work in so many different prisons. We particularly thank Matthew Anderson, Matthew Bradshaw, Philip Jenkins, Thomas Kidd, Jeff Levin, and George Yancey. We also want to express our heartfelt gratitude to Burl Cain, Mississippi Commissioner of Corrections, for his vision and perseverance in helping the field of corrections reconsider the role of religion as a restorative agent. We thank Dr. John Robson, former director of the New Orleans Baptist Theological Center, at Angola, and former Angola inmate ministers, and now Mississippi State Penitentiary (Parchman) chaplains, Ron Oliver, Maurice Clifton, George King, Sydney DeLoch, and Reginald Watts.

We are indebted to many different faith-based prison ministries for the selfless work of literally thousands of other-minded volunteers. These organizations include Bridges to Life, Good News Jail & Prison Ministry, Kairos Prison Ministry, Prison Fellowship, Prison Fellowship International, Prisoners for Christ, and Restoration Outreach of Dallas.

Thanks especially also to Francis Cullen, Peggy Giordano, Jonathan Simon, Ben Fleury-Steiner, Shawn Bushway, Texas Department of Criminal Justice (TDCJ) Executive Director Bryan Collier, Grove & Brenna Norwood, and the late Ray Paternoster. Dr. Alison Liebling and her colleagues at the Prisons Research Centre at the University of Cambridge proved inspirational and set a high bar. The centrality of forgiveness and redemption at the heart of Professor Shadd Maruna's work has inspired us for 20 years.

We also want to thank Ellen Boyne and Kate Taylor from Routledge, for their assistance in making this book a reality.

We especially are grateful to our understanding and patient wives—Jackie Johnson, Sunmi Jang, and Karin Hallett—for allowing us to spend time in correctional facilities across the United States and around the world.

FOREWORD

About a half century ago, I started the study of corrections in the aftermath of the bloody suppression of the Attica prison insurgency and just before the publication of Robert Martinson's famous essay in *The Public Interest* concluding that "nothing works" in offender rehabilitation. Labeling theory was ascending, and critiques of total institutions were ubiquitous. All of us believed that prisons were inherently defective and inhumane, a view seemingly corroborated by the disquieting revelations of Zimbardo's Stanford Prison Experiment. We called for the deinstitutionalization of wayward populations, something that occurred (quite badly) for mental patients but did not occur (also quite badly) for justice-involved individuals. Seeing prisons as evil, our major policy recommendation was to avoid their use whenever possible. This perspective was accompanied by a collateral judgment: If prisons should be opposed unilaterally, there was no reason to find out how to make them better places. After all, if we succeeded in making institutions more livable and effective, we would give the state a rationale for expanding the use of prisons—the very outcome we opposed.

This decision was consequential. Most criminologists abandoned any efforts to reform prisons and instead spent their time documenting how correctional institutions were defective and damaging. These efforts illuminated real problems, but they did little to provide solutions on how to fix these problems. The "criminology of prison reform" never came to fruition. Inmates were left to fend for themselves. Worse, this divestment in improving institutional life ultimately proved tragic. While our publications showing prison horrors grew, they did nothing to stop the rise of mass imprisonment, which culminated about a decade ago with a daily count of more than 2.3 million people behind bars. We excelled as critics but were powerless to halt a lengthy mean season in corrections.

Importantly, the United States is now at a turning point in corrections. After four decades of the ineluctable rise in prison populations across virtually every state in the Union, around 2010 this growth suddenly stalled and, though unevenly, declined. I was astounded. I thought I would go to my grave witnessing annual increases in incarceration—as I had for 39 straight years. But a confluence of factors—state budgets constrained by the Great Recession, concern about racial disparities in imprisonment, the presence of conservative voices for reform, and decreasing punitiveness among the public—combined to create a perfect storm capable of enabling a historic shift in thinking about corrections.

Not long ago, correctional lexicon was peppered with words such as three-strikes-and-you're-out, truth in sentencing, mandatory minimum sentences, super-max institutions, no frills prisons, and death row. More often today, we hear language such as the Innocence Project, prisoner reentry programs, criminal record expungement, reducing collateral consequences of conviction, drug courts, and The First Step Act. In the Covid-19 pandemic, the response has been to release offenders, often to house arrest. Keeping them in prison to die was frowned upon. I doubt it would have been in 1990.

The point of this account—admittedly a touch hyperbolic since brevity is the bane of nuance—is that we have arrived at a moment of opportunity. The possibility exists to reform prisons. Yes, budgets are always tight and bureaucracies resist change. Still, a desire exists to improve prisons. The goal is no longer to subject inmates to hard time on the premise that misery is deserved and a deterrent. Rather, we all seem to understand now that successful reentry depends on people leaving prison less disposed to crime than when they entered prison. Achieving correctional reform, however, is crippled by the failure of scholars to develop a vibrant criminology of prison reform. I am not sure why correctional officials should listen to most of us about how to make their institutions thrive in the business of changing people. Some scholars from the Commonwealth of Nations have come up with ideas for how to rehabilitate offenders (e.g., the Risk-Need-Responsivity and Good Lives models) and should be consulted. The rest of us do not have much to say that is evidence based.

These considerations tell us precisely why *The Restorative Prison* is a work of consequence. For a few decades, Professors Johnson, Hallett, and Jang have traipsed around all sorts of prisons searching for ways to improve institutional life. They have talked with, cared about, and studied a bunch of wayward souls. This journey has equipped them with a reform paradigm that involves at its core the use of religion as a conduit for offenders' personal improvement and desistance from crime. Unlike most of us, they have a plan about how to make prisons more humane and effective. And it makes sense.

A secular bias versus the sacred is so strong in criminology that those who argue for faith-based programming are suspected of being religious zealots or, in today's political climate, White Christian Nationalists sporting Make American Great Again hats. Nothing can be further from the truth in this case. Professors Johnson, Hallett, and Jang are first-class scholars whose works appear in leading peer-reviewed journals. More than this, they do not attribute desistance to a sudden conversion experience—though that can matter—but to religion serving as a source of social capital that transforms the quality of a person's life. Robert Sampson and John Laub understood how a good marriage and a good job could facilitate crime desistance by the capital that inheres in social bonds. The same can occur with religion.

I will refrain from summarizing the book that awaits, since this is an excursion most enjoyed by seeing freshly novel sights as the trip through the pages unfolds. But I will draw four lessons taught by *The Restorative Prison* about the value of religion relative to the correctional enterprise. I am sure that readers will capture other insights and extend my list quite a bit.

First, I have long told my students that evangelicals spend more time in prisons and jails than do criminologists. As the authors document, religious faith is a robust source of volunteerism, including inspiring efforts to comfort and perhaps save the incarcerated. At the core of these efforts is the conviction that all humans have value and merit dignity. Importantly, this valuing of prisoners constitutes a profound rejection of efforts in recent decades to portray offenders as "the other." As scholars such as David Garland and Jonathan Simon have shown, othering offenders depersonalizes them. They are construed not as individuals but as undifferentiated members of a social category who all possess the potential to be violent predators—a danger that makes caging them sensible.

Importantly, Pope Francis exemplifies the religious impulse to value the wayward, regularly visiting prisons locally and in his trips around the world. On his first Holy Thursday of his papacy in 2013, he departed from the tradition of washing the feet of male clergy in the Mass of the Last Supper, traveling instead to a juvenile detention facility near Rome. While celebrating mass, he washed and kissed the feet of a dozen youthful offenders, including two female and two Muslim inmates. The detainees were joyous and broke into applause. Widely covered in the media, his public embrace of these youths was an explicit effort to reject their othering and marginalization. His message was clear: We share a common humanity and sinfulness. "Each of us," he counsels, "is capable of doing the same thing that that man or that woman in prison did.... They are no worse than you and me!" Pope Francis cautions against the "culture of adjectives" directed toward "finding a label, an adjective, to disqualify people." This is "not God's way" because God's love knows no bounds. "He takes us by the hand, and He helps us to go on," observes Pope Francis. "And this is called hope!"

Second, as Pope Francis' comments poignantly demonstrate, a core religious doctrine is a *belief in redeemability*. Justice-involved people are not seen as cold-hearted super-predators who are incurably wicked. In the Christian faith, for example, Jesus' crucifixion involved two other criminals—one on each side of him. Although one blasphemed Him, the other—the so-called penitent thief—asked to be saved, to which Jesus responded: "Assuredly, I say to you, today you will be with Me in Paradise" (Luke 23:43). The prominence of three crosses rising from Calvary sends a crucial message. Jesus' act of grace showed that redemption could be achieved by all of humankind, even a dying offender attached to a cross. Faith is not naïve—not all offenders will choose a path of reform—but it does nurture seeing in others the potential for growth. Notably, empirical research shows that a belief in redeemability is a robust predictor of correctional policy preferences. Those who embrace the possibility of offender change are less punitive and more supportive of rehabilitation and of efforts to facilitate reentry (e.g., expunge criminal records, remove collateral consequences of conviction).

Third, religion improves the quality of prisoners' lives and fosters desistance from crime. Although some polling suggests that allegiance to religious affiliations and church attendance are declining in the general public, this does not appear to be the case within prisons. One study found that prison chaplains portrayed state penitentiaries as a "bustle of religious activity"; other data concluded that inmates were less likely to be atheists. Prisons can be bleak, marked by idleness, limited access to rehabilitation programs, and the prospect of years behind bars. Religion offers a critical coping mechanism, giving prisoners activity, social relationships, and meaning. Faith-based initiatives are not for all inmates and should not be coerced, even implicitly. But for many of those bereft of hope, rewarding accomplishments, and social supports, religion offers the comfort of being part of a faithful community—inside the institution and extending into the community—where these benefits are made possible.

Evidence also suggests that religious faith and practice comprise a protective factor versus crime. Sometimes, critics seek to delegitimate the prosocial effects of religion among returning prisoners by noting high rates of recidivism. But no faith assumes that religion prevents all sins; indeed, we would not need the confessional or the option to receive forgiveness if this were the case. Religion is not a static variable to be measured at one point in time and inserted into a regression equation. Its practice is ongoing, and its effects can be dynamic, shaping and reshaping offenders as their lives unfold. It must be studied as such. Further, religious involvement is only one source of preventing crime. Offenders may suffer from an array of criminogenic risk factors whose reduction may require more than faith alone (e.g., treatment for substance abuse, programs to increase self-control and anger management). Still, religion can be implicated in encouraging desistance because it penetrates people's thinking and can generate social capital.

Faith has the power to foster a desire for a good life, a belief that redemption is possible, and social bonds with prosocial others. It can evoke a cognitive transformation and ready a person to take a different road in life. No, religion is not a crime panacea, but it can serve as a conduit for positive beliefs and experiences that embed the wayward in a conformist rather than a criminal life-course trajectory.

Fourth, Pope Francis has commented, "It is painful when we see prison systems which are not concerned to care for wounds, to soothe pain, to offer new possibilities." Professors Johnson, Hallett, and Jang teach us that this harsh reality need not be the case. As a total institution with limited funding and amenities, transforming a prison into a restorative society of captives faces daunting challenges. Only so much is feasible to achieve. Nonetheless, like Pope Francis, the authors ask us not to accept the worst of possibilities as inevitable or to assume that nothing can work. They reject this perspective as consigning prisoners to a harmful future. We cannot make institutions perfect, but we can make them better.

In fact, a religious perspective demands that we ensure that everyone behind bars be accorded dignity—for our benefit and theirs—and that every effort be made to create an institution that repairs rather than distributes harm. It is crucial to imagine a different correctional future. The authors do not have a monopoly on how to create such a future, so advocates of other paradigms are welcome to join the conversation. Still, the notion of "the restorative prison" is appealing for two reasons. First, as expert criminologists, the authors use evidence to show how religion might serve to transform the lives of offenders. They understand that science is not the enemy of the criminology of religion but its guide and check. Second, as the authors demonstrate, religious ministries and faith-based initiatives are not utopian visions but ongoing facts of contemporary prison life. A foundation thus exists on which to build an institution that seeks to impart virtues capable of transforming the correctional enterprise.

Let me conclude by reiterating that this is not an occasion for banality—of assuming, as is often the case, that the present is merely a prelude to the future. When taking a historical perspective, it is clear that the United States is at a juncture where change is possible. Past correctional policy and practice are no longer hegemonic for we have escaped the clutches of the mass imprisonment era. Now is the time for bold ideas that imagine a different correctional future. Byron R. Johnson, Michael Hallett, and Sung Joon Jang have lived and studied the past and have accumulated the wisdom to articulate a vision for the prison that is, at once, practical and inspiring. Only they could have written *The Restorative Prison*. It is a gift we should open, study, and treasure for its scientific rigor, its humanity, and its guidance.

Francis T. Cullen
University of Cincinnati

1

THE CONSEQUENCES OF FAILING PRISONS

The Human Drain: How Incarceration Affects Families

US prisons are comprised of convicted offenders largely coming from economically disadvantaged communities where poverty is pervasive and highly concentrated. Many prisoners were raised in broken and dysfunctional homes and may have had a parent that was incarcerated. In urban centers across the country, inner-city youth residing in distressed neighborhoods attend underperforming schools. Along with poor functioning inner-city schools, a disturbingly high percentage of students are dropping out from the educational process altogether. Indeed, the dropout rate in many disadvantaged urban environments can reach 60%—about twice the national average. Moreover, we know from decades of research that school performance and dropping out of school are significant predictors of delinquency and adult criminal behavior as well as the increased likelihood of incarceration.[1] And while many believe that exhausting the limits of our nation's criminal justice system brings resolution to society's crime-related issues, there is considerable evidence that a prison sentence may actually reinforce a cyclical pattern of incarceration.[2] The task before us requires confronting a series of great challenges—even notwithstanding those challenges newly brought about by the COVID-19 crisis. These challenges involve first-and-foremost crises in familial entropy, social division, and a tendency to over-rely upon criminal justice sanctions to resolve social problems—which has only contributed to a further breakdown in "traditional" social assets of family and neighborhood-level civic-resources such as churches, schools, and locally owned businesses.

Beyond the cyclical and individual impact of prison life, the ongoing generational impact of criminal behavior also contributes to the growing prison population epidemic. When a parent is incarcerated, the lives of children can be disrupted in tragic ways.[3] Children of prisoners may end up in foster care placement. Repeated changes in family structure due to parental incarceration can be disruptive in children's lives which often creates instability and insecurity that can be harmful to youth.[4] Consider that children of prisoners are more likely to observe parental substance abuse, perform poorly in school, and experience poverty and disadvantage.[5] As might be expected, youth and adolescents who have an incarcerated parent are also more likely to experience aggression, anxiety, and depression.[6] Children of prisoners, therefore, are at-risk for alcohol and drug abuse, delinquency and crime, gang involvement, and subsequent

DOI: 10.4324/9781003171744-1

incarceration.[7] Regrettably, parental criminality is a key risk factor and an important link between the incarceration of a parent and a variety of antisocial behaviors among their children.[8]

Indeed, research confirms that children of prisoners experience much higher rates of criminal behavior and subsequent incarceration.[9] Thus, the impact of one man's incarceration may be felt by families and communities for decades. The nature of prison life yields a host of negative outcomes for all of society, and the cumulative effect of these outcomes will have important implications for generations to come.

Rather than providing offenders with the opportunities and resources necessary to achieve positive life-transformation, incarceration often merely further abuses and isolates inmates. America's prisons are often today profoundly bereft of rehabilitation programming and inundated with violence. Amid reports of staff-coerced "gladiator fights," broomstick rapes, and high staff turnover, Florida Department of Corrections Secretary Mark Inch recently highlighted the fact that only 6% of Florida's inmates received any programming.[10] Florida State Senator Jeff Brandeis, the Republican Chair of the Corrections Oversight Committee, stated "This is not a prison system that anybody can look you in the eye and tell you a person will be safe in the state's care."[11] In short, America's prison inmates often live in fear of physical harm, while experiencing few opportunities for self-improvement. Within a short period of time after release, many ex-offenders find themselves back in the same communities and circles of influence that enabled, if not encouraged, their criminal activity in the first place.

The Financial Drain: The Economic Impact of Overreliance on Incarceration

According to the Sourcebook of Criminal Justice Statistics,[12] the total estimated US prison population increased by 377% (from 319,598 to 1,524,650) between 1980 and 2009, when it reached an all-time peak (see Figure 1.1). Using a more recent estimate of the 2009 prison population

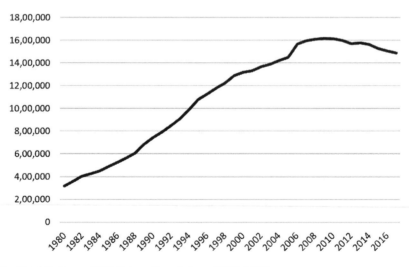

FIGURE 1.1   Total Estimated US Prison Population, 1980–2017.

Source: The Sourcebook of Criminal Justice Statistics Online (https://www.albany.edu/sourcebook/). Section 6. Table 6.1.2011, "Adults on probation, in jail and prison, and on parole, United States, 1980–2011" (https://www.albany.edu/sourcebook/pdf/t612011.pdf); Kaeble and Cowhig (2018). Table 1, "Number of persons supervised by U.S. adult correctional systems, by correctional status, 2000 and 2006–2016"; Bronson and Carson (2019). Table 1.1, "Prisoners under jurisdiction of stat or federal correctional authorities, by jurisdiction and sex, 2007–2017."

(1,615,500),[13] the 30-year increase was even more dramatic (405%). After the peak, the US prison population began to decline and continued a downward trend through 2017 as Figure 1.1 shows, while the federal prison population (which made up about 12% to 14% of the total prison population between 2007 and 2017) peaked three years later (i.e., 2012).[14] Despite the declining trend, almost 1.5 million (1,489,363) persons were incarcerated in prison in 2017.[15]

To state the obvious, it is expensive to keep such a large number of people in correctional institutions. For example, between 1982 and 2001, total state expenditures on corrections increased annually from 15.0 billion to 53.5 billion dollars before they fluctuated between 53.4 billion and 48.4 billion dollars until 2010, when the expenditures totaled 48.5 billion dollars.[16] The total amount a state spends on prisons increases when costs paid by other state agencies (e.g., employee health insurance, pension contributions, and inmate hospital care) are added to correctional budgets.[17] According to a survey focusing on fiscal year of 2010, the total tax payer cost of prisons in 40 states that participated in the survey was 13.9% higher than the costs represented by their combined correctional budgets.

Although an increase in prison population does not always increase prison expenditures,[18] the amount of state correctional expenditures seem to have roughly followed the trends of the total state prison population. Stated differently, the more offenders are sentenced to prison, the more state correctional expenditures increase.[19] Specifically, state correctional institutions' operational expenditures increased threefold (298%) from 9.7 billion to 38.6 billion dollars between 1982 and 2009 (see Figure 1.2). In addition, per capita expenditures ranged from $26,036 (in 1982) to $32,459 (in 2001) during the 19-year period with the average annual operating cost per state prisoner in 2009 being $29,270 or $80.19 per day.[20] In 2010, the total annual expenditure per inmate including prison spending outside of corrections departments averaged $31,286, ranging from $14,603 in Kentucky to $60, 076 in New York.[21]

The dramatic growth in the prison population represents an increasing challenge for policy-makers and correctional authorities, and translates into a costly liability for US taxpayers.[22] Economists are now helping us to estimate the total cost per victimization by the number of victimizations in the United States. According to these figures, in 1993, the one-year cost of

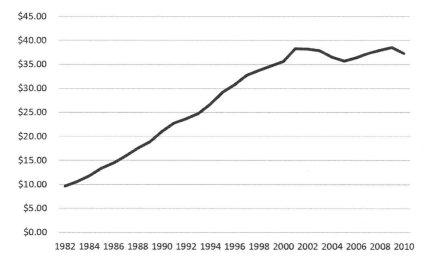

FIGURE 1.2 State Correctional Institutions' Operational Expenditures, 1982–2010.
Source: Kyckelhahn (2012) (Revised 2014). State Corrections Expenditures, FY 1982–2010.

crime to victims totaled $450 billion.[23] Regrettably, scholars, practitioners, and policy-makers alike have largely ignored the enormous cost of victimization to American society.[24]

Prisoner Recidivism in the United States

If prisons fully functioned as truly *correctional* institutions, a majority of prisoners would be rehabilitated and would be unlikely to reoffend after being released from prison. However, in reality, to the extent that prisons fail to perform as such, a certain percentage of prisoners will most certainly relapse into criminal behavior after they return to the community. As a result, a majority of ex-prisoners will likely be rearrested, reconvicted, and reincarcerated. Alternatively, if prisoners are released on probation or parole, a technical violation of their release can result in a revocation of probation or parole and ultimately land them back in prison. Each of these outcomes is known as recidivism, which is typically measured in terms of the percentage of inmates rearrested, reconvicted, and/or reincarcerated during a certain period of time following their release. The recidivism rate varies depending on the type and number of offenses considered, the compositional characteristics of prisoners released, and the length of observation period as well as the result of reoffending (i.e., rearrest, reconviction, and reincarceration).

An early Bureau of Justice Statistics (BJS) study of recidivism among state prisoners was conducted based on a sample of 16,355 prisoners released in 1983.[25] The sample was 89% of 18,374 prisoners in the original sample, representative of an estimated 108,580 prisoners who were released in 11 states (California, Florida, Illinois, Michigan, Minnesota, New Jersey, New York, North Carolina, Ohio, Oregon, and Texas) and remained alive in 1987. A total of 2,019 prisoners were excluded from the original sample because state and federal "rap sheets" were not found for them, or died during a three-year follow-up period. No systematic difference between prisoners with complete records and those lacking either a state or federal rap sheet was found.

Within three years, the study reported, about six of ten (62.5%) released prisoners were rearrested for a felony or serious misdemeanor, almost half (46.8%) of them were reconvicted, and four of ten (41.4%) returned to prison or jail. The recidivism rates were highest in the first year (39.3% rearrested, 23.1% reconvicted, and 18.6% reincarcerated) and increased by about 15% by the end of the second year (i.e., 54.5%, 38.3%, and 32.8%, respectively), whereas the rate of increase between the second and third year decreased by about a half, 8%–9%. That is, larger percentages of prisoners released were rearrested (62.9%), reconvicted (49.4%), and reincarcerated (44.9%) during the first year than the second (24.3%, 32.5%, and 34.2%, respectively) and third years (12.8%, 18.2%, and 20.8%). In other words, while recidivism rates increased over the three years, the rate of increase decreased.

A subsequent BJS study of recidivism among state prisoners tracked 272,111 former inmates discharged from prisons in 15 states (Arizona, Delaware, Maryland, and Virginia in addition to the 11 states included in the previous study) for three years after release in 1994.[26] While the study population of state prisoners released in 1983 and 1994 were different in terms of number (i.e., 108,580 vs. 272,111) and composition (e.g., 11 vs. 15 states participating in the study), the trends and patterns of recidivism were generally consistent with those found in the previous study of state prisoners released about ten years earlier (see Figure 1.3).[27]

Two more recent BJS studies of recidivism were based on a larger dataset collected to track 404,638 prisoners released in 30 states[28] in 2005 for up to five[29] and nine years.[30] More than half (56.7%) of released prisoners were arrested for a new crime by the end of the first year, and about two thirds (67.8%) of them were rearrested within three years. The rate increased to 76.6% and 83.4% by the end of fifth and ninth year, respectively. As found in the previous BJS studies, using the five-year follow-up period, a majority (52.6%) of rearrests for a new crime

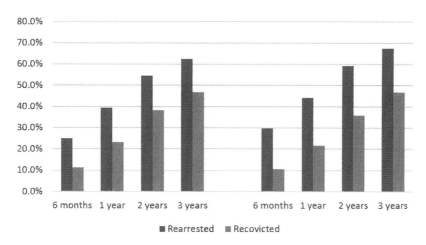

FIGURE 1.3 Cumulative Recidivism Rates among Prisoners Released in 1983 (left) and 1994 (right).
Source: Beck and Shipley (1989). Recidivism of Prisoners Released in 1983; Langan and Levin (2002). Recidivism of Prisoners Released in 1994.

occurred during the first year, and the percentage gradually declined in subsequent years (i.e., 19.4%, 10.0%, 6.1%, 4.2%, 2.9%, 2.0%, 1.6%, and 1.2% during the second through ninth year).

The three-year rearrest rate of prisoners released in 2005 (67.8%) was not much different from the rate of those released in 1983 (62.5%) and 1994 (67.5%), while the one-year rearrest rate (56.7%) was higher among the "2005 prisoners" than their 1983 and 1994 counterparts (39.3% and 44.1%). After the three-year rates were adjusted for two key differences between prisoners released in 1994 and 2005 (i.e., the number and composition of states included in the study and sociodemographic and offending characteristics of released prisoners),[31] the observed difference remained minimal.[32]

The comprehensive cost of incarceration in the context of the efficacy of the US prison system is unfortunately far more pervasive and consequential than many scholars and policy-makers have understood. Consequently, understanding and maximizing the effective use of the human and financial capital expended within the criminal justice system is of utmost importance.

Why Is Prisoner Rehabilitation So Elusive?

Previous studies of prisoners released from state and federal prisons tend to report high rates of recidivism observed consistently across the past several decades, implying that American prisons have not been on the winning side when it comes to prisoner rehabilitation. According to research on state prisoners (whose offenses better represent "street crimes" than federal prisoners'), about four out of ten released prisoners are arrested for a new crime within a year, and about two thirds and three quarters of all prisoners released are arrested by the end of third and fifth year, respectively. Although the high recidivism is attributable to what happens after prison as well as in prison, it is difficult to make a case for American prisons functioning as *correctional* institutions when about three out of ten ex-prisoners return to prison for a new sentence or a technical violation within the first year after release and over half return to prison five years after release.[33]

Demographic group differences in recidivism remain the same across multiple studies of state and federal prisoners. Men and non-whites (Blacks and Hispanics) are more likely to be rearrested than women and whites, and younger prisoners at release are at a higher risk of recidivism than their older counterparts. It is worth noting that the demographic group differences in recidivism are consistent with those in criminal offending, which implies a common underlying theme—an inability to escape criminal justice involvement. Indeed, prior criminal history has been found to be a strong predictor of recidivism: "The number of times a prisoner has been arrested in the past is a good predictor of whether that prisoner will continue to commit crimes after being released."[34] In sum, prior criminality's predictive ability demonstrates the ineffectual role American prisons play in helping prisoners change as a result of their incarceration. Indeed, data reveals that the longer offenders spend in prison the more likely it is they will reoffend.[35]

Although the "nothing works" doctrine asserted the ineffectiveness of correctional interventions,[36] meta-analyses conducted after the publication of Martinson's 1974 essay revealed that some programs in fact do work. Specifically, a group of Canadian psychologists identified the factors likely to increase treatment effectiveness, called "principles of effective correctional intervention."[37] According to the principles, while targeting the known predictors of crime and recidivism for change, interventions should be behavioral in nature, employing the cognitive behavioral and social learning techniques, such as modeling, reinforcement, and cognitive restructuring.[38] For example, the most common forms of behavioral programs, known as "cognitive-behavioral," aim to cognitively restructure the distorted or erroneous cognition of an offender and to assist him or her to learn new, adaptive cognitive skills. The principles also suggest that interventions should be more effective when used with high-risk than low-risk offenders and conducted in the community as opposed to in an institutional setting. For example, "multisystemic therapy"[39] that conforms closely to the principles has been found to be a promising intervention.[40]

Bonta and Andrews developed the principles of effective treatment into the "RNR model," which focuses on three core principles of risk (R), need (N), and responsivity (R).[41] First, the risk principle suggests that treatment should be provided to high-risk rather than low-risk offenders. Second, the need principle emphasizes the importance of addressing offenders' "needs" or risk factors for offending. Treatment should focus on "dynamic" risk factors—criminogenic factors that are malleable—as opposed to "static" ones—characteristics associated with crime that cannot be changed, such as age and race. Third, the responsivity principle highlights the importance of targeting the true cause that would be "responsive" to the problem in question. "General responsivity" concerns the use of cognitive-behavioral, social learning-based programs, whereas "specific responsivity" involves delivery of individualized treatments that would take into account the characteristics of offenders. The RNR model recommends that "correctional interventions focus on high-risk offenders, target empirically strong and malleable predictors of recidivism, and use treatments that are responsive to or capable of changing these dynamic risk factors."[42]

In contrast to the RNR model, a new alternative framework for approaching offender rehabilitation is the "Good Lives Model," developed by Tony Ward and colleagues.[43] The Good Lives Model prioritizes first meeting offenders' *needs*, rather than prioritizing "risk," as key to successfully motivating offender self-change. By noting the life-course differences produced by well-documented structural inequalities operative in the lives of many inmates, the Good Lives Model conceptualizes offending as a byproduct of environmental and social conditions often beyond the control of offenders. Early life experiences and lack of robust opportunity structures for prosocial behavior often hinders the life-course trajectories of citizens who end up in the American prison system. Utilizing a developmental framework similar to that of Abraham Maslow's Hierarchy of Needs, the Good Lives Model (GLM) conceptualizes optimal behavior as built upon a foundation of basic needs (called "primary goods") having first been met. In many cases, the GLM asserts, the "primary goods" necessary for building successful prosocial lives are dramatically missing from the lives of many offenders. Primary goods such as health, safety, and long-lasting interpersonal relationships that are nurturing, form the true foundations of prosocial behavior. Only when these foundational needs are consistently met, can "secondary goods" such as quality education, persistent employment, and self-development be fully cultivated and capitalized upon.

Referred to as a "strengths based" approach, the Good Lives Model operationalizes by seeking first to incentivize good behavior early on through providing adequate resources, rather than disincentivize bad behavior through after-the-fact punishments. The GLM places chief emphasis upon how to reward and encourage conformity, rather than discourage and punish deviance. After all, proponents of the GLM argue, crime is low in low-crime neighborhoods not because these neighborhoods are inundated with saturation policing and high incarceration rates, but because residents have robust opportunity structures that both encourage and reward good behavior. As prosocial opportunities multiply, residents more deeply invest in prosocial identities. In short, residents of low-crime neighborhoods have many more prosocial opportunities to which they will gladly say "yes," rather than simply a proliferation of opportunities to which they must "just say no." Similarly, in a process we identify as "religiously-motivated identity transformation," inmates in America's largest maximum security prison who received gratis opportunities for voluntary religious education, developed "religious counter-narratives" to their status as "inmates," scored higher on assessments of personal wellness, and eventually came to pride themselves upon "giving back to the prison" through personal service.[44] Misconduct rates for these inmates fell dramatically and stayed low. A growing body of research supports GLM approaches to offender treatment, including work with sex-offenders, drug addicts, and violent juveniles.[45] Society's lack of forgiveness and punitive response to offending is counter-productive and often ignores the social context of offending.

In sum, principles and empirical evidence of effective treatment exist, and promising models of correctional intervention are available. However, according to Cullen and Gendreau, a majority of prison programs are not based on either restorative principles or empirical evidence: "In fact, ... only a minority of treatment programs in corrections are rooted in the existing research on 'what works.' ... much of what is done within the field is a matter of correctional quackery."[46] More than a decade later, Cullen still made a similar assessment: "The norm that interventions should be based on evidence is now widely shared, [but] its use in agencies remains spotty."[47] In other words, programs in American prisons tend to be limited not only in number but also in effectiveness, and this may partly explain the high recidivism of ex-prisoners. In addition, we believe that American prison programs would have more success in rehabilitating prisoners if they more intentionally addressed the issue of human agency as well as human capital, motivating prisoners to change and choose to live a prosocial life. For example, while clearly helpful, educational, and vocational skills themselves are unlikely to lead prisoners to live a prosocial life. With the benefit of empirical evidence, we argue that religion enhances the likelihood of rehabilitation as well as helping prisoners to become more virtuous and prosocial.

Religion and Prosocial Corrections: Toward Restoration

Rehabilitation is a principal goal of the correctional system in the United States. While it is one of four traditional goals of corrections along with retribution, incapacitation, and deterrence, rehabilitation is more closely related to how the system is referred to, *corrections*, than the other goals. Also, rehabilitation is complementary to the most recently added fifth goal, restoration, in that the former focuses on individual offenders to rehabilitate, whereas the latter emphasizes restoring broken relationships between those offenders and the community. Restorative Justice looks beyond the mere guilt or innocence of individual offenders to examine more holistically how social relationships might be restored for both victims and offenders.

The goal of rehabilitation is based on the assumption that offenders can be treated to desist from crime and eventually live a crime-free life. The object of treatment includes various factors expected to be causally related to crime. Thus, rehabilitation involves various treatment programs intended to address the presence of risk factors for offending (e.g., mental illness, drug abuse, and anger problem) and the absence of protective factors (e.g., education, job skills, and cognitive functioning). While these issues are all important to address, when people ask whether offenders *change*, that is, are rehabilitated during incarceration, it concerns not only such treatment as helping them recover from drug addiction or complete General Educational Development (GEDs) but also fundamental change or transformation of the offender. Relevant to such change is the concept of self-identity and its transformation.

Identity Theories of Desistance from Crime

The anticipated key outcome of prisoner rehabilitation is post-release desistance from crime, which is a process rather than a discrete event: specifically, a developmental process of declining criminality, which is driven by various factors and eventually leads to the termination of offending.[48] While factors that contribute to the process of criminal desistance can be biological, psychological, or social, scholars explain the process focusing on either external or internal factors. That is, some posit that offenders desist from crime as a result of social (relational or role-related) or structural (institutional or opportunity-related) changes, whereas others emphasize psychological (cognitive and affective) or agentic (volitional) changes as a prerequisite for criminal desistance.

For example, Sampson and Laub explain post-adolescent desistance as a result of structural "turning points" associated with institutions of informal social control during a transition to young adulthood.[49] Specifically, they posit and empirically demonstrate how entering into a "good" marriage relationship, getting a "quality" job, and joining the military decrease crime in adulthood because those changes function as turning points of institutional control.[50] Although they later recognize the importance of internal as well as external factors,[51] their primary focus remains on structural factors and what they call "desistance by default," which is "not necessarily a conscious or deliberate process" on the part of a desisting offender.[52]

However, other scholars emphasize the very "conscious or deliberate process" of human agency in explaining desistance. First, while acknowledging that environmental catalysts are necessary for change, Giordano, Cernkovich, and Rudolph (2002) posit that four types of inter-related "cognitive transformations" are essential to desistance. They include: (1) one's openness to change (a general cognitive readiness for change); (2) one's exposure to a particular "hook (or set of hooks) for change" and its perceived meaning or importance for the individual; (3) one's construction of a conventional new identity, "replacement self"; and (4) one's perception of crime and deviance to be negative, unviable, or even personally irrelevant.[53] Based on the neo-Meadian view of the interconnectedness between human cognitions and emotions, Giordano later added the concept of "emotional self" because a motivation for change involves not only cognitive but also "emotional transformations."[54] That is, offenders in emotional transformation are more likely to be able to regulate and manage their emotions, thereby identifying themselves with socially acceptable positive emotions, and less likely to identify themselves with negative emotions than those who are not in the process of desistance from crime.

Second, from a rational choice perspective, Paternoster and Bushway proposed an identity theory of desistance based on "a distinction between... one's current or working identity and... the kind of person that one wishes to be—and, more importantly, not be ['feared self']—in the future: one's *possible self*."[55] A current or working identity as a criminal offender is fine as long as the criminal identity is perceived to be beneficial than harmful to them. However, it becomes problematic as offenders increasingly perceive diverse kinds of failures in their lives to be not only linked together but also attributable to the criminal identity itself.

The cognitive linking of previously isolated dissatisfactions and failures in life, called "crystallization of discontent," leads to a general sense of dissatisfaction with crime and gradually weakens commitment to an offender's existing life and existing identity. This weakening provides offenders with the initial motivation to consider the benefits of adopting a non-criminal possible self in the future and engage in a deliberate act of intentional self-change. Therefore, offenders who engage in a crystallization of discontent are more likely to be conscious of their feared selves and thus intentional about changing themselves to achieve their possible selves than those who do not engage in the cognitive process.

In sum, existing theories, particularly, those focusing on internal factors contributing to desistance emphasize the importance of human agency as well as structural catalysts (e.g., turning points or "hooks for change") in explaining desistance. While they posited that an ideal typical sequence of cognitive transformations begins with a prisoner's openness to change, Giordano et al. are not clear about what motivates prisoners to be open to change.[56] On the other hand, for Paternoster and Bushway, it is a crystallization of discontent that motivates offenders to consider changing identity.[57] So, when the cognitive process leads prisoners to conclude that their failures and dissatisfactions in life are not isolated incidences but interconnected outcomes of a common source, criminal identity, they are likely to be willing to consider a conventional identity.

Religion and Identity Transformation

Besides a crystallization of discontent, what would motivate prisoners to change, adopting a new, conventional identity in place of a current, criminal one? This question has a practical significance since once we identify the source of motivation, it can be incorporated into prison programming and correctional policy. We propose an identity crisis that prisoners are likely to face in prison may lead them to seek a new meaning in life to cope with the crisis and, as a result, consider adopting a conventional identity to replace their criminal identity. Specifically, it is an "existential crisis" where prisoners question the meaning of their lives that may lead to identity transformation.

We assume that offenders (like non-offenders) are existential beings in the sense that they have an innate need for meaning in life. Meaning is defined as "the sense made of, and significance felt regarding, the nature of one's being and existence."[58] According to Frankl, humans have an inborn desire of "will to meaning" and, if the desire is not fulfilled, they are likely to experience an "existential vacuum" or emptiness inside, resulting in "existential frustration."[59] While meaning could be claimed based on anything, Frankl suggests that the "true meaning of life" should be self-transcendent (i.e., discovered outside of an individual).[60] For example, research shows that meaning is found in close relationship with family and other loved ones or a sense of belonging or mattering to them.[61] Conversely, social exclusion and loneliness are inversely related to the perception of life as meaningful.[62] Since prisons are known to be places of exclusion and isolation from society, it is understandable that offenders would come to perceive their lives as meaningless. Moreover, the loss of social bonds is another possible by-product of incarceration which may also reinforce the perception of meaningless.

The pains of loss and deprivation prisoners experience in prison are not simply physical as the very foundation of their existence, such as a sense of self-worth, is threatened.[63] Upon entrance, prisoners are stripped of supports taken for granted in the outside world and their identity becomes mortified as a result of a series of degradations of self in the "total institution."[64] The mortification of self, along with a sense of guilt and shame, is also likely to throw prisoners into an existential crisis in which they are confronted with the reality that their lives lack meaning and purpose. In this crisis, prisoners are also likely to question their current self-identity as the "divided self"[65]—"a contrast between what is and what might be me"[66] or between "one's current or working identity and ... one's *possible self*"[67]—looms large.

This process of existential struggle might motivate prisoners to search for answers about their existence and its meaning by adopting a new interpretive system that offers not only meaning and guidance but also forgiveness and hope. Religion, which involves a transcendent being, can be a rare source of meaning readily available to prisoners.[68] As a new system of meaning, religion enables prisoners to adopt a new "living narrative" that offers new identity (e.g., a child of God), new life goals or "calling," and a new hope for the future, which is generated by a sense of meaning in life.[69] Moreover, religion can provide a "second chance" at redemption that may further motivate prisoners to keep living a meaningful and purpose-driven life because the belief that they can now live meaningful lives energizes the self and motivates goal-directed, prosocial behavior, which further provide meaning in life.[70]

Prisoners who found new meaning and purpose in life come to have a new identity as they consider their existence as meaningful despite their criminal past and current incarceration. In other words, they come to have a new, "meaningful self"[71] or "existential identity" as they identify themselves with the newly discovered existential meaning of life. Replacing an old, meaningless self with a new, meaningful self can be called "existential identity transformation." Identity transformation via religion (i.e., existential identity transformation) is a cognitive process in that it involves a change in worldview and self-concept, which may lead a prisoner to see and interpret reality in a fundamentally different way, as a result of a new living narrative. It is also an affective process because it includes dealing with the prisoner's guilt and shame stemming from a criminal past and their associated emotions, such as anger and the feelings of depression.[72] Therefore, it is necessary to examine existential identity transformation in relation to both cognitive and emotional identity transformations, proposed by Giordano et al. and Paternoster and Bushway.[73] One recent study examined those relationships.

In their study of inmates at the Louisiana State Penitentiary (a.k.a. Angola), Jang et al. conceptualized identity transformation as a *process* of developing a new self-identity rather than a discrete event of abrupt self-change.[74] Thus, if observed at any point in time, inmates were expected to be different in their progress in identity transformation. That is, inmates who have advanced ahead of others in the process are more likely to show signs of identity transformation than those who are behind, slow, or not even in the process. Using survey data from 2,249 inmates, they constructed measures of an inmate's religiousness (individual religiosity, religious conversion, and congregational participation), existential (identity) transformation, cognitive transformation, crystallization of discontent, and transformation in positive and negative affect.[75] Results from estimating a latent-variable structural equation model (SEM) showed: (1) religious conversion and, to a lesser extent, individual religiosity were positively related to existential and cognitive transformations and crystallization of discontent; (2) both existential and cognitive transformations were positively related to transformation in positive affect; and

(3) individual religiosity was also positively related to transformation in positive affect. In sum, religion seemed to have contributed to existential, cognitive, and emotional identity transformations and crystallization of discontent among inmates.

In two subsequent studies, Jang and his colleagues examined the relationship between inmate religiosity and a sense of meaning and purpose in life, which is an indicator of existential identity. In a first study, using the same measure of religiosity (perceived closeness to God, perceived importance of religion, religious service attendance, praying outside of religious services, and reading a sacred book in private) that was used in their earlier study,[76] Jang et al. found an inmate's religiosity was positively associated with his perceived presence of meaning in life as hypothesized: that is, more religious inmates tended to have a clear sense of meaning and purpose in life compared to their less or not religious peers.[77] While this study was based on data collected from male prisoners in Texas, a second study employed data from male and female prisoners in a non-Western country, South Africa.[78] Using the data collected from a survey with 425 inmates, (245 males and 180 females), housed in four prisons, Jang et al. replicated the positive relationship between religiosity and presence of meaning among inmates: that is, the more religious, the more likely to have a sense of meaning and purpose in life. In addition, the positive relationship was found among both males and females, indicating that religion's contribution to existential identity transformation was applicable to both male and female inmates. This finding based on non-Wetern data also shows that the religiosity-meaning relationship may be cross-culturally applicable.

Finally, we report results from a preliminary analysis of two-wave panel data collected from survey with 424 male inmates in two prisons in Colombia to assess the effects of a faith-based program of Prison Fellowship International (PFI), called "The Prisoner's Journey (TPJ)," on offender rehabilitation in prison.[79] TPJ is an eight-week course, run by more than 650 prisons in about 40 countries including Colombia and South Africa. A half of the sample (i.e., 212 inmates) participated in TPJ (treatment group), and the other half did not (control group). A pretest survey was administered to the total sample ($n = 424$) before inmates of the treatment group participated in TPJ, and 253 of them (97 TPJ inmates and 156 non-TPJ inmates) participated in a posttest after the participating inmates completed the program. Although the program was an eight-week course, it took, on average, about three months due to prison lockdown and other interruptions of program administration. The program was run in small groups (10–15 inmates per group), and time interval between pretest (Time 1) and posttest (Time 2) varied among those groups. So, the interval (in days) was controlled for in analysis.

A manifest-variable SEM was constructed to examine whether the effects of participation in TPJ on a sense of meaning and purpose in life (search for as well as presence of meaning) and identity transformations (replacement self, negative emotional self, and crystallization of discontent) were mediated by religiosity. In other words, the faith-based program was hypothesized to increase religiosity, which, in turn, enhanced a sense of meaning and purpose in life. It was also hypothesized that an increase in presence of meaning contributed to cognitive and emotional identity transformations and crystallization of discontent.[80] Besides the time interval between pretest and posttest, inmate's self-reported spiritual transformation and participation in other prison programs were controlled for to avoid estimating confounding effects.

Results from model estimation are presented in Table 1.1. As expected, an inmate's participation in TPJ increased religiosity (.138) between Times 1 and 2, and the increase in

TABLE 1.1 Existential Effects of Participation in The Prisoner's Journey (TPJ) on Self-Identities among Prison Inmates in Colombia (n = 424)

	Religiosity T2		Spiritual transform T2		Non-TPJ programs T2		Search for meaning T2		Presence of meaning T2		Replacement self T2		Neg. emotional self T2		Crystal. of discontent T2	
	β	(S.E.)	β	(S.E.)	β	(S.E.)	β	(S.E.)	β	(S.E.)	β	(S.E.)	β	(S.E.)	β	(S.E.)
Survey interval (days)	.001	(.073)	-.027	(.110)	-.310*	(.138)	-.115	(.116)	.058	(.100)	-.143	(.128)	.200	(.119)	-.057	(.137)
Search for meaning T1	.081	(.066)	.007	(.095)	.190+	(.100)	.313*	(.081)	-.072	(.073)	-.017	(.065)	-.002	(.098)	-.053	(.064)
Presence of meaning T1	.152*	(.062)	.076	(.081)	-.099	(.095)	-.043	(.072)	.468*	(.078)	-.021	(.091)	.104	(.079)	-.058	(.080)
Replacement self T1	-.039	(.077)	-.092	(.080)	-.126	(.102)	-.108+	(.059)	.056	(.070)	.290*	(.082)	-.090	(.080)	.024	(.072)
Neg. emotional self T1	.053	(.045)	.050	(.060)	-.066	(.091)	.025	(.058)	-.051	(.052)	-.036	(.057)	.349*	(.063)	-.002	(.060)
Crystal. of discount. T1	.023	(.049)	.041	(.078)	.061	(.093)	.217*	(.076)	.137*	(.067)	.135*	(.064)	-.005	(.070)	.491*	(.061)
Religiosity T1	.473*	(.073)	.219*	(.091)	-.030	(.108)	.119	(.083)	.000	(.080)	.002	(.071)	-.017	(.087)	-.106	(.069)
Spiritual transform. T1	.116+	(.070)	.273*	(.093)	.005	(.129)	-.027	(.109)	-.032	(.084)	-.080	(.075)	.031	(.084)	-.078	(.070)
Non-TPJ programs T1	.154*	(.077)	-.031	(.077)	.330*	(.128)	.027	(.096)	-.213*	(.082)	.082	(.097)	-.181	(.114)	-.044	(.111)
Participation in TPJ	.138*	(.080)	.085	(.120)	-.312*	(.149)	-.131	(.122)	.039	(.105)	-.111	(.135)	.142	(.121)	-.026	(.128)
Religiosity T2	.290*	(.074)					.006	(.082)	.336*	(.081)	-.054	(.073)	.026	(.092)	.188*	(.088)
Spiritual transform. T2	-.015	(.104)	.043	(.098)			.059	(.092)	-.059	(.063)	.120+	(.062)	-.010	(.074)	.030	(.055)
Non-TPJ programs T2							.226*	(.109)	.128	(.088)	.201*	(.102)	.241*	(.095)	.074	(.083)
Search for meaning T2							.216*	(.065)			.124	(.095)	.033	(.085)	.027	(.086)
Presence of meaning T2											.189*	(.082)	-.162+	(.088)	.074	(.092)
Replacement self T2																
Neg. emotional self T2											.053	(.070)				
Crystal. of discount. T2											.416*	(.095)	.030	(.063)		
R-square	.465*	(.070)	.205*	(.071)	.165*	(.074)	.268*	(.066)	.447*	(.063)	.331*	(.076)	.205*	(.055)	.302*	(.062)

p < .05 (one–tailed test), * p < .05 (two–tailed test).

religiosity enhanced the inmate's perceived presence of meaning in life (.336). In addition, the increase in presence of meaning was found to have significant effects on cognitive and emotional transformations, that is, replacement self (.189) and negative emotional self (–.162) in the expected direction. Although the perception of meaning in life had no significant effect on crystallization of discontent (.074, $p > .05$), religiosity was found to have a direct effect on it (.188).

In sum, consistent with the previous findings,[81] overall results indicate that the faith-based program helped inmates develop a sense of meaning and purpose in life by increasing their involvement in religion. The new belief in existential meaning and life's purpose, in turn, led inmates not only to be open to change and willing to have themselves changed completely but also to replace their old bad self with a good new self. There was also an indication of emotional identity transformation: that is, inmates with a new sense of meaning and purpose in life were less likely to identify themselves with the feelings of depression, anger, frustration, and anxiety. In addition, inmates who increased their religious involvement were more likely to engage in a crystallization of discontent.

Conclusion

While the US prison population has been declining since 2009, about 1.5 million persons are incarcerated in state and federal prisons. It annually costs, on average, more than $30,000 to keep each inmate in state prison. Despite the high taxpayer cost of state prisons, recidivism among released state prisoners remains high for the past several decades. For example, about 40% of released state prisoners are arrested for a new crime within a year, and about 75% of all prisoners released are arrested by the end of fifth year. Recidivism is lower among federal prisoners (e.g., about 45% of prisoners are rearrested within five years after release), but the difference is likely to be attributable mainly to differences in sociodemographic and offending characteristics between federal and state prisoners released.

The high recidivism rate indicates that American prisons are not doing a good job in reforming prisoners, which means their protection of public safety generally stops at the moment prisoners are released back into the community. American prisons are not to be solely blamed for the high recidivism because various factors and circumstances prisoners encounter after release also contribute to their reoffending. However, they are not without blame, either, to the extent that they fail to help prisoners change through rehabilitative programming during their incarceration whether the failure is due to policy-makers' reluctance to be "soft on crime," retributive correctional policies, or financial constraints.[82]

The "nothing works" doctrine has been debunked, and the principles of effective correctional intervention have been developed. Those principles provide a theoretical basis for achieving efficacious treatment of offenders. Empirical research shows what works for prisoner rehabilitation, so we can be smart to maximize the utility of limited resources. For example, interventions that provide learning opportunities where antisocial cognitions and behaviors are replaced with prosocial cognitions and behaviors tend to be effective. As mentioned above, while the RNR model has gained some preliminary empirical support, it has also been criticized for its failure to address social context. As much of criminological research has demonstrated, the fact that such profoundly high disproportions of citizens "at risk" for offending come from socioeconomically disadvantaged backgrounds cannot be ignored. Through an over-fixation on individual-level traits, the RNR model ignores the other half of the equation: social and environmental conditions.

Critics have also maintained that while the RNR model is grounded empirically, it offers little practical utility to practitioners seeking to motivate people to change and offers little to help people access "good lives." Rather than merely understanding what works to reduce offending, Ward and Maruna (2007) argue that the system should find "what helps" people live good lives. They draw on positive and humanistic psychology that emphasizes the "whole person" and assume that all people have certain basic needs in common that are necessary for fulfilling lives, such as affection, meaningful purpose and security.[83]

While these principles are crucial to the creation of programs that work, the effectiveness of correctional intervention ultimately depends on whether prisoners are open to change. We maintain that religion offers incarcerated individuals both a blueprint and an opportunity for (re)examination of their lives and valuable tools useful for living "good lives." If inmates have little opportunity and maintain no interest in changing themselves or do not want to change, programs proven to be effective are unlikely to have the intended impact on them. Prisoners may sign up for programs to earn points for early release, but the programs won't affect their rehabilitation. For successful rehabilitation, we need not only effective programs but also a change of heart on the part of prisoners, where they come to desire to end their criminal life and start a new life. Such change was the focus at the beginning of American corrections. That is, in the 1820s reformers in Pennsylvania invented the "penitentiary" based on the Christian idea that correctional intervention should reform prisoners, changing who they are, because they believed that a change of heart through penance was the very first step toward prisoner rehabilitation. Nearly all reform efforts were justified as religiously informed undertakings, and religion was considered as the most important because of its impact on human heart and life.[84]

However, by the latter part of the 1800s, the religious ideal of reforming prisoners through an inner change of heart had lost its appeal and was replaced by an increasing emphasis on outer factors like human capital, such as education and industrial training, which were believed to encourage prisoners to redeem their character and regain their lost position in society.[85] In addition, prisoner's outer, behavioral change was sought by offering more rewards than punishments via indeterminate sentencing rather than encouraging their inner change of heart. The trend continued in the first two decades of the 20th century, called "the Progressive Era," when the emerging social sciences identified external factors to be treated, whether the harsh environments of poor inner cities, dysfunctional families, criminal influence of peers, or individual pathologies. For the next 50 years, the rehabilitation ideal continued to dominate until the 1970s that saw the publication of Martinson's "nothing works" study, criticisms of correctional interventions for their harmful effects on offenders and prisons as "total institutions," and a decline in public support for rehabilitation. Although the rehabilitation ideal gained support again from both the policy-makers and the public after empirical refutation of the Martinson's study and the identification of effective correctional intervention principles in the latter part of 20th century, the religious ideal of prisoner's change of heart for rehabilitation never regained the position it once had in American corrections two centuries ago.

While being locked up and isolated from the outside world, prisoners are likely to experience existential identity crisis as they are confronted with a reality that their lives lack meaning and purpose. Although the crisis could be simply ignored and suppressed, prisoners who have an innate need for existential meaning for life like any human beings are likely to be pressured to address the crisis. Religion can help prisoners struggling with the crisis by offering a well-established meaning and purpose in life. The newly found meaning and purpose in life leads prisoners to replace an old, criminal identity with a new, prosocial one. Empirical research provides evidence of religion increasing a sense of meaning and purpose in life among prison inmates, which is, in turn, likely to lead to their cognitive and emotional identity transformations.

Religion is widely available for prisoners in America, and their participation in religion is protected by the US Constitution. Although financial challenges and budget cuts put a limit on the number and scope of programs American prisons can offer, faith-based programs do not cost taxpayers' money because they operate largely through using religious volunteers. Thus, as long as an inmate's participation remains voluntary, religion in prison could become a turning point for American correctional efforts to rehabilitate prisoners.

Notes

 1 Farrington (1998), Catalano and Hawkins (1996), Hawkins, Farrington, and Catalan (1998).
 2 Turney and Wildeman (2013).
 3 Johnson and Waldfogel (2002).
 4 Johnston (1995), Turney (2018).
 5 Hagan and Dinovitzer (1999).
 6 Turney and Goodsell (2018).
 7 Krisberg (2001).
 8 Sack and Seidler (1978).
 9 Gabel and Johnston (1995).
10 Mahoney (2019).
11 Mahoney (2019).
12 See Section 6's Table 6.1.2011, "Adults on probation, in jail and prison, and on parole, United States, 1980–2011" (https://www.albany.edu/sourcebook/pdf/t612011.pdf).
13 Kaeble and Cowhig (2018).
14 Bronson and Carson (2019).
15 Bronson and Carson (2019).
16 Kychelhahn (2012).
17 Henrichson and Delaney (2012).
18 Mai and Subramanian (2017).
19 State correctional expenditures consist of capital outlay and operational expenditures. The former expenditures include "spending on construction, renovations, and major repair of institutions; purchase of land, rights-of-way, and existing structures; title searches and related costs; and purchase of equipment having a useful life of more than 5 years" (Kychelhahn, 2012, p. 2), whereas the latter include "compensation of officers and employees and supplies, materials, and contractual services exclusive of capital outlay" (p. 5).
20 Kychelhahn (2012).
21 Hendrichson and Delaney (2012).
22 Wildeman (2013), Wildeman, Andersen, Lee, and Karlson (2014), Turney and Wildeman (2013).
23 Miller (1996).
24 The Office for Victims of Crime (OVC) is one of seven components within the Office of Justice Programs, US Department of Justice, and was established in 1988 to enhance the Nation's capacity to assist crime victims and to provide leadership in changing attitudes, policies, and practices to promote justice and healing for all victims of crime.
25 Beck and Shipley (1989).
26 Langan and Levin (2002).
27 Beck and Shipley (1989).
28 They were *Alaska*, *Arkansas*, California, *Colorado*, Florida, *Georgia*, *Hawaii*, *Iowa*, *Louisiana*, Maryland, Michigan, Minnesota, *Missouri*, *Nebraska*, *Nevada*, New Jersey, New York, North Carolina, *North Dakota*, Ohio, *Oklahoma*, Oregon, *Pennsylvania*, *South Carolina*, *South Dakota*, Texas, *Utah*, Virginia,

Washington, and *West Virginia* with 18 states not included in the study of prisoners released in 1994 being *italicized*. Three states included in the 2002 study but not in this study were Arizona, Delaware, and Illinois.
29 Durose, Cooper, and Snyder (2014).
30 Alper, Durose, and Markman (2018).
31 Durose et al. (2014).
32 Another factor important to keep in mind, though not controlled for the comparison of population-adjusted rates, was improvements to the national criminal history records and reporting of arrests and prosecutions (i.e., the rap sheets of prisoners released). "These improvements would have resulted in higher observed recidivism rates in 2005 than in 1994, even if the two samples had the same true recidivism rates" (Durose et al., 2014, p. 5).
33 Alper et al. (2018).
34 Langan and Levin (2002, p. 10).
35 Cullen, Jonson, and Stohr (2014, pp. 238–240). "The failure of prisons."
36 Martinson (1974).
37 Andrews (1995), Gendreau and Goggin (1996).
38 Cullen and Gendreau (2000).
39 Henggeler (1997, 1999), Henggeler, Schoenwald, Borduin, Rowland, and Cunningham (2009).
40 Cullen and Gendreau (2000).
41 Bonta and Andrews (2016).
42 Cullen (2013, p. 343).
43 Ward and Gannon (2005).
44 Hallett, Hays, Johnson, Jang, and Duwe (2017).
45 See Casey, Day, Vess, and Ward (2013, pp. 33–46).
46 Cullen and Gendreau (2000, p. 157).
47 Cullen (2013, p. 346).
48 Bushway, Piquero, Broidy, Cauffman, and Mazerolle (2001).
49 Sampson and Laub (1993, 1996).
50 Sampson and Laub (1993, 1996), see also Uggen (2000).
51 Laub and Sampson (2001), Sampson and Laub (2005).
52 Laub and Sampson (2003, p. 278).
53 For Giordano et al., cognitions and human agency are crucial for any intentional, sustained behavioral change to take place. But, from their symbolic interactionist perspective, they also suggest that an individual's cognitive shifts and agentic moves for desistance should be explained in the context of the structural and cultural forces as well as the individual's immediate social world. One's identity is "social" in that it is a result of symbolic interaction between an individual and a society, whether other people in an immediate environment or a distant context of structure and culture.
54 Giordano, Schroeder, and Cernkovich (2007, p. 1610).
55 Paternoster and Bushway (2009, p. 1105, *emphasis* in original).
56 Giordano et al. (2002).
57 Paternoster and Bushway (2009).
58 Steger, Frazier, Oishi, and Kaler (2006, p. 81).
59 Frankl (1984, p. 121).
60 Frankl (1984).
61 Costin and Vignoles (2020), Lambert et al. (2013), Routledge (2020).
62 Stillman et al. (2009).
63 Sykes (2007).
64 Goffman (1961).
65 James (2007).
66 Maruna, Wilson, and Curran (2006, p. 17).
67 Paternoster and Bushway (2009, p. 1105, *emphasis* in original).
68 Batson and Stocks (2004), Fry (2000), Martos, Thege, and Steger (2010).
69 Mascaro and Rosen (2005), Smith (2003).
70 Routledge (2020), Van Tongeren, Green, Davis, Hook, and Hulsey (2016).
71 Farrall (2005).
72 Clear, Hardyman, Stout, Lucken, and Dammer (2000).
73 Giordano et al. (2002, 2007), Paternoster and Bushway (2009).
74 Johnson (2011).
75 Giordano et al. (2002), Paternoster and Bushway (2009), Giordano et al. (2007).

76 Jang, Johnson, Hays, Hallett, and Duwe (2018b).
77 Jang, Johnson, Hays, Hallett, and Duwe (2018a).
78 Jang, Johnson, Anderson, and Booyens (2019).
79 It was "preliminary" analysis because the National Penitentiary and Prison Institute (INPEC: Instituto Nacional Penitenciario y Carcelario) had not provided data on participating inmates' sociodemographic and criminal backgrounds at the time of writing this chapter. INPEC is the Colombian central government agency responsible for the incarceration and rehabilitation of convicted criminal offenders, and administration of the penitentiary institutions in the country.
80 Giordano et al. (2002, 2007), Paternoster and Bushway (2009).
81 Jang et al. (2018a, 2018b, 2019).
82 Johnson and Jang (2020).
83 Goshe (2019).
84 Cullen and Gendreau (2000), Cullen (2013).
85 Cullen (2013).

References

Alper, M., Durose, M. R., & Markman, J. (2018). *2018 update on prisoner recidivism: A 9-year follow-up period (2005–2014)*. Washington, DC: US Department of Justice, Office of Justice Programs, Bureau of Justice Statistic.

Andrews, D. A. (1995). The psychology of criminal conduct and effective treatment. In J. McGuire (Ed.) *What works: Reducing re-offending: Guidelines from research and practice*. Chichester, UK: Wiley.

Batson, C. D., & Stocks, E. L. (2004). Religion: Its core psychological functions. In J. Greenberg, S. L. Koole & T. Pyszczynski (Eds.), *Handbook of experimental existential psychology* (pp. 141–155). New York, NY: Guilford Press.

Beck, A. J., & Shipley, B. E. (1989). *Recidivism of prisoners released in 1983*. Washington, DC:US Department of Justice, Office of Justice Programs, Bureau of Justice Statistic.

Bonta, J., & Andrews, D. A. (2016). *The psychology of criminal conduct*. London, UK: Routledge.

Bronson, J., & Carson, E. A. (2019). Prisoners in 2017. U.S. Department of Justice, Office of Justice Programs, Bureau of Justice Statistics, NCJ 252156.

Bushway, S. D., Piquero, A. R., Broidy, L. M., Cauffman, E., & Mazerolle, P. (2001). An empirical framework for studying desistance as a process. *Criminology, 39*(2), 491–515.

Casey, S., Day, A., Vess, J., & Ward, T. (2013). *Foundations of offender rehabilitation*. New York, NY: Routledge.

Catalano, R. F., & Hawkins, J. D. (1996). The social development model: A theory of antisocial behavior. In J. D. Hawkins (Ed.), *Delinquency and crime: Current theories* (pp. 149–197). New York, NY: Cambridge University Press.

Clear, T. R., Hardyman, P. L., Stout, B., Lucken, K., & Dammer, H. R. (2000). The value of religion in prison an inmate perspective. *Journal of Contemporary Criminal Justice, 16*(1), 53–74.

Costin, V., & Vignoles, V. L. (2020). Meaning is about mattering: Evaluating coherence, purpose, and existential mattering as precursors of meaning in life judgments. *Journal of Personality and Social Psychology, 118*(4), 864–884. doi:10.1037/pspp0000225; 10.1037/pspp0000225.supp (Supplemental).

Cullen, F. T. (2013). Rehabilitation: Beyond nothing works. *Crime and Justice, 42*(1), 299–376.

Cullen, F. T., & Gendreau, P. (2000). Assessing correctional rehabilitation: Policy, practice, and prospects. *Criminal Justice, 3*, 109–175.

Cullen, F. T., Jonson, C. L., & Stohr, M. K. (2014). *The American Prison: Imagining a Different Future*. Los Angeles, CA: Sage.

Durose, M. R., Cooper, A. D., & Snyder, H. N. (2014). *Recidivism of prisoners released in 30 states in 2005: Patterns from 2005 to 2010*. Washington, DC: US Department of Justice, Office of Justice Programs, Bureau of Justice Statistic.

Farrall, S. (2005). On the existential aspects of desistance from crime. *Symbolic Interaction, 28*(3), 367–386.

Farrington, D. P. (1998). Predictors, causes and correlates of male youth violence. In M. Tonry & M. H. Moore (Eds.), *Youth Violence, Crime and Justice: A Review of Research*, vol. 24. Chicago, IL: University of Chicago Press.

Frankl, V. E. (1984). *Man's search for meaning.* New York, NY: Pocket Books.

Fry, P. S. (2000). Religious involvement, spirituality and personal meaning for life: Existential predictors of psychological wellbeing in community-residing and institutional care elders. *Aging & Mental Health, 4*(4), 375–387.

Gabel, K., & Johnston, D. (eds.) (1995). *Children of incarcerated parents.* New York, NY: Lexington Books.

Gendreau, P., & Goggin, C. (1996). Principles of effective correctional programming. *Forum on Corrections Research, 8,* 38–41.

Giordano, P. C., Cernkovich, S. A., & Rudolph, J. L. (2002). Gender, crime, and desistance: Toward a theory of cognitive transformation. *American Journal of Sociology, 107*(4), 990–1064.

Giordano, P. C., Schroeder, R. D., & Cernkovich, S. A. (2007). Emotions and crime over the life course: A neo-Meadian perspective on criminal continuity and change. *American Journal of Sociology, 112*(6), 1603–1661.

Goffman, E. (1961). On the characteristics of total institutions. The inmate world. In D.R. Cressey (Ed.), *The Prison: Studies in Institutional Organization and Change* (pp. 15–67). New York, NY: Hold, Rinehart and Winston.

Goshe, S. (2019). How contemporary rehabilitation fails youth and sabotages the American juvenile justice system: A critique and call for change. *Critical Criminology,* 27, 559–573.

Hagan, J., & Dinovitzer, R. (1999). Collateral consequences of imprisonment, communities and prisoners. In M. Tonry & J. Petersilia (Eds.), *Crime and justice,* vol. 26. Chicago, IL: University of Chicago Press.

Hallett, M., Hays, J., Johnson, B., Jang, S. J., & Duwe, G. (2017). *The Angola prison seminary: Effects of faith-based ministry on identity transformation, desistance, and rehabilitation.* New York, NY: Routledge.

Henggeler, S. W. (1997). *Treating serious anti-social behavior in youth: The MST approach.* Washington, DC: US Department of Justice, Office of Justice Programs, Office of Juvenile Justice and Delinquency Prevention.

Henggeler, S. W. (1999). Multisystemic therapy: An overview of clinical procedures, outcomes, and policy implications. *Child Psychology and Psychiatry Review, 4*(1), 2–10.

Henggeler, S. W., Schoenwald, S. K., Borduin, C. M., Rowland, M. D., & Cunningham, P. B. (2009). *Multisystemic therapy for antisocial behavior in children and adolescents.* New York, NY: Guilford Press.

Henrichson C., & Delaney, R. (2012). *The price of prisons: What incarceration costs taxpayers.* Vera Institute of Justice, New York, NY.

James, W. (2007). *The varieties of religious experience: A study of human nature.* Charleston, SC: BiblioBazaar.

Jang, S. J., Johnson, B. R., Anderson, M. L., & Booyens, K. (2019). The effect of religion on mental health among prisoners in South Africa: Explanations and gender differences. *Justice Quarterly,* doi:10.1080/07418825.2019.1689286.

Jang, S. J., Johnson, B. R., Hays, J., Hallett, M., & Duwe, G. (2018a). Existential and virtuous effects of religiosity on mental health and aggressiveness among offenders. *Religions, 9*(6), 182.

Jang, S. J., Johnson, B. R., Hays, J., Hallett, M., & Duwe, G. (2018b). Religion and misconduct in "Angola" prison: Conversion, congregational participation, religiosity, and self-identities. *Justice Quarterly, 35*(3), 412–442.

Johnson, B. R. (2011). *More god, less crime: Why faith matters and how it could matter more.* Conshohocken, PA: Templeton Foundation Press.

Johnson, B. R., & Jang, S. J. (2020). Connecting in-prison programs to prisoner reentry and aftercare: A case study of Restoration Outreach of Dallas Ministries. Waco, TX: Baylor Institute for Studies of Religion.

Johnson, E., & Waldfogel, J. (2002). *Children of incarcerated parents: Cumulative risk and children's living arrangements.* JCPR Working Paper #306. Chicago: Joint Center for Poverty Research, Northwestern University/University of Chicago. Retrieved from http://www.jcpr.org/wp/wpprofile.cfm. id=364.

Johnston, D. (1995). Effects of parental incarceration. In K. Gabel and D. Johnston (Eds.), *Children of incarcerated parents.* New York, NY: Lexington Books, 59–88.

Kaeble, D., & Cowhig, M. (2018). *Correctional populations in the United States, 2016.* Ncj 251211. Washington, DC: US Department of Justice.

Krisberg, B. (2001). *The plight of children whose parents are in prison.* Oakland, CA: National Council on Crime and Delinquency, Focus.

Kyckelhahn, T. (2014). State corrections expenditures, FY 1982–2010. Washington, DC: Bureau of Justice Statistics.

Lambert, N. M., Stillman, T. F., Hicks, J. A., Kamble, S., Baumeister, R. F., & Fincham, F. D. (2013). To belong is to matter: Sense of belonging enhances meaning in life. *Personality and Social Psychology Bulletin, 39*(11), 1418–1427.

Langan, P. A., & Levin, D. J. (2002). *Recidivism of prisoners released in 1994.* Washington, DC: US Department of Justice, Office of Justice Programs, Bureau of Justice Statistic.

Laub, J. H., & Sampson, R. J. (2001). Understanding desistance from crime. *Crime and Justice: A Review of Research, 28,* 1–69.

Mahoney, E. (2019). Florida corrections secretary seeks help from lawmakers to curb prison violence. *Tampa Bay Times.* September 18. Retrieved from https://www.tampabay.com/florida-politics/buzz/2019/09/18/florida-corrections-secretary-seeks-help-from-lawmakers-to-curb-prison-violence/.

Mai, C., & Subramanian, R. (2017). The price of prisons. *Vera Institute of Justice.*

Martinson, R. (1974). What works? Questions and answers about prison reform. *The Public Interest, 35,* 22.

Martos, T., Thege, B. K., & Steger, M. F. (2010). It's not only what you hold, it's how you hold it: Dimensions of religiosity and meaning in life. *Personality and Individual Differences, 49*(8), 863–868.

Maruna, S., Wilson, L., & Curran, K. (2006). Why god is often found behind bars: Prison conversions and the crisis of self-narrative. *Research in Human Development, 3*(2&3), 161–184.

Mascaro, N., & Rosen, D. H. (2005). Existential meaning's role in the enhancement of hope and prevention of depressive symptoms. *Journal of Personality, 73*(4), 985–1014.

Miller, T. R. (1996). *Victim costs and consequences: A new look.* National Institute of Justice Research Report, NCJ-155282. Retrieved from http://www.ncjrs.org/pdffiles/victcost.pdf.

Paternoster, R., & Bushway, S. D. (2009). Desistance and the "feared self": Toward an identity theory of criminal desistance. *Journal of Criminal Law and Criminology, 99*(4), 1103–1156.

Routledge, C. (2020). Why meaning matters for freedom and flourishing. Retrieved from https://www.archbridgeinstitute.org/2020/05/28/why-meaning-matters-for-freedom-and-flourishing/.

Sack, W. A. & Seidler, J. (1978). Should children visit their parents in prison? *Law and Human Behavior, 2,* 261–266.

Sampson, R. J., & Laub, J. H. (1993). *Crime in the making: Pathways and turning points through life.* Cambridge, MA: Harvard University Press.

Sampson, R. J., & Laub, J. H. (1996). Socioeconomic achievement in the life course of disadvantaged men: Military service as a turning point, circa 1940–1965. *American Sociological Review, 61*(3), 347–367.

Sampson, R. J., & Laub, J. H. (2005). A life-course view of the development of crime. *Annals of the American Academy of Political and Social Science, 602,* 12–45.

Smith, C. (2003). *Moral, believing animals: Human personhood and culture.* New York, NY: Oxford University Press.

Steger, M. F., Frazier, P., Oishi, S., & Kaler, M. (2006). The meaning in life questionnaire: Assessing the presence of and search for meaning in life. *Journal of Counseling Psychology, 53*(1), 80–93.

Stillman, T. F., Baumeister, R. F., Lambert, N. M., Crescioni, A. W., DeWall, C. N., & Fincham, F. D. (2009). *Alone and without purpose: Life loses meaning following social exclusion.* doi: 10.1016/j.jesp.2009.03.007.

Sykes, G. M. (2007). *The society of captives: A study of a maximum security prison.* Princeton, NJ: Princeton University Press.

Turney, K. (2018). Adverse childhood experiences of incarcerated parents. *Children & Youth Services Review, 89,* 218–225.

Turney, K., & Goodsell, R. (2018). Parental incarceration and children's wellbeing. *Future of Children, 28,* 147–164.

Turney, K., & Wildeman, C. (2013). Redefining relationships: Explaining the countervailing consequences of paternal incarceration for parenting quality. *American Sociological Review, 78,* 949–979.

Uggen, C. (2000). Work as a turning point in the life course of criminals: A duration model of age, employment, and recidivism. *American Sociological Review, 65*(4), 529–546.

Van Tongeren, D. R., Green, J. D., Davis, D. E., Hook, J. N., & Hulsey, T. L. (2016). Prosociality enhances meaning in life. *The Journal of Positive Psychology, 11*(3), 225–236.

Ward, T., & Gannon, T. (2005). Rehabilitation, etiology, and self-regulation: The comprehensive good lives model of treatment for sexual offenders. *Aggression and Violent Behavior, 11*, 77–94.

Ward, T., & Maruna, S. (2007). *Rehabilitation*. New York, NY: Routledge.

Wildeman, C. (2013). Parental incarceration, child homelessness, and the invisible consequences of mass imprisonment. *Annals of the American Academy of Political and Social Science, 165*(1), 74–96.

Wildeman, C., Andersen, S. H., Lee, H., & Karlson, K. B. (2014). Parental incarceration and child mortality in Denmark. *American Journal of Public Health, 104*(3): 428–433.

2

CAN PRISONS MODEL VIRTUOUS BEHAVIOR?

There is fairly wide consensus, even among politicians, that the United States incarcerates too many people. However, claims that the United States incarcerates more people per capita than any country in the world, lack adequate documentation. For example, many of the countries the United States is compared with do not publish reliable or verifiable data that would even allow valid comparisons to be made. Being highly critical of mass incarceration in the United States, criminologists generally agree that imprisonment should be reserved to sanction only a particular type of offender, that is, to incapacitate violent, career criminals who are seemingly beyond redemption or to serve "just deserts" to those who committed truly heinous crimes.[1] A growing consensus among scholars who study prisons, moreover, is that they have become dysfunctional and counter-productive.[2]

The widespread support for less reliance on incarceration has brought together lawmakers from both sides of the political aisle to address the issue. A recent example is the First Step Act (FSA), which President Trump signed into law in December 2018 with bipartisan support despite the highly strained relationship between the Trump administration and the Democrat-controlled House. The FSA is designed to decrease the size of the federal prison population by reducing mandatory minimums, allowing eligible inmates to earn more good time credits for early release, placing certain elderly and terminally ill prisoners on home confinement, and lowering the chance of prisoners' post-release returning to prison via the assessment of prisoners' recidivism risk and criminogenic needs and a placement of prisoners in recidivism-reducing programs and productive activities to address their needs and reduce the risk.[3]

Despite widespread consensus on the problem of the overreliance on incarceration, criminologists tend to disagree on the primary goal and function of prisons. According to Cullen and his colleagues, two major positions on what prisons should be like or two models of prison emerged after the attack on rehabilitation in the 1970s.[4] One model, called "the legal prison," was the position criminologists on the left took, whereas the other, "the painful prison," was advocated by those on the right.

The Legal Prison and the Painful Prison[5]

Embracing the view that prison is a "total institution"[6] and thus *inherently* inhumane, by the early 1970s, politically progressive criminologists argued that any effort to make prison environments

DOI: 10.4324/9781003171744-2

more humane would be futile and, worse, legitimate the oxymoronic notion of a "humane prison." Progressive criminologists shifted from an optimistic view of government playing an important part role in addressing the crime problem (which they held dear just a decade earlier), to a critical view that any intervention to solve the crime problem was a disguised attempt for social control on the part of the government. Furthermore, they argued, any governmental response to crime, whether the punishment or rehabilitation of criminals, would subsequently worsen the crime problem because it stigmatized offenders. Thus, according to this politically progressive view, the goal of the criminal justice system should not be to "do good" but to "do the least harm possible," which was well illustrated by a "radical non-interventionism"—do nothing whenever possible approach—that labeling theorists advocated.[7]

Within the prison system, the main target of progressives on the left, was the discretion exercised by correctional staff and by parole boards, which was intended to provide prisoners incentives for rehabilitation. For them, however, the incentive was simply a way to control prisoners. Thus, advocating for a "justice model," progressives argued that all indeterminacy in sentencing, parole decisions, and mandatory therapy should be eliminated. They also believed that maximizing legal rights of prisoners would protect them against abuses by correctional staff and from being forced to live in the inherently inhumane environment of prison. In sum, they wished to construct a "legal prison": "an institutional community built on the principles of restraining state power and of according inmates every legal right available to them in a free society."[8]

This model of prisons was also referred to as a "citizenship model of corrections" as those who favored the legal prison model argued that once inmates could enjoy and exercise the rights of citizens, the prison would become more orderly and a better place overall. This model suggests that citizenship learned inside prison is likely to have a rehabilitative effect on prisoners by making them more responsible when they returned to the community. In other words, for those on the political left, the law was a key instrument for making changes in both prisoners and the prison itself. In fact, prison litigation made it possible to improve basic standards of living within prisons and allow prisoners to exercise legal rights including their religious rights, protecting them from "cruel and unusual" prison environments. As it turns out, success would be rather limited due to the "hands off" doctrine of conservative courts at that time, which took a minimalist approach to the legal matters involving the prison system.

What then, one might ask, was the legal prison supposed to do to help prisoners change in order that they might not reoffend and return to prison in the months or years following release? Regrettably, the answer to this question is—not much, other than ensuring prisoners' exercise of the rights of citizens. Advocates of this model suggested that prisoners' "voluntary rehabilitation" and learning of "citizenship" *might* address their criminality. In the spirit of non-interventionism, having criticized rehabilitation as coercive and ineffective, they would not argue that prisoners *should* change let alone suggest that prisons should facilitate their change. Not surprisingly, proponents of the legal prison model were perceived to be not only "weak on crime," but silent about how prisons could be used for the protection of innocent citizens.

In contrast to the legal prison perspective of "doing the least harm possible" to prisoners, some criminologists advocated for "the painful prison model" which would support the "penal harm movement."[9] The premise being it is necessary to inflict an increasing amount of pain on prisoners, in order to make their life in prison physically uncomfortable. This approach was called the policy of "penal austerity."[10] For example, in his "punishment manifesto," embracing a retributivist position, Newman made a case for corporal punishment of criminals, which he argued should be used more often than imprisonment. Moreover, this philosophy claims prisons should be reserved for punishing only the most serious and/or repeat offenders.[11] Newman thought we should envision "prisons as purgatory," where inmates necessarily suffer, but also must be given the opportunity to atone for their sinful acts to in order to save their souls.

Disagreeing with Newman on the idea of "prisons as purgatory" and causing physical pain to inmates, Logan and Gaes proposed a milder version of the painful prison.[12] They believed that prison conditions and operation should not violate the Constitutional standards of safety and decency, but, their "confinement model" based on retribution or just deserts saw imprisonment as a means of punishing criminals. Although they wanted prison to be humane, the guiding principle of their model of "punitive confinement" was retribution and just deserts. Furthermore, they viewed rehabilitation and treatment in prison as a way to foster institutional order rather than changing offenders.

While concurring with Logan and Gaes' desire to hold offenders morally responsible, Cullen, Sundt, and Wozniak were critical of their confinement model for neglecting the influence of society on the criminal choices individual offenders make and having inmates' time in prison wasted, not being used for their reformation. In addition, for Cullen et al., they were oblivious to the potential for abuse and a lack of restraint on the impulse to create a "no frills" prison. Another problem is that the painful prison is based on "the utilitarian and criminologically ill-conceived notion that exposing offenders to dreadful living conditions will deter their future wrongdoing. There is no evidence to support the view that the painful prison ... reduces reoffending."[13]

In sum, the legal and the painful prisons were proposed by criminologists on the political left and the right, respectively, after their common attack on rehabilitation in 1970s. The proponents of the legal prison argued that the primary task of prison is to ensure that inmates exercise Constitutional rights they are entitled to for their protection from inhumane treatment in prison and, possibly, a reduction of their criminality. On the other hand, based on the correctional philosophy of retribution, the advocates of the painful prison argued for a punitive approach to the treatment of inmates not only to hold them accountable for their crimes but also to have their experience of pain in prison keep them from reoffending. From a rehabilitation perspective, however, both models neglect or even avoid suggesting how we can make the most of inmates' time in prison without wasting tax dollars spent on their imprisonment. Therefore, Cullen and his colleagues proposed an alternative model, "the virtuous prison."

The Virtuous Prison

"The mission of the virtuous prison is to use offenders' time of incarceration to cultivate moral awareness and the capacity to act virtuously."[14] The virtuous prison model rejects the legal prison's claim that prison is *inherently* inhumane and thus, other than protecting their legal rights, should do little, if anything, to change or reform inmates. The virtuous prison model rejects the painful prison as its goal of causing pain to inmates makes it more difficult to rehabilitate them, and its retributive approach has little interest in crime control through offender reformation.[15] For Cullen et al., the legal and painful prisons take a minimalist approach and are unacceptable because they both squander an opportunity they could take advantage of for prisoner rehabilitation.

Cullen et al. proposed an alternative model of prison, called "the virtuous prison," which differs from these two models in approaching the treatment of inmates based on different assumptions about human nature and society in relation to criminal offending. For example, the legal prison model tends to assume that humans are essentially subject to external factors, such as surrounding environments, and their behaviors are determined by those factors, portraying offenders as victims of various criminogenic forces. To the contrary, the virtuous prison model assumes that humans are moral agents in that they choose to engage in behaviors that have moral consequences with some of them being in violation of the society's moral order including the law, particularly, criminal law.[16] In this sense, offenders are moral beings as much as non-offenders, some of whom committed crime but did not get caught, and thus morally responsible for their criminal behaviors. For this reason, inmates' accepting their responsibility for crime is an important first step toward their rehabilitation.

On the other hand, unlike the painful prison model that focuses exclusively on an individual offender's moral failing, the virtuous prison model emphasizes the importance of recognizing society's role in criminal choices offenders make because crime is not a free and autonomous choice. For Cullen et al., acknowledging how society contributes to an offender's criminal behavior and thus holds a secondary responsibility for the behavior does not weaken the idea that offenders should be held accountable for their behaviors. That is, they must not only recognize damages they caused to the commonwealth but also repair the damages, whether through an offender's apology to the victims of crime or via restitution. An offender making amends, however, is not a sufficient, though necessary, condition for restoring the broken relationship between an offender and society. Restoration also requires the victim to eventually forgive and reconcile with the offender. Additionally, in order to achieve successful community reintegration for the repentant offender. The state needs to play a role as an arbiter to help all involved parties reach the goal of restoration.

In sum, the virtuous prison is to be built on two principles, the rehabilitative ideal and restorative justice, which involves both the individual offender and the community. To achieve the correctional goal of *restorative rehabilitation* of inmates, the prison needs to create a virtuous environment, where inmates are surrounded by positive moral influences. Specifically, Cullen et al. proposed seven "prison particulars" for consideration.[17]

"*First, inmate idleness would be eliminated.*" The virtuous prison would create a productive environment, where inmates can produce something useful or serve others. Engaging in productive activity and service to others is likely to generate a sense of fulfillment among inmates as they see how their lives could be used for something positive. It would also foster a sense of meaning and purpose in life among inmates, which prior research shows tends to be positively associated with virtuous characteristics.[18]

"*Second, the activities in which inmates engage would have a restorative purpose.*" Productive activities inmates are encouraged to participate in would have a larger purpose beyond the inmate's own self-interest, such as earning money or acquiring job skills for future employment. For example, inmate wages from prison employment might be used to compensate victims with inmates writing and sending the checks to victims. In addition, inmates might participate in activities that produce something for the needy, like toys for disadvantaged children. Various types of community service inside (e.g., training dogs for the blind and holding bake sales for the needy) and outside of the prison (e.g., building or repairing a playground in a poor neighborhood) would serve the same function. From a "wounded healer" perspective, training peer mentors to help other inmates and become positive role models for them is likely to accomplish the goal of moral development among both mentors and mentees. Regardless of which activities are encouraged, they should provide opportunities to help inmates develop virtuous characteristics.

"*Third, contact with virtuous people would be encouraged.*" To the extent that the security of prison is not compromised, the virtuous prison should proactively have upstanding community people, including members of faith community, lead or participate in prison programs, mentor inmates, and spend time with inmates to encourage and challenge inmates to become virtuous.

Ideally, those community volunteers would continue to serve as mentors after inmates return to community given that aftercare is generally disconnected from in-prison ministry.[19]

"*Fourth, inmates would participate in rehabilitation programs that are based on criminological research and the principles of effective correctional intervention.*"[20] To achieve the goal of restorative rehabilitation of inmates, the virtuous prison would provide quality treatment programs that maximize the chance of inmate restoration. Therefore, the virtuous prison would distinguish between programs shown to work (e.g., cognitive-behavioral interventions) and those that do not work (e.g., boot camps), and subsequently implement only those programs found to be efficacious. Those programs might need some modification so they could give inmates the values, understanding of the world, and skills to live a productive and virtuous life.

"*Fifth, the standard of inmate living would be as high as possible.*" A low standard of living intended to inflict pain on inmates serves no purpose in the virtuous prison, which takes on the maxim that "virtue begets virtue." That is, treating inmates in a humane way and protecting their dignity as human beings is essential to encouraging them to become virtuous. Inmates are often seen as undeserving to receive social welfare "entitlements," but they might be viewed as more "deserving" if they engage in restorative activities to give back victims and the community.

"*Sixth, prison guards would be encouraged to function as 'correctional' officers.*" In the virtuous prison, guards would be professionals who deliver various types of human services. Although they would still involve the tasks of maintaining order, ensuring custody, and enforcing rules, they would also foster virtue in inmates. That is, they would have a dual function, custodial and treatment. It is not easy to balance between the two roles correctional officers are supposed to play because they might be perceived to be contradictory to each other, so they would need proper training to avoid any unnecessary tensions between the two functions. In addition, prison guards should be brought into the planning of how best to achieve the virtuous prison's central mission for their ownership.

"*Seventh, the virtuous prison would not be for all inmates.*" While Cullen et al. are confident that it would work and be effective with enough experimentation and organizational development, they are realistic enough to know that the virtuous prison would not work for certain types of inmates, like the intractably recalcitrant, violent, or mentally disturbed inmate. They call, therefore, for an experiment to determine for whom the virtuous prison would be most appropriate. While this empirical question cannot be fully addressed until an actual experiment is conducted, some support for the virtuous prison can be drawn from the current experimentation with "faith-based prison programs."

A Faith-Based Prison: The InnerChange Freedom Initiative

Although a prison that incorporates all the features proposed above has yet to be tried, Cullen et al. found the InnerChange Freedom Initiative (IFI) established by the Prison Fellowship Ministries, a Christian ministry organization for prison reform, came close to what they had in mind except for the religious component. Unlike traditional, evangelistic programs in prison that typically operate small groups that lead Bible studies or prayer meetings or large gatherings for a worship service, IFI intends to reform not only prisoners but also prison culture by creating a faith-based community within prisons. Also, unlike traditional prison ministries that depend exclusively on outside volunteers visiting prison, the IFI offered programs in prison virtually around the clock. IFI's programs are also comprehensive in that they promote adult basic education, vocational training, life skills, mentoring, and aftercare. In this respect, IFI is a faith-saturated program whose mission is to "create and maintain a prison environment that fosters respect for God's law and rights of others, and to encourage the spiritual and moral re-generation of prisoners."

IFI was officially launched in April of 1997 at the Carol Vance Unit, a 378-bed prison in Richmond, Texas.[21] The Vance Unit was selected because of its custody level (i.e., a minimum-security prison) as a pre-release facility and its proximity to the Houston area, the focus of aftercare resources and volunteer recruitment. Only offenders from Houston or surrounding counties were eligible for voluntary participation in the program. More than a half of beds in the Vance Unit, to be precise, 200 beds were reserved for IFI.

Anchored in Biblical teaching, life-skill education, and group accountability, IFI established a three-phase program involving prisoners in 16–24 months of in-prison programs and 6–12 months of aftercare while on parole. Phase I, which lasts about 12 months, focuses on rebuilding the inmate's spiritual and moral foundation that the rest of the program is based on as well as providing educational and survival skills. Six months into Phase I, IFI participants are matched with a mentor, who meets with a participating inmate one-on-one for a minimum of two hours per week. Phase II, which lasts 6–12 months, continues the educational, work, and support group aspect of the program. To test the inmate's value system in real-life settings, IFI participants are allowed to perform community service work during the day at off-site location (e.g., Habitat for Humanity). During this phase, participants will begin to take on leadership roles within the program. Phase III, which lasts 6–12 months, is the reentry component of IFI and is designed to help assimilate the inmate back into the community through productive and supportive relationships with family, local churches, and the workplace.

For Cullen et al., except for the religious aspect, the IFI created a prison that incorporated key features of their virtuous prison. For example, IFI largely embraces the virtuous prison's two principles of moral restoration and rehabilitation. It also has inmates participate in productive activities, not only eliminating inmate idleness but also using their time of incarceration to cultivate moral awareness and the capacity to act virtuously. Through mentoring, inmates have regular contacts with religiously inspired, virtuous people who make positive impact on their moral restoration. In addition, IFI creates a faith-based community of strong bonds and love, where inmates are treated with dignity, and rejects the painful prison's goal to inflict pain on inmates. Finally, IFI's aftercare program intends to achieve the goal of reintegrating offenders into community, particularly, a supportive religious community.

Did IFI work? Previous studies evaluating the program tend to answer this question in the affirmative. For example, Johnson and Larson examined differences in two-year post-release recidivism (arrest and incarceration) rates between the total sample of IFI participants and three comparison groups: "matched," "screened," and "volunteered" groups.[22] The IFI participants were 177 prisoners who met the selection criteria, entered the program between April 1997 and January of 1999, and were released from prison prior to September 1, 2000. The matched group included 1,754 prisoners selected from the records of inmates released during the evaluation period that met program selection criteria but did not enter the program, whereas the screened group consisted of 1,083 prisoners selected from the records of inmates released during the evaluation period that met program selection criteria and were screened as eligible but did not volunteer or were not selected for program participation. Finally, the volunteered group refers to 560 prisoners selected from the records of inmates released during the evaluation period that actually volunteered for the IFI program, but did not participate either because they did not have a minimum-out custody classification, their remaining sentence was not between the required length (18–30 months) to be considered, or they were not planning to return to the Houston area following release.

The comparison groups were generally similar to IFI participants in terms of race (African-American, Hispanic, and Anglo), age (35 or younger and older than 35), offense type (violent, property, and drug), and risk score (high, medium, and low). However, since prisoners could not be randomly assigned to these groups as originally planned, results should be interpreted with potential selection bias in mind. For example, since the program was "Christ-centered," Christian prisoners might have gotten preferential treatment in the selection process, although Johnson and Larson found little evidence of such bias based on their observation of the selection process and interviews with hundreds of prisoners eventually selected for the program. Similarly, most religiously committed prisoners might have volunteered for IFI, and, as a result, positive findings about the IFI participants might have been due to their preexisting motivation or determination for change rather than the program per se. Although this concern was reasonable, interviews with correctional officers, correctional administrators, and prison chaplains indicated that volunteering of prisoners who simply tried to "con" the system for an early release was also likely that the direction of selection bias was difficult to predict.

Cross-tabulation analysis initially revealed non-significant difference in the two-year post-release arrest rate between IFI participants (36.2%) and the three comparison groups—matched (35.0%), screened (34.9%), and volunteered groups (29.3%), and difference in reincarceration rate was not significant, either (24.3% vs. 20.3%, 22.3%, and 19.1%, respectively). However, when 75 IFI graduates (who completed all three phases of the program) were separated from 102 IFI non-completers, the former were found to show significantly lower rates of post-release arrest (17.3%) and reincarceration (8.0%) than the latter (50.0% and 36.3%, respectively) as well as the three comparisons groups. In sum, it was the *completion* of program that made a difference in recidivism, not program participation.

Another research evaluating IFI was conducted by Duwe and King for a reentry program that was implemented at the Minnesota Correctional Facility-Lino Lakes, beginning in 2002.[23] The program was an improved version of what was launched at the Carol Vance Unit in Texas because it augmented some of the biblical instruction with values-based programming that specifically addressed the criminogenic needs of program participants for evidence-based intervention.[24] Specifically, the researchers examined differences in recidivism between IFI participants and non-participants, released from Minnesota prisons between August 2003 and December 2009. Recidivism was measured by rearrest, reconviction, reincarceration for a new sentence, and revocation for a technical violation with the first three outcomes measuring new criminal offenses. Recidivism data were collected on offenders through December 31, 2010 so those included in their study could have at least the follow-up period of one year.

It was found that 421 of 18,883 male inmates released between August 2003 and December 2009 had participated in IFI, whereas the remaining 18,462 had not participated. Since it was imperative to control for recidivism risk in matching non-participants with IFI participants, those who had no risk assessment data were excluded, leaving 366 IFI participants and 13,188 non-participants eligible for matching. So, based on propensity scores calculated using 27 sociodemographic (i.e., age at release, race—being non-white, and religious affiliation) and justice system-related variables (e.g., prior convictions, offense type, length of stay, etc.), 366 non-participants were matched with the 366 participants for a total sample of 732 inmates.

As expected, recidivism rates were lower among IFI participants than non-participants in all recidivism outcomes: rearrest (42.1% vs. 51.1%), reconviction (25.4% vs. 34.2%), reincarceration (8.7% vs. 13.1%), and, to a lesser extent, revocation (33.1% vs. 36.3%). Among the participants, inmates who completed the in-prison portion of the program ($n = 212$) showed lower recidivism rates than those who dropped out ($n = 154$): rearrest (33.0% vs. 54.5%), reconviction (17.9%

vs. 35.7%), reincarceration (2.4% vs. 17.5%), and revocation (23.6% vs. 46.1%). In addition, IFI participants who had mentoring in both prison and community tended to show lower recidivism than those who had mentoring only in prison as well as those who had no mentoring: rearrest (29.8% vs. 50.0% and 48.7%), reconviction (14.5% vs. 38.1% and 30.1%), reincarceration (0.8% vs. 7.1% and 14.5%), and revocation (19.1% vs. 33.3% and 42.5%).

Multivariate analysis (using a Cox regression model) showed that participation in IFI significantly reduced the hazard ratio for all the three recidivism rates that measured new criminal offenses (specifically, by 26% for rearrest, 35% for reconvictions, and 40% for reincarcerations), though not for the rate of technical violation revocation. Furthermore, the significant impact of IFI on recidivism was observed only among participants who had mentoring in both prison and community, which confirmed the importance of continued mentoring before and after release from prison as found in Johnson and Larson's study.

In sum, both studies that evaluated IFI provided positive evidence, indicating that the virtuous prison is not an unrealistic idea. Making a separate community within prison by setting aside a number of beds for the program participants was necessary for creating a virtuous milieu that surrounds offenders with positive moral influences. IFI's mission "to encourage the spiritual and moral regeneration of prisoners" is consistent with the virtuous prison's principle of moral restoration, and its conscious effort to incorporate programs that empirical research found effective was essential to achieve the goal of inmate rehabilitation. The finding that mentoring in prison and community was crucial to IFI reducing recidivism illustrates the importance of having inmates regularly contact with virtuous people. Although it is not a necessary condition for the virtuous prison, religion would make it easier to build one because religious community is generally willing to provide financial and human resources (i.e., volunteers including mentors) for prisoner reform. In addition, religion promotes virtues and teaches living virtuously. Thus, religion-promoted virtues among IFI participants are likely to lower their recidivism.

Religion, Virtue, and Crime

Different religious traditions promote virtue, a trait of "persisting excellence in being for the good" or "excellence of moral character,"[25] such as self-control, forgiveness, gratitude, and compassion. For example, forgiveness is central to five world religions.[26] In Judaism, God Himself is forgiving, so His followers must be forgiving as well, as the Torah demands (e.g., Exodus 34:6). Not only God's forgiveness but also human forgiveness occupies a central place in Judaism. Similarly, God's forgiveness of human sins, offered through Jesus Christ who asked His Father to forgive his crucifiers, enables and inspires Christians to forgive. Consequently, forgiveness is at the core of Christian tradition. In Islam, the Qur'an (e.g., 3:133–136 and 7:199–200) and Hadith provide the theological basis of forgiveness, which is important for happiness and good relations with people in this world as well as one's afterlife. Being a nontheistic religion, Buddhism has no "theological" basis of forgiveness but promotes it indirectly by teaching against resentment (the opposite of forgiveness) that causes suffering. Finally, despite a number of different traditions and viewpoints found in Hinduism, many examples of divine forgiveness are found in Hindu sacred texts, so forgiveness is considered to be important in the Hindu tradition.

Gratitude is also a virtue in many religions, which encourage their adherents to be grateful toward God and others.[27] In Judaism, gratitude is an essential element of worship. For example, the prayer during Passover (*dayenu*) and the prayer during Sabbath (*Nishmat*) are prayers of thanksgiving. The Hebrew Scriptures, particularly, the Psalms are full of gratitude to God (e.g., Psalm 136). Thanksgiving for everything in Judaism is appropriate because all things came from God, whether good or bad. Judaism also emphasizes gratefulness toward others. In Christianity, gratitude to God is a central virtue because He, the Creator and Sustainer, is the source of life and all good gifts. Christians gives thanks to God for Jesus Christ, the Savior. Christians are called to pray to God with thanksgiving even when they are anxious about something (Philippians 4:6). In Islam, the Qur'an emphasizes the importance of gratitude to Allah for blessings (e.g., Sura 14:7, "If you are grateful, I will give you more."). Two "pillars" of Islam, the daily prayers and fasting during the month of Ramadan, are to express gratitude, praising Allah for life and mercy. Buddhism also promotes gratitude. For example, Theravada Buddhist narratives include highly grateful exemplars for others to follow and stories of great sacrifices by the Buddha and other bodhisattvas, which instill gratitude toward them. Gratitude is a highly prized virtue in Hindu as well as Jewish, Christian, Muslim, and Buddhist traditions.[28]

Compassion is also an important virtue in the world's major religions.[29] In Judaism, compassion is one of the characteristics of the Holy One: "… just as God is compassionate, you too must be compassionate" (Psalms 145:17).[30] In Christianity, Jesus commanded his followers to love one another as themselves and to be compassionate to others in need, which is the lesson in the parable of Good Samaritan (Luke 10:25–37). Islam's emphasis on compassion is well illustrated by one of the five pillars of Islam, Zakat, a religious duty for all Muslims to donate a certain portion of wealth each year to charitable causes. In Buddhism, compassion and forbearance are considered "perfections" (*paramitas*), moral qualities to be cultivated to a maximum degree. The Hindu concept of *karma*, the law of cause and effect, is developed by compassionate caring for the poor and seeking the good for others, whereas the concept of *dharma*, living according to a cosmic law that underlies right behavior and social order, emphasizes doing good to others.

Since all major religions place a high value on virtues, it makes sense to assume that an individual's involvement in religion is expected to increase personal virtue. There are several ways in which religion contributes to the development of virtue. First, religion not only emphasizes but also *sanctifies* virtue, teaching adherents to adopt and practice divine-like qualities.[31] In theistic religions, for example, forgiveness is a way to imitate God who forgives, carry out God's plan beyond self-pity and resentment, and enhance one's relationship with God (e.g., Matthew 6:14, "For if you forgive other people when they sin against you, your heavenly Father will also forgive you."; the Qur'an 64:14, "But if you pardon [your spouses' and children's faults], and forbear, and forgive—then, behold, Allah is Forgiving, Merciful."), and it is a way to become divinity or reach nirvana in non-theistic religions.

Second, religion provides adherents with a spiritual or self-transcendent narrative, in which virtue (e.g., self-sacrifice or forgiveness) has meaning even when it goes against human instincts (e.g., self-preservation) or counteract a natural tendency (e.g., vengefulness). While spiritual transcendence—the "capacity of individuals to stand outside of their immediate sense of time and place to view life from a larger more objective perspective"[32]—is not unique to religion and found in various secular venues as well (e.g., patriotism and secular humanism), religion provides the contexts (religious communities), where narratives and orientation toward the divine or supernatural are easily fostered.[33] Thus, the transcendent narrative and identity motivates an individual to strive for the development of virtue as it has an obvious spiritual and moral significance.

Third, religious communities stimulate virtue development as they collectively engage in practices (e.g., worship and prayer/meditation) that promote the connection between the transcendent narrative and virtuous behavior. For example, it was found that when people prayed for relationship partners or friends, the transcendent element of prayer (i.e., activating transcendent identity) was essential to build the virtue of forgiveness.[34] Religion also provides role models of virtuous individuals, opportunities to serve and lead, which reinforces the development of virtue, and emotional resources beyond the self that are potentially fertile ground for virtue development.[35] In addition, religion generates a conviction that one's behavior is being monitored by an omniscient deity, who administers rewards and punishments, and co-religionists, who provide and withhold social support, depending on how an individual behaves. It also requires self-discipline to be regularly involved in public and private religious rituals and practice. These mechanisms explain how religion promotes virtue, such as self-control.[36]

These explanations of how religion promotes virtue and why religious involvement contributes to virtue development have been offered by scholars, especially those within the positive psychology movement, as well as other social scientists interested in religion, personality, and emotions. Criminologists, on the other hand, have largely overlooked the concept of virtue as a key to explaining crime, particularly, the religion-crime relationship despite their increasing research on the religious influence on crime.[37] An exception is Gottfredson and Hirschi's "general theory" of crime, which explains crime as an outcome of a lack of virtue, self-control, coupled with criminal opportunity.[38] According to this theory, self-control decreases crime because criminal acts are inconsistent with people with high self-control tend to do or be like.

Specifically, they tend to: (1) defer gratification (vs. seeking immediate gratification of desires), (2) have diligence, tenancy, or persistence in a course of action (vs. seeking easy or simple gratification of desires), (3) be cautious, cognitive, and verbal (vs. being adventuresome, active, and physical, thereby engaging in exciting, risky, or thrilling acts), (4) commit themselves to long-term benefits (vs. seeking quick or instant benefits), (5) possess or value cognitive skills or planning (vs. lacking manual skills that require training or apprenticeship), and (6) care about the pain or loss of others (vs. being self-centered, indifferent, or insensitive to the suffering and needs of others). Therefore, people with high self-control are less likely to commit crime or use drugs, whether licit or illicit, than those with low self-control. Prior research provides empirical evidence for Gottfredson and Hirschi's low self-control theory, except for their argument that an individual's level of self-control is fully established prior to adolescence (before the age of 10) and not malleable after childhood.[39]

Like self-control, other virtues are likely to be inversely related to criminal acts as they are incompatible with the nature of those acts. For example, while there is no agreed-upon definition of forgiveness, one definition relevant to the explanation of crime is "a willingness to abandon one's right to resentment, negative judgment, and indifferent behavior toward one who unjustly hurt us, while fostering the undeserved qualities of compassion, generosity, and even love toward him or her."[40] Similarly, essential to forgiving is reductions in avoidance and revenge motivations.[41] In other words, forgiveness refers to "*intraindividual, prosocial change toward a perceived transgressor that is situated with a specific interpersonal context.*"[42]

Criminological theory most relevant to the concept of forgiveness is general strain theory, which conceptualizes crime as behavioral coping of strain, which is defined as "*events or conditions that are disliked by individuals,*"[43] and has three major types: (1) the failure to achieve positively valued goals, (2) the removal of positively valued stimuli from the individual, and (3) the presentation of negative stimuli.[44] Specifically, strain (e.g., being assaulted on the street or bullied at school) generates negative emotional states (e.g., anger and frustration), which, in turn, motivate the victim to commit crime and delinquency (e.g., physically hurt the victimizer or bully) to cope with the strain and negative emotions (e.g., getting even or removing the source of strain). That is, crime is an antisocial method of coping in response to strain and its resultant negative emotions. Forgiveness is a coping method, too, though a prosocial method of coping. It is also a religious method of coping because practically all religious traditions encourage their adherents to forgive to return good for evil, providing models, methods, and resources for forgiving.[45] If one forgives a wrongdoer instead of revenging him or her, crime as a vengeful act would be unlikely even when the forgiveness would not have the victim of wrongdoing go an extra mile to love the wrongdoer. Forgiveness, which restores broken relationships with other people, would not lead the forgiver to commit crime against them, which "results in pain or discomfort for the [other people]."[46]

Compassion can be defined as "being moved by the suffering of others *and* having the desire to alleviate that suffering."[47] It is also defined as "an attitude toward all people that involves feelings and cognitions that are focused on caring and concern *coupled with* a proclivity toward supporting, helping, and understanding the plight of those who are in need."[48] That is, whether universal or tribal, compassion consists of two related virtues, empathy, and altruism.[49] Either constituent virtue of compassion is antithetical to crime, which is a product of being "self-centered, indifferent, or insensitive to the suffering and needs of others"[50] and taking advantage of other people with a malicious intent. Thus, individuals with high levels of compassion are less likely to commit crime than those with low levels of compassion.

Gratitude has been conceptualized as an emotion, an attitude, a habit, a personality trait, and a coping response as well as a virtue. As a result, gratitude has been defined in various ways. For example, it is defined as "a positive emotional reaction to the receipt of a benefit that is perceived to have resulted from the good intentions of another."[51] Gratitude is an interpersonal virtue but could be a response to receiving a gift from an impersonal benefactor (e.g., a moment of peaceful bless evoked by natural beauty).[52] Gratitude as an affective trait is defined as "a generalized tendency to recognize and respond with grateful emotion to the roles of other people's benevolence in the positive experiences and outcomes that one obtains."[53] To define gratitude as a virtue, Roberts writes: to experience gratitude is to "gladly construe some person as a giver of some benefice (gift) to oneself, and thus gladly to construe oneself as a recipient of some benefice from a benefactor, and thus as a kind of debtor."[54] The gift is *undeserved merit*. Thus, the most essential feature of gratitude as a virtue is that it is a response to perceived benevolence and a sense of being indebtedness.

Gratitude motivates people to behave in a prosocial manner after receiving benefits intended for them as it entails thanking one's benefactor and generating a fitting and appropriate response, including altruistic action. For example, gratitude to God is likely to lead individuals to engage in virtuous acts as a proper response because the Benefactor commands them to do. Gratitude may motivate prosocial behavior by influencing psychological states that support generosity. For instance, a study found that individuals who felt grateful toward someone tended to trust other people more than those who felt angry or guilty toward someone.[55] In sum, individuals with the disposition to gratitude are more likely to engage in prosocial behavior and thus less likely to commit crime than those without such disposition.

Prior Research

Previous studies on the relationships between religiosity and self-control tend to provide empirical evidence that religion is likely to promote the virtue.[56] Specifically, intrinsic religiosity is positively associated with individual differences in self-control, although extrinsic religiosity is either inversely related or unrelated to self-control. Those studies, mostly cross-sectional, also report that an individual's religious upbringing or background is positively associated with self-control. For example, it was found that religious parents and families tend to raise children with higher levels of self-control compared to their non-religious counterparts. Consistent with these findings, longitudinal studies show that religiosity was related to an increase in personality traits related to self-control, Agreeableness (which reflects the ability to control oneself out of concern for the feelings and desires of others) and Conscientiousness (a trait that subsumes self-control). Furthermore, they indicated that the causal relationship between religiosity and self-control was likely to be reciprocal over time.

Some criminologists have examined whether self-control mediates the effect of religion on crime and drug use. Analyzing the first two waves of data from a nationally representative sample of adolescents, one study found not only a positive relationship between religiosity and self-control (i.e., the higher the religiosity, the higher the self-control) but also a partial mediation of self-control between religiosity and drug use (drinking and marijuana use). Based on survey data from a random sample of adult residents in a Southwestern city, another study reported that religiosity was inversely related to the self-reported probability of committing offenses (assault, illegal gambling, DUI, petty theft, and tax evasion). When self-control was added to the model, the inverse relationship was found to reduce in size, while remaining significant, which indicated self-control's partial mediation of the relationship.[57] Unlike these studies that estimated relationships among between-individual differences in religiosity, self-control, and crime/drug use using data from a sample of a general population, one longitudinal study examined the relationships in terms of within-individual differences among juvenile offenders.[58] It found first that a short-term, within-individual increase in religiosity predicted a decrease in future criminal behavior and then that the inverse relationship was partly attributable to an increase in self-control, the mediator. It was also observed that the reversed relationship between religiosity and self-control was not significant, implying that the relationship was not reciprocal, unlike what was found in psychological studies above.[59]

Prior research has also found religiosity to be positively related to people's perceived importance of (or positive attitudes toward) forgiveness, self-reported dispositions to forgive, and willingness to forgive in a hypothetical situation, though not significantly or, at best, weakly related to transgression-specific forgiveness.[60] In other words, religious people appear convinced or believe that they *should be* forgiving people but are not necessarily more forgiving than their non-religious peers if it is measured by self-reports of people's forgiveness of specific offenders for specific transgression (e.g., self-reported forgiveness for one's spouse for a particular transgression).[61]

A meta-analysis of empirical studies on religion/spirituality (R/S) and forgiveness found 64 independent samples reporting an effect size (Pearson product-moment correlation) of the relationship between R/S and trait forgivingness, 50 for R/S and state forgiveness, and 23 for R/S and self-forgiveness.[62] The analysis revealed that the overall effect sizes between R/S and forgiveness were positive as expected: that is, the higher the R/S, the higher the chance of forgiveness. Specifically, the effect size for R/S and trait forgiveness was .29 (95% CI [.26, .32]), and that for R/S and state forgiveness was .15 (95% CI [.10, .19]). The effect size between R/S and self-forgiveness was .12 (95% CI [.06, .19]). These findings show that the relationship between R/S and trait forgiveness (which measures forgiveness as a virtue), though moderate in size, tended to be larger than that between R/S and situational, state forgiveness.

Previous studies tend to show a positive association between religiosity and compassion although there is some evidence that it might be circumscribed. For example, experimental studies of college students revealed that intrinsic religiosity was positively related to compassion, measured in terms of behavioral intention to help others in need, when those in need were in-group, but not out-group, members.[63] In other words, compassion observed among religious people seems to be tribal compassion rather than universal compassion.

Some researchers have examined whether compassion partly mediates relationships between religiosity and subjective well-being or aggression. Based on data from samples of college students and community residents, one study found intrinsic religiosity was inversely related to depressive symptoms and perceived stress but positively to satisfaction with social support (perceived to be available), marital adjustment, and marital commitment.[64] When compassionate attitude and compassionate behavior were controlled for, the observed relationships became not significant or reduced in size, remaining significant. This finding provides evidence that compassion, at least, partly explains the religious influence on emotional and relational health. Similarly, another study of a national sample of adults in the United States found that religious individuals (who reported frequent attendance at worship services and commitment to faith) are more likely to be compassionate, providing support to others, and thus happier than their less or not religious counterparts.[65] A longitudinal study of religiousness and aggression among adolescents showed that an inverse relationship between religiousness (the extent to which adolescents followed their religious values, beliefs, and practices) and aggression (direct and indirect) was partly mediated by compassion (the extent to which people feel caring and concern for others and a motivation to help others in need).

An individual's involvement in religion has also been found to be positively related to gratitude.[66] For example, a study of a national sample of older adults (65 or older) in the United States found that frequent church attendance tended to increase a sense of gratitude over time because church attendance was likely to enhance their perception of "God-mediated control" (e.g., "I rely on God to help me control my life.").[67] Based on data from a national sample of American adolescents and young adults, another study examined the relationship between religiosity and gratitude, using various measures of religiosity: participation in organized religious activities (e.g., attending religious services and religious education), private devotion (praying and reading the religious scriptures alone), religious salience (perceived importance of religion and making a decision to live for God), "religious efficacy" (experiencing answered prayers and a miracle from God), otherworldly beliefs (e.g., judgment day, the afterlife, etc.), and religious friends.[68] These measures of religiosity were all positively related to general feelings of gratitude when they were examined individually. When they were analyzed simultaneously, two of them remained significant in relation to gratitude: religious salience and religious friends. One study found the relationship between religiosity and gratitude to God was mediated partly by other religious virtues, like humility and compassion.[69]

Gratitude is likely to mediate the relationship between religiosity and psychological and behavioral consequences of gratitude, such as subjective well-being and prosocial behavior. For example, previous studies show that people who feel grateful for a benefit they received are more likely to engage in prosocial behaviors toward not only the benefactor but also a third party because of gratitude's moral motive function.[70] This would help explain why religiosity contributes to prosocial behaviors, like helping others. In the same vein, gratitude is unlikely to lead to deviant and criminal acts against other people as well as the benefactor. Thus, gratitude is expected to mediate the effect of religiosity on crime and drug use, though the mediation has not been examined yet.

In sum, prior research provides evidence of religion promoting virtues, empirically demonstrating that an individual's involvement in religion tends to be positively related to virtues, like self-control, forgiveness, compassion, and gratitude. A small number of longitudinal studies show that religiosity has causal effect on virtues, while findings about the reversed causal effect are mixed. Psychologists and health researchers have examined not only the relationship between virtues and their health, mental and physical, and prosocial behavioral outcomes but also the mediation of virtues between religiosity and those outcomes. However, criminologists have paid little attention to the concept of virtue, except for self-control à la low self-control, to explain crime and delinquency. For example, we do not know if the well-established inverse relationship between religiosity and crime is in part attributable to virtues promoted by religion with the exception of criminological research on religion and self-control. To address this issue, we recently conducted research based on survey data collected from prisoners in the United States and a non-US country, South Africa.

The "Virtuous" Effect of Religion on Prisoners

First, we analyzed cross-sectional data from an anonymous survey with a random sample of 163 male inmates housed at three maximum-security prisons in Texas to test first whether individual religiosity was inversely related to negative emotions and aggressiveness among those inmates and then whether the inverse relationship was mediated by religion-associated virtues.[71] Estimated structural equation models showed that inmates who not only frequently attended religious services, prayed alone, and read a sacred text in private but also perceived closeness to God and importance of religion tended to report lower levels of state depression and anxiety than those who reported relatively low scores on those indicators of religiosity. Religious inmates were also less likely to say that they would get into an argument with another inmate who took his seat while taking a restroom break during an NFL game than their less or not religious counterparts.

More importantly, mediation analysis revealed that religiosity was positively related to compassion, forgiveness, gratitude to other people, and gratitude to God, which were, in turn, inversely associated with negative emotional states and intended aggression, though not all of the indirect effects of religiosity via virtue were statistically significant. This result provides some evidence of religion's "virtuous" effect on emotional well-being and behaviors among inmates. That is, religious prisoners were likely to report higher scores on virtues, thereby reporting a lower risk of interpersonal aggression as well as better mental health, compared to less or not religious peers. This finding implies that the virtuous effect of religion is likely to reduce prison misconduct, which is a function of inmate's criminality and negative emotions.

Second, the virtuous effect of religiosity (which was measured by the same five indicators of religious involvement that were used in our study of Texas prisons) was tested again in relation to negative emotions, not only state depression and anxiety but also state anger and frustration, using data from prisoners in South Africa.[72] For virtue, we examined self-control as well as forgiveness and gratitude. Consistent with findings from the study of prisoners in Texas, inmate religiosity was positively associated with all three measures of virtue, while only self-control was significantly related to negative emotional states in the expected (i.e., negative) direction. The indirect effect of religiosity on negative emotions via self-control was found statistically significant. The findings provided evidence that religion promotes virtue, which tends to explain the salutary effect of religion on mental health among prisoners. Supplemental analysis revealed that the virtuous effect of religiosity applied to not only both outer-directed (i.e., anger and frustration) and inner-directed negative emotions (feelings of depression and anxiety) but also males and females.

To advance this line of inquiry, we conducted a preliminary analysis of panel data from samples of prisoners in Colombia (South America) and South Africa. The data were collected to evaluate an international faith-based prison program, called "The Prisoner's Journey (TPJ)," which was described in Chapter 1.[73] The combined sample of 861 prisoners (691 males and 170 females) consisted of 424 inmates (all male) housed at two prisons in Colombia and 437 inmates (267 males and 170 females) at five correctional centers in South Africa.

A pretest survey was administered to 524 inmates (401 males and 123 females) in the treatment group and 337 inmates (290 males and 47 females) in the control group before the treatment group inmates began to participate in TPJ. Almost 60% (58.8%, 506) of the total sample (i.e., 861)—53.2% (279) of the treatment group inmates and 67.4% (227) of the control group inmates—participated in the posttest, conducted after they completed the eight-session program, with 60.1% (255) of the Colombian inmates and 57.4% (251) of the South African inmates completing the survey. The average interval between the surveys was 130.69 days (median = 118 days) with the standard deviation of 54.85 days. That is, although the TPJ was designed to be completed over an eight-week period, covering one session per week, the posttest was conducted about four months after the pretest was administered due to various interruptions and delays, such as lockdown or sudden cancellation of space reserved for the program.[74]

The main purpose of this analysis was to replicate the above two studies on the virtuous effect of religion on emotional well-being and aggressiveness among prison inmates, using longitudinal data that allow *causal* interpretation of estimated relationships. Specifically, we hypothesized that an *increase* in religiosity leads to an *increase* in virtue, which, in turn, results in a *decrease* in negative emotions and aggression. We employed practically the same items as used in the two previous studies to measure religiosity, virtues (forgiveness, gratitude, and self-control), negative emotional states (anger, frustration, depression, and anxiety), and a likelihood of aggressive behavior (using the vignette method).

To test the hypothesis, we examined (1) whether the key exogenous variable, inmate's participation in the faith-based program, TPJ, increased the inmate's religiosity between the pretest and posttest, (2) whether the increase in religiosity was positively associated with an increase in forgiveness, gratitude, and self-control, and (3) whether the increase in virtue was significantly related to a decrease in negative emotional states and intended aggression. To examine these relationships among changes, we estimated associations among religiosity, virtues, negative emotions, and intended aggression observed at the posttest, controlling for those variables measured at the pretest along with survey interval and gender (being male). Also controlled for in the model were inmate's experience of "spiritual transformation, like being 'born again' ... or religious conversion" and participation in prison programs other than TPJ. Missing data were treated using the method of full-information maximum likelihood (FIML), which tends to produce unbiased estimates, like multiple imputation.[75]

Table 2.1 summarizes results from estimating a manifest-variable structural equation model, presenting standardized coefficients and correlations among endogenous variables (shown in boxes). First, as expected, we found participation in TPJ increased religiosity (.128): that is, inmates who completed TPJ reported an increase in religious involvement after the completion compared to before the participation. Second, the change in religiosity observed between the pretest and posttest was found to be positively related to changes in all three measures of virtue: that is, as hypothesized, treatment group inmates whose religiosity increased between the surveys tended to report increased levels of forgiveness (.341), gratitude (.296), and self-control at the posttest (.209). Third, the increases in gratitude and self-control were related to a decrease in negative emotional states (−.091 and −.387, respectively), whereas the increases in forgiveness and self-control were associated with a reduction in the likelihood of aggressive behavior in an annoying situation (−.192 and −.181).[76] Finally, the indirect effect of participation in TPJ on forgiveness, gratitude, and self-control via religiosity were all significant (.044, .038, and .027, respectively). The program participation also decreased negative emotional states and intended aggression by increasing self-control either directly (−.055 and −.026) or indirectly via religiosity (−.010 and −.055), whereas it lowered the probability of aggression by increasing forgiveness through religiosity (−.088). In addition, religiosity was found to decrease negative emotional states by increasing self-control (−.081) and intended aggression by increasing self-control (−.038) and forgiveness (−.065).

In sum, overall results are consistent with the previous findings about the virtuous effect of religiosity on emotional well-being and aggressiveness among prison inmates: that is, religious

TABLE 2.1 Virtuous Effects of Participation in The Prisoner's Journey (TPJ) on Negative Emotions and Intended Aggression among Prisoners in Colombia and South Africa (n = 861; 691 males and 170 females)

	Religiosity T2	Spiritual Transform. T2	Other Programs T2	Forgiveness T2	Gratitude T2	Self-control T2	Negative Emotions T2	Intended Aggression T2
Survey interval (in days)	.108	.075	-.125	.016	-.146	.259*	.040	.097
Male	-.051	-.056	.046	-.135*	-.114	-.078	-.016	.126*
Forgiveness T1	-.004	.020	.061	.342*	-.011	.039	.045	.061
Gratitude T1	.064	.107	.024	.054	.310*	-.006	.023	-.049
Self-control T1	.063	.033	.047	.015	.019	.401*	-.018	-.060
Religiosity T1	.521*	.113*	-.029	-.099	-.111*	-.085	.061	.018
Spiritual transformation T1	.118*	.346*	-.018	-.009	-.019	-.095	-.047	-.005
Other programs T1	.077	.004	.344*	-.019	-.017	.056	-.078	-.019
Negative emotions T1	.005	.068	-.062	-.004	-.047	-.108*	.258*	.002
Intended aggression T1	-.080	.019	.030	-.041	.028	-.090	.055	.248*
Colombia	.161	-.014	-.122	-.047	.069	.176	-.049	.032
Participation in TPJ	.128*	.107	-.104	.019	-.072	.141*	-.026	.057
Religiosity T2				.341*	.296*	.209*	-.020	-.044
Spiritual transformation T2	.208*			.027	-.013	-.012	.035	-.005
Other programs T2	.005	.058		.056	.089	-.103*	-.019	.032
Forgiveness T2							-.065	-.192*
Gratitude T2				.200*			-.091+	.123*
Self-control T2				.059	.004		-.387*	-.181*
Negative emotions T2								
Intended aggression T2							.072	
R-square	.402	.142	.226	.318	.245	.296	.342	.228
Indirect effects								
TPJ → Religiosity T2 →				.044*	.038+	.027*		
TPJ → Self-control T2 →							-.055*	-.026*
TPJ → Religiosity T2 → Self-control T2 →							-.010*	-.005*
TPJ → Religiosity T2 → Forgiveness T2 →								-.008*
Religiosity T2 → Self-control T2							-.081*	-.038*
Religiosity T2 → Gratitude T2 →								.036*
Religiosity T2 → Forgiveness T2 →								-.065*

Note. Standardized coefficients are presented.
+ $p < .05$ (one-tailed test), * $p < .05$ (two-tailed test).

involvement is likely to promote personal virtues, which are, in turn, likely to decrease negative emotional states and aggressiveness among inmates, which tend to affect their misconduct in prison.[77] Furthermore, based on longitudinal data, the results provide evidence that the virtuous effect is likely to be causal rather than simply correlational.

Conclusion

Cullen and his colleagues' proposed model of virtuous prison might have come as an outrageous idea if you do not consider offenders who committed crime serious enough to be incarcerated as "moral beings" as they are assumed to be qualitatively different from non-offenders in the general population. However, if you think of crime as a moral failure, that is, an outcome of an individual's wrong choices, the idea is not necessarily unusual but rather makes sense. Immoral choices are due in part to the individual's lack of personal virtues, while it is also affected by other criminogenic factors, whether interpersonal, situational, or structural. For example, individuals with low self-control are more likely to commit crime for immediate gratification of desires than those with high self-control who tend to defer gratification. When someone hurt physically or mentally, people who have a disposition to be resentful are more likely to retaliate, repaying crime with crime, than those who are forgiving. Also, people who tend to be ungrateful are more likely to engage in criminal behavior than those of gratitude.

To the extent that crime is a function of personal virtue (or lack thereof), it logically follows that one way to help prisoners to achieve rehabilitation is "to use offenders' time of incarceration to cultivate moral awareness and the capacity to act virtuously."[78] To achieve this goal, Cullen et al. proposed, for example, that prisoners should be encouraged to engage in virtuous activities with a restorative purpose and to have contact with virtuous people. Such activities can be created without any religious component, and virtuous people do not have to come from a faith community. However, Cullen et al. recognized that religious institutions are readily available to help create virtuous activities and provide virtuous people who would volunteer to regularly visit prison and spend time with prisoners as their mentor. Furthermore, those institutions are willing to pay the cost of their contribution to prisoner rehabilitation without adding any financial burden to already tight correctional budget. Therefore, working with religious institutions to achieve prisoner rehabilitation would seem to provide a win-win situation for prison administrators. In this context, Cullen et al. illustrated the possibility of a virtuous prison using the case of a faith-based prison, such as Prison Fellowship's InnerChange Freedom Initiative (IFI), implemented first in Texas and then Minnesota. Evaluation research revealed that inmates who participated and completed the program tended to show lower rates of recidivism than those who did not participate or participated but failed to complete the program, though it did not examine whether the rates were lower because the program increased the participants' religiosity, which, in turn, may have enhanced their virtue.

Prior research provides empirical evidence that religiosity is positively related to virtue, and virtue is associated positively with emotional well-being and prosocial behavior. A small number of longitudinal and experimental studies tend to suggest that the observed relationships are likely to be causal, while their reciprocity remains to be examined. In our own studies of prison inmates, we found the same pattern of relationships. That is, inmates' religiosity was positively associated with self-control, forgiveness, and gratitude, whereas these virtues were inversely related to negative emotional states—both inner-directed (depression and anxiety) and outer-directed (anger and frustration)—and the likelihood of interpersonal aggression. Consistent with the previous longitudinal and experimental studies, our analysis of two-wave panel data indicated that the observed relationships are likely to be causal rather than correlational.

Despite this empirical evidence, it would not be easy to help prisoners change and become virtuous given that they are likely to be repeated offenders who developed a habit of making a morally wrong choice throughout their lives. Cullen et al. acknowledge that "the virtuous prison would not be for all inmates,"[79] although they are optimistic that the virtuous prison could work for most inmates except those who stubbornly refuse any help with change or are mentally disturbed. The virtuous prison could be built without religion, but religion has a unique ability to help build a prison where inmates are challenged and encouraged to have their identity transformed and become virtuous as religion provides a basis of identity transformation and leads to its resultant character change. Becoming virtuous is not only a personal choice but also a religious mandate, so, once they make a commitment to religion or God, inmates are likely to stay the course of virtue development and overcome obstacles or setbacks with support and help from coreligionists, whether their mentor or other inmates who share the same faith. Of course, religion should be incorporated into building the virtuous prison within the Constitutional boundaries without violating inmate's rights, but it would be unwise if it is not taken seriously. While it is still in infancy, the faith-based, virtuous prison would release inmates who are likely to not only desist from crime but also have become men and women of excellence in being for the good.

Notes

1 Cullen, Sundt, and Wozniak (2014).
2 Liebling (2017), Cullen et al. (2014).
3 Federal Bureau of Prisons "An Overview of the First Step Act" Retrieved June 22, 2020, from https://www.bop.gov/inmates/fsa/overview.jsp#:~:text=The%20First%20Step%20Act%20 requires,needs%20and%20reduce%20this%20risk.
4 Cullen et al. (2014).
5 This section is largely a summary of Cullen et al.'s (2014) description of the two models of prison.
6 Cressey (1961).
7 Schur (1973).
8 Cullen et al. (2014, p. 69).
9 Clear (1994).
10 Sparks (1996).
11 Newman (1983).
12 Logan and Gaes (1993).
13 Cullen et al. (2014, p. 73).
14 Cullen et al. (2014, p. 74).
15 For this reason, it also rejects the idea of incapacitation because crime control "works" only when offenders are locked up inside the prison and is likely to be weakened to the extent that they become worse without the benefit of treatment during incarceration.
16 Smith (2003).
17 Cullen et al. (2014, pp. 76–78).
18 Jang, Johnson, Hays, Hallett, and Duwe (2018a), Jang, Johnson, Anderson, and Booyens (2019).
19 Johnson and Jang (2020).
20 Bonta and Andrews (2017).
21 The description of IFI programs is based on Johnson (2014).
22 Johnson and Larson (2008).
23 Duwe and King (2012).
24 Cullen and Gendreau (2000).
25 Adams (2006, p. 14).
26 Rye et al. (2000).
27 Emmons and Crumpler (2000), Tsang and Martin (2016).
28 Peterson and Seligman (2004).
29 Steffen and Masters (2005).
30 Rye et al. (2000).
31 Rye et al. (2000).
32 Piedmont (1999, p. 988).
33 Schnitker, Houltberg, Dryness, and Redmond (2019).
34 Schnitker et al. (2019).
35 Rye et al. (2005).
36 McCullough and Willoughby (2009).
37 Johnson and Jang (2010).
38 Gottfredson and Hirschi (1990).
39 Na and Paternoster (2012), Pratt and Cullen (2000).
40 Enright and Coyle (1998).
41 McCullough et al. (1998).
42 McCullough, Pargament, and Thoresen (2000, p. 9).

43 Agnew (2006, p. 4).
44 Agnew (1992).
45 Pargament and Rye (1998).
46 Agnew (2006), Gottfredson and Hirschi (1990, p. 89), Krause (2018).
47 Steffen and Masters (2005, p. 218).
48 Krause and Hayward (2015p. 195, cited from Sprecher and Fehr, 2005, p. 630, *emphasis* added).
49 Batson, Floyd, Meyer, and Winner (1999), Batson, Eidelman, Higley, and Russell (2001).
50 Gottfredson and Hirschi (1990, p. 89).
51 Tsang, Schulwitz, and Carlisle (2012, p. 41, cited from Tsang, 2006, p. 139).
52 Peterson and Seligman (2004, p. 554).
53 McCullough, Emmons, and Tsang (2002, p. 112).
54 Emmons and Crumpler (2000, p. 57).
55 McCullough, Kimeldorf, and Cohen (2008).
56 McCullough and Willoughby (2009).
57 Welch, Tittle, and Grasmick (2006).
58 Pirutinsky (2014).
59 McCullough and Willoughby (2009).
60 McCullough and Worthington (1999).
61 This discrepancy has several potential explanations. It might be due to social desirability bias: that is, religious people tend to overreport their forgiveness or report what they should do rather than what they actually do. The reliability and specificity of measures may contribute to the discrepancy. For example, general measures of religiosity are likely to be weakly related compared to a measure of beliefs regarding what religion specifically teaches about forgiveness. Another possibility is that more proximate conditions for forgiveness than religiosity may affect the relationship between religiosity and forgiveness.
62 Davis, Worthington, Hook, and Hill (2013).
63 Batson et al. (1999); Batson et al. (2001).
64 Steffen and Masters (2005).
65 Krause, Ironson, and Hill (2018).
66 Emmons and Crumpler (2000), Peterson and Seligman (2004), Tsang and Martin (2016), Tsang, Schulwitz, and Carlisle (2012).
67 Krause (2009).
68 Kraus, Desmond, and Palmer (2015).
69 Krause and Hayward (2015).
70 McCullough and Tsang (2004).
71 Jang, Johnson, Hays, Hallett, and Duwe (2018).
72 Jang et al. (2019).
73 This analysis was "preliminary" in that the data had not included inmates' information about sociodemographic and justice system-related backgrounds yet since we were waiting for the data to be made available by the National Penitentiary and Prison Institute (INPEC: Instituto Nacional Penitenciario y Carcelario) of Colombia and the South Africa Department of Correctional Services (DCS).
74 We also conducted a follow-up survey about a year after the posttest, while the interval between the surveys varied. Almost a quarter (23.9%) of the 861 pretest participants and about 40% (206) of the 506 posttest participants (61 in the treatment group and 145 in the control group; 157 Colombian inmates and 49 South African inmates) were available for the follow-up. The response rate was affected by not only the number of transfers and refusals but also the level of prison authority's cooperation (or lack thereof). In addition to the three surveys, we conducted personal interviews with randomly selected 113—43 Colombian and 60 South African—inmates (which consisted of 73 treatment and 40 control group inmates) at the pretest, while we re-interviewed only treatment group inmates, 38.4% (28) of the 73 pretest interviewees (16 Colombian and 12 South African inmates), at the posttest.
75 Baraldi and Enders (2010), Graham (2009).
76 One unexpected finding was the positive association between changes in gratitude and intended aggression (.123): that is, an increase in the virtue of gratitude was found to increase, not decrease, the likelihood of interpersonal aggression. This finding is puzzling given that the same variable was, as expected, inversely related to the other ultimate endogenous variable, negative emotional states (−.091). This counter-intuitive result is difficult to even speculate without additional data, while this anomalous relationship was found among both Colombian and South African inmates when their data were analyzed separately.
77 Beijersbergen, Dirkzwager, Eichelsheim, Van der La, and Nieuwbeerta (2015), Jang (2020).

78 Cullen et al. (2014, p. 74).
79 Cullen et al. (2014, p. 78).

References

Adams, R. M. (2006). *A theory of virtue: Excellence in being for the good*. Oxford, UK: Oxford University Press.

Agnew, R. (1992). Foundation for a general strain theory of crime and delinquency. *Criminology, 30*(1), 47–88.

Agnew, R. (2006). *Pressured into crime: An overview of general strain theory*. Los Angeles, CA: Roxbury Publishing Company.

Baraldi, A. N., & Enders, C. K. (2010). An introduction to modern missing data analyses. *Journal of School Psychology, 48*(1), 5–37.

Batson, C. D., Eidelman, S. H., Higley, S. L., & Russell, S. A. (2001). "And who is my neighbor?" II: Quest religion as a source of universal compassion. *Journal for the Scientific Study of Religion, 40*(1), 39–50.

Batson, C. D., Floyd, R. B., Meyer, J. M., & Winner, A. L. (1999). "And who is my neighbor?": Intrinsic religion as a source of universal compassion. *Journal for the Scientific Study of Religion, 38*(4), 445–457.

Beijersbergen, K. A., Dirkzwager, A. J. E., Eichelsheim, V. I., Van der Laan, P. H., & Nieuwbeerta, P. (2015). Procedural justice, anger, and prisoners' misconduct: A longitudinal study. *Criminal Justice and Behavior, 42*(2), 196–218. doi:10.1177/0093854814550710.

Bonta, J., & Andrews, D. A. (2017). *The psychology of criminal conduct* (6th ed.). New York, NY: Routledge.

Clear, T. R. (1994). *Harm in American penology: Offenders, victims, and their communities*. New York, NY: SUNY Press.

Cressey, D. R. (1961). *The Prison: Studies in Institutional Organization and Change*. New York, NY: Holt, Rinehart and Winston.

Cullen, F. T., & Gendreau, P. (2000). Assessing correctional rehabilitation: Policy, practice, and prospects. *Criminal Justice, 3*, 109–175.

Cullen, F. T., Sundt, J. L., & Wozniak, J. F. (2014). The virtuous prison: Toward a restorative rehabilitation. In F. T. Cullen, C. L. Jonson, & M. K. Stohr (Eds.), *The American prison: Imagining a different future* (pp. 61–84). Thousand Oaks, CA: Sage.

Davis, D. E., Worthington, E. L., Hook, J. N., & Hill, P. C. (2013). Research on religion/spirituality and forgiveness: A meta-analytic review. *Psychology of Religion and Spirituality, 5*(4): 233–241.

Duwe, G., & King, M. (2012). Can faith-based correctional programs work? An outcome evaluation of the InnerChange freedom initiative in Minnesota. *International Journal of Offender Therapy and Comparative Criminology, 57*(7), 813–841.

Emmons, R. A., & Crumpler, C. A. (2000). Gratitude as a human strength: Appraising the evidence. *Journal of Social and Clinical Psychology, 19*(1), 56–69.

Enright, R. D., & Coyle, C. T. (1998). Researching the process model of forgiveness within psychological interventions. In E. Worthington, Jr. (Ed.), *Dimensions of forgiveness: Psychological research and theological perspectives* (pp. 139–161). Radnor, PA: Templeton Foundation Press.

Gottfredson, M. R., & Hirschi, T. (1990). *A general theory of crime*. Stanford, CA: Stanford University Press.

Graham, J. W. (2009). Missing data analysis: Making it work in the real world. *Annual Review of Psychology, 60*, 549–576.

Jang, S. J. (2020). Prison strains, negative emotions, and deviance among prisoners in South Korea: A latent-variable modeling test of general strain theory. *International Journal of Offender Therapy and Comparative Criminology, 64*(15), 1607–1636.

Jang, S. J., Johnson, B. R., Anderson, M. L., & Boyens, K. (2019). The effect of religion on mental health among prisoners in South Africa: Explanations and gender differences. *Justice Quarterly,* doi:10.1080/07418825.2019.1689286.

Jang, S. J., Johnson, B. R., Hays, J., Hallett, M., & Duwe, G. (2018a). Existential and virtuous effects of religiosity on mental health and aggressiveness among offenders. *Religions, 9*(6), 182.

Jang, S. J., Johnson, B. R., Hays, J., Hallett, M., & Duwe, G. (2018b). Religion and misconduct in "Angola" prison: Conversion, congregational participation, religiosity, and self-identities. *Justice Quarterly, 35*(3), 412–442.

Johnson, B. R. (2014). The faith-based prison. In F. T. Cullen, C. L. Jonson, & M. K. Stohr (Eds.), *The American prison: Imagining a different future* (pp. 35–60). Los Angeles, CA: Sage.

Johnson, B. R., & Jang, S. J. (2010). Crime and religion: Assessing the role of the faith factor. In R. Rosenfeld, K. Quinet, & C. Garcia (Eds.), *Contemporary issues in criminological theory and research: The role of social institutions* (pp. 117–149). Belmont, CA: Wadsworth.

Johnson, B. R., & Jang, S. J. (2020). *Connecting in-prison programs to prisoner reentry and aftercare.* Waco, TX: Institute for Studies of Religion.

Johnson, B. R., & Larson, D. B. (2008). *The InnerChange freedom initiative.* Waco, TX: Institute for Studies of Religion.

Kraus, R., Desmond, S. A., & Palmer, Z. D. (2015). Being thankful: Examining the relationship between young adult religiosity and gratitude. *Journal of Religion and Health, 54*(4), 1331–1344.

Krause, N. (2009). Religious involvement, gratitude, and change in depressive symptoms over time. *The International Journal for the Psychology of Religion, 19*(3), 155–172.

Krause, N. (2018). Assessing the relationships among religion, humility, forgiveness, and self-rated health. *Research in Human Development, 15*(1), 33–49.

Krause, N., & Hayward, R. D. (2015). Humility, compassion, and gratitude to god: Assessing the relationships among key religious virtues. *Psychology of Religion and Spirituality, 7*(3), 192.

Krause, N., Ironson, G., & Hill, P. (2018). Religious involvement and happiness: Assessing the mediating role of compassion and helping others. *The Journal of Social Psychology, 158*(2), 256–270.

Logan, C. H., & Gaes, G. G. (1993). Meta-analysis and the rehabilitation of punishment. *Justice Quarterly, 10*(2), 245–263.

McCullough, M. E., Emmons, R. A., & Tsang, J. (2002). The grateful disposition: A conceptual and empirical topography. *Journal of Personality and Social Psychology, 82,*(1), 112–127.

McCullough, M. E., Kimeldorf, M. B., & Cohen, A. (2008). An adaptation for altruism? The social causes, social effects, and social evolution of gratitude. *Current Directions in Psychological Science, 17*(4), 281–285.

McCullough, M. E., Pargament, K. I., & Thoresen, C. E. (2000). The psychology of forgiveness. In M. E. McCullough, K. I. Pargament, & C. E. Thoresen (Eds.), *Forgiveness: Theory, research, and practice* (pp. 1–14). New York, NY: Guilford Press.

McCullough, M. E., Rachal, K. C., Sandage, S. J., Worthington Jr, E. L., Brown, S. W., & Hight, T. L. (1998). Interpersonal forgiving in close relationships: II theoretical elaboration and measurement. *Journal of Personality and Social Psychology, 75*(6), 1586.

McCullough, M. E., & Tsang, J. (2004). Parent of the virtues? The prosocial contours of gratitude. In R. A. Emmons & M. E. McCullough (Eds.), *The psychology of gratitude* (pp. 123–141). New York, NY: Oxford University Press.

McCullough, M. E., & Willoughby, B. L. (2009). Religion, self-regulation, and self-control: Associations, explanations, and implications. *Psychological Bulletin, 135*(1), 69.

McCullough, M. E., & Worthington, E. L. (1999). Religion and the forgiving personality. *Journal of Personality, 67*(6): 1141–1164.

Na, C., & Paternoster, R. (2012). Can self-control change substantially over time? Rethinking the relationship between self- and social control. *Criminology, 50*(2), 427–462. doi:10.1111/j.1745-9125.2011.00269.x.

Newman, G. R. (1983). *Just and painful: A case for the corporal punishment of criminals.* New York, NY: Macmillan.

Pargament, K. I., & Rye, M. S. (1998). Forgiveness as a method of religious coping. In Everett L. Worthington, Jr. (Ed.), *Dimensions of Forgiveness: Psychological Research and Theological Perspectives* (pp. 59–78). Philadelphia, PA: Templeton Foundation Press.

Peterson, C., & Seligman, M. E. (2004). *Character strengths and virtues: A handbook and classification.* Oxford, UK: Oxford University Press.

Piedmont, R. L. (1999). Does spirituality represent the sixth factor of personality? Spiritual transcendence and the five-factor model. *Journal of Personality, 67*(6), 985–1013.

Pirutinsky, S. (2014). Does religiousness increase self-control and reduce criminal behavior? A longitudinal analysis of adolescent offenders. *Criminal Justice and Behavior 41*(11): 1290–1307.

Pratt, T. C., & Cullen, F. T. (2000). The empirical status of Gottfredson and Hirschi's general theory of crime: A meta-analysis. *Criminology, 38*(3), 931–964.

Rye, M. S., Pargament, K. I., Ali, M. A., Beck, G. L., Dorff, E. N., Hallisey, C., … Williams, J. G. (2000). Religious perspectives on forgiveness. In M. E. McCullough, K. I. Pargament, & C. E. Thoresen (Eds.), *Forgiveness: Theory, research, and practice* (pp. 17–40). New York, NY: The Guilford Press.

Rye, M. S., Pargament, K. I., Pan, W., Yingling, D. W., Shegren, K. A., & Ito, M. (2005). Can group interventions facilitate forgiveness of an ex-spouse? A randomized clinical trial. *Journal of Consulting and Clinical Psychology, 73*, 880–892.

Schnitker, S. A., King, P. E., & Houltberg, B. (2019). Religion, spirituality, and thriving: Transcendent narrative, virtue, and telos. *Journal of Research on Adolescence, 29*(2), 276–290.

Schur, E. M. (1973). *Radical nonintervention: Rethinking the delinquency problem.* Englewood Cliffs, NJ: Prentice Hall.

Smith, C. (2003). *Moral, believing animals: Human personhood and culture.* New York, NY: Oxford University Press.

Sparks, R. (1996). Penal "austerity": The doctrine of less eligibility reborn? In R. Matthews & P. Francis (Eds.), *Prisons 2000: An international perspective on the current state and future of imprisonment* (pp. 74–93). London, UK: Palgrave MacMillan.

Sprecher, S., & Fehr, B. (2005). Compassionate love for close others and humanity. *Journal of Social and Personal Relationships, 22*(5), 629–651.

Steffen, P. R., & Masters, K. S. (2005). Does compassion mediate the intrinsic religion-health relationship? *Annals of Behavioral Medicine, 30*(3), 217–224.

Tsang, J., & Martin, S. R. (2016). A psychological perspective on gratitude and religion. In D. Carr (Ed.), *Perspectives on gratitude: An interdisciplinary approach* (pp. 154–168). New York, NY: Routledge.

Tsang, J., Schulwitz, A., & Carlisle, R. D. (2012). An experimental test of the relationship between religion and gratitude. *Psychology of Religion and Spirituality, 4*(1), 40.

Welch, M. R., Tittle, C. R., & Grasmick, H. G. (2006). Christian religiosity, self-control, and social conformity. *Social Forces 84*, 1605–1623.

3

HOW RELIGION CONTRIBUTES TO VOLUNTEERISM, PROSOCIAL BEHAVIOR, AND POSITIVE CRIMINOLOGY

Religious Freedom and Other-Mindedness in Early America

Alexis de Tocqueville, a French political scientist, visited the United States in 1831, to research and study the American penal system. Over the course of his visit to America, he was inspired to write about a number of intriguing factors that seemed to distinguish the workings of American society, including the uniquely American tendency toward volunteerism. He wrote extensively about the American phenomenon of forming associations of all types including professional, religious, social, civil, and political.

Tocqueville's observations of the role of volunteerism have continued to be played out in the civic life and culture of America. Tocqueville also observed the critical role that religion played in American society. He drew a connection between the formation and effectiveness of associations in solving social problems. Often times bolstered by the influence of religion and religious awakenings, the rise of social reform movements around issues like poverty, temperance, and the abolition of slavery would be mobilized by a new generation that had not previously been involved in civic life, including women and young people. Tocqueville witnessed that associating with other like-minded people to improve the common welfare requires personal sacrifice. What contemporary social scientists refer to as the virtue of other-mindedness, Tocqueville observed and wrote about in the 1830s.

Tocqueville also noted associating for the common good is not done without concern for one's own self-interest. He referred to this as the doctrine of self-interest, properly understood. In regard to prisons, however, he noted a concern that lingers to this day: "while society in the United States gives the example of the most extended liberty, the prisons of the same country offer the spectacle of the most complete despotism."[1] Tocqueville argued that Americans do not claim to sacrifice oneself for another because it is a good thing to do, but because such sacrifices are as necessary to the person who makes them as to those who gain from them. Moreover, Tocqueville claimed that Americans were unique in going beyond the call of duty to prove that it is in each man's interest to be virtuous.

Since America's founding, a host of important organizations driven largely by volunteers have sought to address difficult to solve problems that plagued society. Moreover, the majority of these organizations were founded by individuals motivated by faith to pursue acts of service to others. In their highly regarded book, *The Churching of America, 1776–2005*, Roger Finke

DOI: 10.4324/9781003171744-3

and Rodney Stark examine how religious freedom allowed religious congregations to compete for adherents and to subsequently grow and thrive in the great American experiment.[2] Using historical and sociological data, they were able to document the dramatic growth experienced by many religious denominations in early America. Thus, Finke and Stark provide evidence that tracks with Tocqueville's observation some 175 years earlier; the growth of American religion was very much connected to the important and positive contribution of faith-motivated volunteers in providing acts of service that lifted their neighbors and subsequently advanced the common good.[3] In short, religion and religious practice contributes to American life by adding tremendous amounts of social capital to the public sphere.

The influence of America's houses of worship for more than 200 years has been unprecedented and profoundly consequential, ultimately leading to the founding of organizations like the YMCA, Salvation Army, and the American Red Cross (to mention just a few), associations that were formed primarily to connect volunteers to the delivery of social services to improve the life prospects of others.[4] But the impact of religion and religious freedom in America would be felt far beyond the realm of social service delivery. Indeed, the history of medicine and hospitals in America has also been inextricably tied to religious freedom and the rise of religious pluralism. When Benjamin Franklin promoted the founding of the Pennsylvania Hospital in the 1750s, he made an explicitly Christian argument for why it was needed. Citing Matthew 25:36, Franklin reminded readers that Jesus commended those who visited the sick, as if they were visiting Jesus himself. Even though Franklin was not by any means a traditional believer, he certainly endorsed the Christian ethic of serving those who were suffering.[5] Many American hospitals and health systems today remain visibly connected with the Catholic, Jewish or Protestant traditions out of which they were born.[6]

In many ways, the growth of religion in America resembles the rise of Christianity two millennia earlier. As documented in the book, *The Rise of Christianity: How the Obscure, Marginal Jesus Movement Became the Dominant Religious Force in the Western World in a Few Centuries*, Rodney Stark brings to light the historical accounts associated with the early Christian church and the rapid rise of Christianity in the decades following Jesus' resurrection—documenting how Christianity taught adherents to be concerned for the welfare of others.[7] Conversely, Stark shows that the dramatic growth of early Christianity was fueled by pagan leaders who did not have adequate answers or responses to why a devastating epidemic (probably smallpox) swept through the Roman Empire in the year 165, taking the lives of roughly one-fourth of the population. Fewer than 100 years later, another equally lethal epidemic (probably measles) again ravaged the empire. Christianity offered a more satisfactory account of why these epidemics happened. It also projected a more hopeful and optimistic picture of the future. Christian values of love and charity were translated into norms of social service and community solidarity. Care for widows and orphans became an essential part of the rise of Christianity. As Stark documents, Christians were able to better cope with the epidemics than other religious groups, which resulted in higher rates of survival. In other words, caring for one's neighbor was a feature linked to religious freedom as well as the churching of America.

Religion and Volunteerism in Contemporary American Society

Social scientists have noted that volunteerism continues to play a significantly larger role in enhancing American life than it does in other countries.[8] According to the Bureau of Labor Statistics, volunteerism peaked between 2003 and 2005, when 28.8% of Americans reported having volunteered the previous year. The nonprofit sector, which relies heavily on volunteers as a strategic resource, has become increasingly important in the engagement of local communities.

This is particularly the case in the human services sector, which relies heavily on the support of volunteers to fill the gaps in federal, state, and local funding. To state the obvious, the contribution volunteers make to civil society and civic engagement is profound.[9]

In general terms, volunteers are people who perform unpaid work "without coercion" for the benefit of the community. We know that many Americans volunteer and that volunteers make critical contributions to American civil society. For example, volunteers provide a host of community services that the formal sector is either unwilling or unable to effectively provide, such as, remedial education, sporting and recreational programs, medical and health services, mentoring of at-risk youth, shelters for the homeless, substance abuse counseling, offender treatment programs, educational programs for prisoners, and prisoner reentry initiatives.

According to a study by the Corporation for National and Community Service (CNCS), more Americans than ever are volunteering.[10] The 2018 *Volunteering in America* study found that more than 77 million adults volunteered their time through an organization in the previous year. In total, Americans volunteered nearly 6.9 billion hours, worth an estimated $167 billion in economic value.[11] These extraordinary figures do not even account for the millions of Americans—some 43%—who voluntarily serve and support friends and family, or more than half of American adults (51%) who do favors for their neighbors; what might be called acts of "informal volunteering." In sum, volunteers provide a staggering economic benefit to American society.

In addition, the contribution of volunteering goes beyond the value of services provided. Volunteering has been linked to with the formation of social capital—social connections that help to build trust and collective action within the community.[12] Robert Putnam argues that a community that is more connected is likely to have a greater level of trust and reciprocity among its citizens, leading to a more cohesive and stable society with economic as well as social benefits.[13] For example, high levels of connectivity and trust can reduce transaction costs, improve information flows and enhance workplace cooperation.[14]

Barbara Stewart, CEO of the Corporation for National and Community Service, summed up the role of volunteers in making a difference nicely:

> Each and every day, ordinary Americans are stepping up to support their fellow citizens to help with needs both great and small because they understand the power service has to change communities and lives for the better…The fabric of our nation is strengthened by the service of its volunteers. When we stand side-by-side to help others, our differences fade away and we learn that Americans have more in common than we realize.[15]

This research also found that Americans are generous with more than just their time. Volunteers donate to charity at twice the rate as non-volunteers. Nearly 80% of volunteers donated to charity, compared to 40% of non-volunteers. Overall, half of all citizens (52.2%) donated to charity last year. Across all categories in the study, volunteers engage in their communities at higher rates than non-volunteers. They more frequently talk to neighbors, participate in civic organizations, fix things in the community, attend public meetings, discuss local issues with family and friends, do favors for neighbors, and vote in local elections.[16]

Here are some of the key findings of the *Volunteering in America* study:

- Parents volunteer at rates nearly 48% higher than non-parents and working mothers give more time than any other demographic, with a volunteer rate of 46.7%.
- Generation X has the highest rate (36.4%) of volunteering, while Baby Boomers are giving more hours of service (2.2 billion).

- Veterans are among the most neighborly Americans. They do something positive for the neighborhood, spend time with and do favors for their neighbors, and donate to charity at higher rates than their civilian counterparts.
- Americans most frequently gave their time to religious groups (32%), a quarter volunteered most often with sports or arts groups (25.7%); with another nearly 20% supporting education or youth service groups.

But what factors predict the likelihood that one will volunteer in the first place? As it turns out, religion is considered to be one of the key predictors of volunteer participation, in both religious and secular organizations. Numerous studies have documented a positive relationship between various measures of religion as an independent variable and social and civic outcomes such as philanthropic giving, community group membership, and volunteering.[17] Indeed, the more religious people are, the more likely they are to volunteer.[18]

Joseph Johnston found that increased religious belief and attendance were both associated with greater service to others in a study examining religion and volunteering throughout adulthood.[19] The study offers longitudinal evidence that religious motivation, attendance and involvement matter to increased volunteering behavior over time. In analyzing four waves of the Americans' Changing Lives study from 1986 to 2002, Johnston found that increased religious beliefs made it more likely that individuals would volunteer in religious institutions. Moreover, volunteering in religious institutions increased the chances that people would move on to other forms of volunteering.[20]

Utilizing data from more than 37,000 in the 2008–2009 US Congregational Life Survey, Jennifer McClure measured which factors of congregational life were associated with attenders providing social support to non-family members.[21] She found having close friends in the congregation made a difference, but the most consistent association with social support came from private devotional activities. Adherents who spend more time in prayer, meditation, or Bible reading were more likely to give a loan, care for the sick and help someone find a job.[22]

Americans who volunteer for religious groups are two or three times as likely to also volunteer for secular groups as Americans who do not volunteer for religious groups, according to the Faith Matters surveys led by Robert Putnam of Harvard University and David Campbell of the University of Notre Dame. In their book, *American Grace: How Religion Divides and Unites Us*, they note:

> Religiously observant Americans are more generous with time and treasure than demographically similar secular Americans…This is true for secular causes (especially help to the needy, the elderly and young people) as well as for purely religious causes. It is true even for most random acts of kindness.

We recently interviewed a group of faith-motivated volunteers who regularly travel to a correctional facility in a rural area where they work with prisoners in a faith-based trauma and healing program, supported by the American Bible Society.[23] The volunteers were all senior citizens and some of them would drive several hours just to get to the facility. They stayed in a local hotel for several days a week working with inmates before driving home. The expenses of this weekly routine were covered by the volunteers themselves. Without exception, the volunteers claimed that they were the real beneficiaries of working with these prisoners.[24]

A major reason cited by Putnam and Campbell and other researchers for the heightened volunteerism of religious individuals is the social networks that people form at houses of worship. Churches, synagogues, and mosques are places that encourage volunteerism and other-mindedness, and expose individuals to secular as well as religious opportunities for ser-vice that create social bonds making it more likely individuals will respond to requests to vol-unteer. Indeed, these ties can extend beyond houses of worship. There is empirical evidence that non-religious people with strong ties to people that are highly active within a congregation, increases the likelihood that they will be encouraged to volunteer.[25] This is important because volunteerism means a great deal to America in ways that are consequential as well as positive, and if religion can help expand volunteerism, society stands to be the beneficiary of this good will.

Out of a concern for the welfare of others, religion can be seen as a catalyst that stimulates or generates volunteers. For example, when people attend religious congregations they tend to get connected to different social networks. Whether through classes, retreats, small groups, mis-sion trips, church-sponsored volunteer work, or any number of related group functions, these activities connect people to multiple networks of social support that have the potential to be meaningful. Research documents that social support in congregations has been linked to better coping skills,[26] increased life expectancy,[27] stress reduction,[28] and better self-reported health.[29] In fact, according to Harvard scholar Robert Putnam, churches are enormous repositories of good will and social capital.[30]

Houses of worship build and sustain more social capital—and social capital of more var-ied forms—than any other type of institution in America. Churches, synagogues, mosques, and other houses of worship provide a vibrant institutional base for civic good works and a training ground for civic entrepreneurs. Nearly half of America's stock of social capital is reli-gious or religiously affiliated, whether measured by association memberships, philanthropy, or volunteering.[31]

If Putnam's estimation is close to accurate, houses of worship can certainly be viewed as a training ground for good works and civic engagement. More recently, Putnam goes a bit further in his assessment, arguing that people with religious affiliations are more satisfied with their lives mainly because they attend religious services more frequently and build social networks with people who share their faith and religious experience, thus building a strong sense of be-longing to a community of religious faith.[32] So significant are faith-based networks, Putnam argues, they generate unique effects that cannot be explained in any other way. Simply put, these faith-infused networks of support—in and of themselves—are powerful independent pre-dictors of beneficial outcomes.[33]

In sum, religious freedom has been catalytic to the growth of religious congregations in America, which continues to be linked to other-mindedness and concern for neighbor. A tan-gible expression of this concern is manifested in the varied and ubiquitous acts of service pro-vided everyday by countless volunteers in America. Putnam's assessment of the contribution of religious congregations to America's overall repository of social capital and good will is nothing short of colossal.

The Role of Religion in Prosocial Behavior

Prosocial behaviors are those actions that are intended to help other people. Prosocial behavior is characterized by a concern for the rights, feelings, and welfare of other people. Behaviors that can be described as prosocial include not just feeling empathy and concern for others, but actually behaving in ways that help or benefit other people. In *The Handbook of Social Psychology*, C. Daniel Batson explains that prosocial behaviors refer to "a broad range of actions intended to benefit one or more people other than oneself—behaviors such as helping, comforting, sharing and cooperation."[34]

The term prosocial behavior originated during the 1970s and was introduced by social scientists as an antonym for the term antisocial behavior, but in recent years the term has come to mean far more than the opposite of antisocial behavior. As criminologists, we have argued that the field of criminology has been preoccupied with only "half" of a field.[35] Its general focus has largely been limited to understanding antisocial behavior, with almost no attention given to prosocial activities. That is, criminologists tend to ask why people commit crimes; they rarely ask why people do good deeds. Rather than neglecting "half" of human behavior, we think criminologists should also be interested in studying a number of important questions that focus on positive and prosocial factors. For example, positive criminology is interested in understanding: (1) Why do the vast majority of Americans choose to obey rather than break laws? (2) Why do most of the people reared in disadvantaged neighborhoods turn out not only to be law-abiding but to be good citizens? (3) How is it that offenders who previously exhibited antisocial patterns of behavior, can undergo transformations that result in consistent patterns of positive behavior, accountability, and other-mindedness? (4) What is the role of religion in not only guiding individual behavior in positive ways, but the role of faith-based groups and organizations in fostering prosocial activities?

The motivation for organized prosocial helping behaviors can often be traced to religious practice. The world's three primary monotheistic traditions—Islam, Judaism, and Christianity—teach that helping the less fortunate is a religious obligation. The compulsory alms tax, or zakat, is one of the five pillars of Islam. There are also numerous examples of God commanding Jews to aid the poor throughout the Old Testament. In the parable of the "Good Samaritan," Jesus instructs to follow the example of the good neighbor who aided a poor beaten man previously ignored by other passers-by, including a priest. The emphasis on giving and helping within the Judeo-Christian religions is a primary reason prosocial behavior is considered a social norm in Western culture.[36] The concept of prosocial behavior and its psychological and sociological foundations are extremely important in furthering research and practice in a number of fields, including education, social work, criminal justice, and law.

Involvement in religious practices and related activities can foster the development of and integration into personal networks that provide both social and emotional support.[37] When such personal networks overlap with other networks, it is reasonable to expect these networks will not only constrain illegal behavior but may also protect one from the effects of living in disadvantaged areas.[38] In other words, an individual's integration into a community-based religious network actually weakens the effects of other factors that might otherwise influence deviant behavior. Thus, religious networks can buffer or shield one from the harmful effects of negative influences.[39]

It makes sense, therefore, that those who regularly attend church and participate in religious activities would be more likely to internalize values modeled and taught in such settings. These faith-filled networks may encourage appropriate behavior as well as emphasize concern for others' welfare. Such processes can contribute to the acquisition of positive attributes that give those attending a greater sense of empathy toward others, which, in turn, makes them less likely to commit acts that harm others. Perhaps this influence is why research confirms that religiosity can help people to be resilient even in the midst of poverty, unemployment, or other social ills.[40] Churches and communities of faith provide instruction and the teaching of religious beliefs and values that, if internalized, may help individuals make good decisions.

This influence may explain why church-attending youth from disadvantaged communities are less likely to use illicit drugs than youth from suburban communities who attend church less frequently or not at all.[41] In a similar vein, preliminary research has examined intergenerational religious influence and finds parental religious devotion is a protective factor for crime.[42] Taken together these findings suggest that the effect of church attendance is compelling in and of itself. Either through the networks of support they provide, the learning of self-control through the teaching of religious moral beliefs, or the condemning of inappropriate behavior, regular church attendance may foster each of these possibilities.

Over the last several decades scholars have produced an impressive and mounting body of evidence that has helped to highlight the many ways in which religious participation is linked to religious practices and beliefs that are consequential for a variety of important outcomes. These include overall flourishing and well-being,[43] social integration and support,[44] delivery of social services to disadvantaged populations,[45] mental and physical health,[46] forgiveness,[47] voluntary activities,[48] crime reduction,[49] prisoner rehabilitation,[50] family relations,[51] substance use/abuse,[52] sobriety,[53] health care utilization,[54] coping strategies for stressful conditions,[55] and even longevity/mortality.[56] Thus, efforts to restrict religious freedom will unnecessarily curtail the effort of faith-motivated volunteers, acts of service, reduce social capital, and come with a staggering cost to society. According to a 2016 study that quantifies the economic value of religion and religious individuals, and businesses, as well as the contribution of faith-based organizations, religion adds 1.2 trillion dollars to the US economy each year.[57]

We live in an age when discussions about inequality and discrimination and the need to correct injustice in all its manifestations are clearly front and center in contemporary society. Examples of injustice receive ample attention—and it is good that they do. Receiving far less attention, however, is the empirical evidence documenting that many people are working diligently in an effort to remedy many of the injustices and social problems found in our society. It is one thing to complain about injustice, inequality, or various social problems, it is quite another to intentionally work to reduce or even eliminate these problems. Stated differently, there are those who spend a great deal of time *looking* for justice, while there are others who spend a great deal of time actively and quietly *doing* justice. Oswald Chambers provides a critical insight when it comes to the issue of justice. He argues that people who *look* for justice can easily become sidetracked by any number of distractions. He goes on to invoke the teaching of Jesus from the Sermon on the Mount, suggesting a better way of correcting injustice is to simply give or do justice at every opportunity. Chambers puts it this way—"Never look for justice in this world, but never cease to give it."[58] One can make a compelling argument that this is the very essence of what countless volunteers—often motivated by faith—do each day without any fanfare.

Religion and Positive Criminology

Recent research in an emerging sub-field labeled "positive criminology,"[59] suggests that more positive and restorative approaches—including those that foster social connectedness and support, service to others, spiritual experience, personal integrity, and identity change—may be more effective than the prevailing punitive tactics.[60] Consistent with traditional and contemporary restorative justice practices, these approaches seek to develop active responsibility on the part of individuals who have been living a lifestyle of irresponsibility.[61] From this perspective, correctional practices should be explicitly designed to promote virtue.[62] Thus, the goal of punishment is not to inflict pain or exact revenge but rather to reconstruct and make better.[63] A clear example of what this paradigm shift looks like is captured in a new study of a faith-based program designed to reduce the trauma that negatively affects so many incarcerated offenders who have experienced long before they are incarcerated.[64] This program is administered through a partnership between the Good News Jail & Prison Ministry and the American Bible Society. By promoting virtues like forgiveness, compassion, and resilience, the Trauma Healing

Program participants were found to have significantly reduced Post Traumatic Stress Disorder trauma-related grief, and negative emotions.[65]

Another important example of an organization that approaches correctional practices with a view to promoting virtue, is Prison Fellowship International (PFI).[66] For more than 40 years, PFI has built programs inside prisons around the world that are designed to restore prisoners, help their families, and integrate them back into the community. Consequently, PFI's work has long been consistent with a positive criminology focus whereby the goal of punishment is not to inflict pain but rather to reconstruct. A new study of one of PFI's prison programs—The Prisoner's Journey—in Colombia, South America, finds that those inmates who completed the program were more likely than non-participants to become increasingly religious.[67] Moreover, this faith-based program was found to increase the motivation to engage in self-change, and to find a sense of meaning and purpose in life, and to experience the virtues of forgiveness, accountability, gratitude, and self-control. Participation in this volunteer-led program also decreased negative emotional states (state depression, anxiety, and anger) and the likelihood of aggression toward other inmates by increasing religiosity, which, in turn, reduced the negative consequences of imprisonment.[68] In an important study of a non-Christian sample, scholars examined the effects of two Jewish-based rehabilitation programs on recidivism in Israel.[69] Compared to non-participants, only those who participated in both programs had a significantly lower risk of recidivism. Comparing participants of the two programs, those from the most intensive program had significantly more positive recidivism outcomes than those from the less intensive program. The authors conclude that, when religious-oriented programs create authentic changes in levels of religiosity, they can have a positive effect on reducing recidivism.[70]

Unfortunately, efforts like this tend to fly under the radar in our current system, but a concrete example has been provided by a program at the Louisiana State Penitentiary (Angola), the largest maximum security prison in the United States. Once known as one of the most violent and corrupt prisons in America, Angola is now known for its many inmate-led churches and a fully operational seminary (launched in 1995 and discussed in detail in Chapter 5). In recent years adjudicated juveniles from New Orleans are being given the option to serve their sentence at Angola and to participate in a unique mentoring project. Rev. John Robson, who formerly led the seminary at Angola, observed that this restorative, faith-based program effectively[71]:

> ...de-institutionalizes the dehumanization of punitive justice [because it gives a person] the responsibility of making the right choices for the right reasons. Whereas dehumanization within a punitive system demands simply making choices for the wrong reasons— because they fear punishment.

[emphasis in the original]

Research now confirms that even visitation can help reduce recidivism. One study examined whether visits from community volunteers—specifically clergy and mentors—had an impact on recidivism by examining 836 offenders released from different prisons in Minnesota. The results show that community visits significantly reduced all three measures of reoffending (rearrest, reconviction, reincarceration). The salutary effect on recidivism grew as the proportion of community visits to all visits increased. The findings suggest community volunteer visits should be conceptualized as a programming resource to be used with offenders who lack social support.[72]

This highlights Braithewaite's[73] crucial distinction between the passive responsibility inherent in the phrase "serving time," and which implies the state holding a person accountable for their past actions, and the active responsibility at the heart of restorative justice processes which focuses on "taking responsibility for putting things right into the future." This active responsibility is brought about by a "redemption script"[74] that allows a person to claim a "coherent and convincing" narrative supporting a significant identity transformation: from a selfish delinquent and/or addict to a responsible and helpful "new person." Rather than viewing the person as a set of risks to be managed, or a bundle of needs to be met, the person is understood to have strengths that can be deployed for the benefit of self and others.[75] The paradigm case is the "wounded healer:" a former addict who is uniquely effective in helping other addicts precisely because of prior experience in active addiction and addiction recovery.

Though research on how incarcerated offenders can help other prisoners change is rare, the Field Ministry program within the Texas Department of Criminal Justice is one such current example. The program enlists inmates who have graduated from a prison-based seminary to work as "Field Ministers," serving other inmates in various capacities.[76] We have recently examined whether inmate exposure to Field Ministers is inversely related to antisocial factors and positively to prosocial ones at three maximum-security prisons where the Field Ministry program operates. Preliminary results indicate inmates exposed to Field Ministers more frequently and for a longer period tended to report lower levels of criminological risk factors (e.g., legal cynicism) and aggressiveness, and higher levels of virtues (e.g., humility), predictors of human agency (e.g., a sense of meaning and purpose in life), religiosity, and spirituality. We find that prisoners who are the beneficiaries of the inmate-led Field Ministry help other prisoners make positive and prosocial changes. We conclude that inmate ministers play an important role in fostering virtuous behavior,[77] and achieving the goal of offender rehabilitation.[78] Moreover, we find that some offenders in prison should be viewed as potential assets waiting to be reformed with the help of other offenders.[79]

Furthermore, there is empirical evidence that faith-based prison programs are cost-effective. Duwe and Johnson found that participation in the InnerChange Freedom Initiative in Minnesota, a faith-based prisoner reentry program that has operated within Minnesota's prison system since 2002, showed the program is effective in lowering recidivism. A cost-benefit analysis of the program which is privately funded and relies heavily on volunteers, does not exact additional costs to the State of Minnesota. As a result, this study focused on estimating the program's benefits by examining recidivism and post-release employment. The findings showed that during its first six years of operation in Minnesota, InnerChange produced an estimated benefit of $3 million, which amounts to nearly $8,300 per participant.[80]

Finally, the issue of prisoner reentry remains yet another correctional crisis in need of a more restorative approach. One organization that is an exemplar in addressing the prisoner reentry crisis in a way that is restorative and consistent with positive criminology is that of Restoration Outreach of Dallas Ministries.[81] This faith-based prison program promotes hope and restoration through biblically based mentoring and the promotion of various virtues. Most importantly, the program has a robust in-prison component in a number of prisons in Texas, and the in-prison program is intentionally connected to an aftercare component that includes housing, transportation, and job placement. To date, too many of these faith-based prison programs only operate within prisons. Prisoner reentry and aftercare offer challenges that many well-intentioned organizations have been unable to meet. Unfortunately, we have precious few examples like Restoration Outreach of Dallas, that have shown a willingness to build bridges between faith-based programs in prisons that are connected to efforts in the community that take on housing, transportation, job training and employment, and mentoring.

Conclusion

This chapter makes the case that religion and religious congregations play a key role in generating a great deal of good will and social capital in the United States. Indeed, volunteerism has always been a hallmark of the American experiment. The fact that Americans readily volunteer for so many different worthy causes is not just a noteworthy statistic. Though largely overlooked, volunteers play an absolutely critical role in undergirding many of the existing educational, treatment, and religious programs found within correctional institutions. The plight of an already struggling prison and jail system would be immeasurably worse if not for the voluntary labor of thousands of volunteers who visit these facilities every day. Correctional practitioners and administrators are also the beneficiaries of selfless activities of volunteers. The role of volunteers is increasingly important because correctional budgets have tightened in recent years and government-funded programs are often the first to be subject to cuts.

Correctional institutions could obviously use many more volunteers and there is no better place to recruit volunteers than religious congregations. America has somewhere between 350,000 and 500,000 houses of worship, and many of these congregations already have prison ministries of some kind. To greatly expand the reach of faith-based volunteers is not something that would be difficult to achieve. This is especially true for rural communities, where many of our prisons tend to exists.

However, religious congregations should not only be viewed as volunteer-rich communities that can help prisons run better. These houses of worship are also home to a tremendous amount of philanthropic good will. For example, in 2019, Americans gave more than $449 billion to various charities. By far, the largest segment of this generosity stems from religion.[82] Religious congregations are already contributing to various prison-based programs, but there is a great opportunity for more intentional giving in order to underwrite programs that aid the rehabilitation and reform of prisoners.

As discussed in this chapter, prosocial behavior is something every society needs. We also know that involvement in religious activities is linked to increases in prosocial behavior. Many of the faith-based programs we and others have studied, document how participation in such programs increases prosocial behavior among prisoners. This emerging body of empirical evidence is giving rise to a rich sub-field known as positive criminology, which suggests that more positive and restorative approaches—including those that foster social connectedness and support, service to others, spiritual experience, personal integrity, and identity change—may be more effective than the prevailing punitive tactics. Such restorative justice practices seek to develop active responsibility on the part of individuals who have been living a lifestyle of irresponsibility. Though it would be a dramatic shift, it is not far-fetched to imagine correctional practices that could, in fact, be designed to promote virtue among incarcerated offenders.

Notes

1 de Beaumont and De Tocqueville (1833, p. 47).
2 Finke and Stark (2005).
3 Stark (2005).
4 Ellis and Campbell (2006).
5 Kidd (2017).
6 Levin (2020).
7 Stark (1997).
8 Schuck and Wilson (2008).
9 Putnam (2000), Putnam and Feldstein (2003).
10 *2018 Volunteering in America.*
11 This figure is based on the Independent Sector's estimate of the average value of a volunteer hour for 2017.
12 Putnam (1995).
13 Putnam (2000).
14 Productivity Commission (2003).
15 *2018 Volunteering in America.*

16 The Volunteering in America research is produced by CNCS as part of its efforts to expand the reach and impact of America's volunteers. Collected for the past 15 years, the research is the most comprehensive data on American volunteering ever assembled, and it includes a volunteer data profile for all states and major metropolitan areas. The complete report can be accessed at *VolunteeringInAmerica. gov*. The data for the report were collected through a supplement to the Current Population Survey (CPS): the Civic Engagement and Volunteering Supplement. The CPS is a monthly survey of about 60,000 households (approximately 100,000 adults), conducted by the US Census Bureau on behalf of the Bureau of Labor Statistics. The selected supplements collect data on the volunteering, voting, and civic activities of adults age 16 and older. Volunteers are considered individuals who performed unpaid volunteer activities through or for an organization at any point during the 12-month period (from September 1st of the prior year through the survey week in September of the survey year).

17 Lam (2002), Lam (2006), Wuthnow (1991), Putnam and Campbell (2010).

18 Hustinx, Essen, Haers, and Mels (2014).

19 Johnston (2013).

20 Johnston (2013).

21 McClure (2013).

22 McClure (2013).

23 The American Bible Society is a US-based Bible society which for more than 200 years has been publishing and distributing translations of the Protestant Christian version of the Bible and provides study aids and other tools to help people engage with it. American Bible Society pioneered the Bible-based trauma healing program, a ministry equipping churches to help hurting people reconnect with God through Scripture.

24 Interview with volunteers took place at the Riverside Regional Jail, in Prince George County, Virginia, on January 14, 2020.

25 Merino (2013), Lim and MacGregor (2012).

26 Krause (2010).

27 Brown, Neese, Vinokur, and Smith (2003), Krause (2006a).

28 Krause (2006b).

29 Krause (2009).

30 Social capital is the effective functioning of social groups through interpersonal relationships, a shared sense of identity, a shared understanding, shared norms, shared values, trust, cooperation, and reciprocity. Social capital is a measure of the value of resources, both tangible (e.g., public spaces, private property) and intangible (e.g., actors, human capital, people), and the impact that these relationships have on the resources involved in each relationship, and on larger groups. It is generally seen as a form of capital that produces public goods for a common purpose. Social capital has been used to explain the improved performance of diverse groups, the growth of entrepreneurial firms, superior managerial performance, enhanced supply chain relations, the value derived from strategic alliances, and the evolution of communities.

31 Putnam and Feldstein (2003).

32 Putnam and Campbell (2010).

33 Lim and Putnam (2009).

34 Batson (2012).

35 See the mission of the Baylor ISR's Program on Prosocial Behavior: Criminology has always been only "half" of a field. Its focus is limited to antisocial behavior, with almost no attention ever given to prosocial activities. That is, criminologists ask why people do, or do not, commit crimes; they rarely ask why people do, or do not do, good deeds. The Program on Prosocial Behavior emphasizes the neglected "half" of human behavior. For example, why do so many people generously give money to help those in need? Or, why do most of the people reared in "bad" neighborhoods turn out not only to be law-abiding but to be good citizens? Indeed, how are people transformed from antisocial patterns of behavior to positive patterns? In keeping with the overall mission of ISR, the role of religion in promoting prosocial behavior will be the central concern. Not only the role of religiousness in guiding individual behavior but the role of faith-based groups and organizations in fostering prosocial activities. https://www.baylorisr.org/programs-research/program-on-prosocial-behavior/.

36 Stark (1997, 2014), Wilken (2019).

37 Jang and Johnson (2004), Johnson, Larson, Jang, and Li (2000), Johnson, Jang, Larson, and Li (2000), Putnam and Campbell (2010).

38 Krohn and Thornberry (1993).

39 Johnson (2006a, 2006b).

40 Johnson (2011).

41 Johnson and Siegel (2006).

42 Regnerus (2003), Petts (2009).
43 VanderWeele (2017), Makridis (2019).
44 Lim and Putnam (2009), McClure (2013).
45 Cnaan (2008), Johnson and Wubbenhorst (2017).
46 Koenig (2015), Rosmarin and Koenig (2020).
47 McCullough, Bono, and Root (2005), McCullough (2008).
48 Lam (2002), Wilson and Musick (1997).
49 Johnson (2011), Kelly, Polanin, Johnson, and Jang (2015).
50 Hallett, Hays, Johnson, Jang, and Duwe (2016).
51 Edgell (2013), Mahoney, Pargament, Murray-Swank, and Murray-Swank (2003).
52 Bahr and Hoffmann (2008), Bahr and Hoffmann (2010).
53 Lee, Johnson, Pagano, Post, and Leibowitz (2017).
54 Benjamins and Brown (2004).
55 Ellison and Henderson (2011), Makridis, Johnson, and Koenig (2020), Park (2005).
56 Hummer, Rogers, Nam, and Ellison (1999), VanderWeele et al. (2017).
57 Grim and Grim (2016).
58 Chambers (2017).
59 Ronel and Elisha (2011).
60 Ronel and Segev (2015).
61 Braithwaite (2005), Best and Aston (2015).
62 Cullen, Sundt, and Wozniak (2001).
63 Thompson and Jenkins (1993).
64 Johnson, Jang, and Bradshaw (2021).
65 Johnson et al. (2021).
66 PFI partners with more than 100 different prison ministries around the world, in close collaboration with churches and volunteers. See https://pfi.org.
67 Jang, Johnson, and Anderson (2021).
68 Jang et al. (2021).
69 Haviv, Weisburd, Hasisi, Shoham, and Wolfowicz (2020).
70 Haviv et al. (2020).
71 Hallett, Hays, Johnson, Jang, and Duwe (2015).
72 Duwe and Johnson (2016).
73 Braithwaite (2005).
74 Maruna (2001).
75 Maruna and LeBel (2003).
76 Duwe, Johnson, Hallett, Hays, and Jang (2015).
77 Jang, Johnson, Hays, Hallett, and Duwe (2020).
78 Hallett, Hays, Johnson, Jang, and Duwe (2016).
79 Jang, Johnson, Hays, Hallett, and Duwe (2018).
80 Duwe and Johnson (2013).
81 Johnson and Jang (2020).
82 *Giving USA 2020.*

References

Bahr, S. J., & Hoffmann, J. P. (2008). Religiosity, peers, and adolescent drug use. *Journal of Drug Issues*, *38*(3), 743–769.

Bahr, S. J., & Hoffmann, J. P. (2010). Parenting style, religiosity, peers, and adolescent heavy drinking. *Journal of Studies on Alcohol and Drugs*, *71*(4), 539–543.

Batson, C. D. (2012). A history of prosocial behavior research: C. Daniel Batson, Chapter 12. In A. W. Kruglanski & W. Stoebe (Eds.), *Handbook of the history of social psychology*. London, UK: Psychology Press, 243–264.

Benjamins, M. R., & Brown, C. (2004). Religion and preventative health care utilization among the elderly. *Social Science & Medicine*, *58*(1), 109–118.

Best, D., & Aston, E. (2015). Long-term recovery from addiction: Criminal justice involvement and positive criminology. In N. Ronel & D. Segev (Eds.), *Positive criminology* (pp. 177–193). New York: Routledge.

Braithwaite, J. 2005. Between proportionality & impunity: Confrontation, truth, prevention. *Criminology, 43*, 283–305. doi:10.1111/j.0011-1348.2005.00009.x.

Brown, S. L., Neese, R. M., Vinokur, A. D., & Smith, D. M. (2003). Providing social support may be more beneficial than receiving it: Results from a prospective study of mortality. *Psychological Science, 14*(4), 320–327.

Chambers, O. (2017). *My utmost for his highest*, classic ed. (see June 27th entry). Grand Rapids, MI: Our Daily Bread Publishing.

Cnaan, R. A. (2008). *The invisible caring hand: American congregations and the provision of welfare.* New York, NY: NYU Press.

Cullen, F. T., Sundt, J., & Wozniak, J. (2001). The virtuous prison: Toward a restorative rehabilitation. In H. N. Pontell & D. Shichor (Eds.), *Contemporary issues in crime and criminal justice: Essays in honor of Gilbert Geis* (pp. 265–286). Upper Saddle River, NJ: Prentice Hall.

de Beaumont, G., & de Tocqueville, A. (1833). *On the penitentiary system in the United States* (p. 47). Philadelphia, PA: Carey, Lea & Blanchard

Duwe, G., & Johnson, B. R. (2013). Estimating the benefits of a faith-based correctional program. *International Journal of Criminology and Sociology, 2*, 227–239.

Duwe, G., & Johnson, B. R. (2016). The effect of prison visits from community volunteers on offender recidivism. *The Prison Journal, 96*(2), 279–303.

Duwe, G., Johnson, B. R., Hallett, M., Hays, J., & Jang, S.J. (2015). Bible college participation and prison misconduct: A preliminary analysis. *Journal of Offender Rehabilitation, 54*(5): 371–390.

Edgell, P. (2013). *Religion and family in a changing society.* Princeton, NJ: Princeton University Press.

Ellis, S. J., & Campbell, K. H. (2006). *By the people: A history of Americans as volunteers.* Philadelphia, PA: Energize, Inc.

Ellison, C. G., & Henderson, A. K. (2011). Religion and mental health: Through the lens of the stress process. In A. Blasi (Ed.), *Toward a sociological theory of religion and health* (pp. 11–44). Leiden, The Netherland: Brill.

Finke, R., & Stark, R. (2005). *The churching of America, 1776–2005.* New Brunswick, NJ: Rutgers University Press.

Giving USA 2020: The Annual Report on Philanthropy for the Year 2019. Chicago, IL: Indiana University Lilly Family School of Philanthropy.

Grim, B., & Grim, M. (2016). The socio-economic contriubtions of religion to American society: An empirical analysis. *Interdisciplinary Journal of Research on Religion.* Retrieved from http://www.religjournal.com/articles/article_view.php?id=108.

Hallett, M., Hays, J., Johnson, B. R., Jang, S. J., & Duwe, G. (2015). "First stop dying": Angola's Christian seminary as positive criminology. *International Journal of Offender Therapy and Comparative Criminology.* http://dx.doi.org/10.1177/0306624X15598179.

Hallett, M., Hays, J., Johnson, B. R., Jang, S. J., & Duwe, G. (2016). *The Angola prison seminary: Effects of faith-based ministry on identity transformation, desistance, and rehabilitation.* London, UK: Routledge.

Haviv, N., Weisburd, D., Hasisi, B., Shoham, E., & Wolfowicz, M. (2020). Do religious programs in prison work? A quasi-experimental evaluation in the Israeli prison service. *Journal of Experimental Criminology, 16*, 505–533.

Hummer, R. A., Rogers, R. G., Nam, C. B., & Ellison, C. G. (1999). Religious involvement and US adult mortality. *Demography, 36*(2), 273–285.

Hustinx, L., von Essen, J., Haers, J., and Mels, S. (2014). *Religion and volunteering: Complex, contested, and ambiguous relationships.* Cham, Switzerland: Springer.

Jang, S. J., & Johnson, B. R. (2004). Explaining religious effects on distress among African Americans. *Journal for the Scientific Study of Religion, 43*(2), 239–260.

Jang, S. J., Johnson, B. R., & Anderson, M. (2021). The prisoner's journey: Assessing the effectiveness of a faith-based program in Colombian prisons" with Sung Joon Jang, and Matthew Anderson. Retrieved from http://www.BAYLORISR.org.

Jang, S. J., Johnson, B. R., Hays, J., Hallett, M., & Duwe, G. (2018). Religion and misconduct in Angola prison: Conversion, congregational participation, religiosity, and self-identities. *Justice Quarterly, 35*(3): 412–442.

Jang, S. J., Johnson, B. R., Hays, J., Hallett, M., & Duwe, G. (2020). Prisoners helping prisoners change: A study of inmates field ministers within Texas prisons. *International Journal of Offender Therapy and Comparative Criminology, 64*(5), 470–497.

Johnson, B. R. (2006a). *Objective hope – Assessing the effectiveness of religion and faith-based organizations: A systematic review of the literature.* Institute for Studies of Religion (ISR Research Report), Baylor University. Retrieved from http://www.BAYLORISR.org/publications/reports/.

Johnson, B. R. (2006b). *The great escape: How religion alters the delinquent behavior of high-risk adolescents.* Institute for Studies of Religion (ISR Research Report), Baylor University. Retrieved from http://www.BAYLORISR.org/publications/reports/.

Johnson, B. R. (2011). *More God, less crime: Why religion matters and how it could matter more.* Conshohocken, PA: Templeton Press.

Johnson, B. R., & Jang, S. J. (2020). *Connecting in-prison programs to prisoner reentry and aftercare: A case study of restoration outreach of dallas ministries.* Program on Prosocial Behavior, Baylor University. Retrieved from http://www.BAYLORISR.org/publications/reports/.

Johnson, B. R., Jang, S. J., & Bradshaw, M. (2021). *New hope for offender rehabilitation: Assessing the trauma healing program.* Program on Prosocial Behavior, Baylor University. Retrieved from http://www.BAYLORISR.org/publications/reports/.

Johnson, B. R., Jang, S. J., Larson, D. B., & Li, S. (2000). The 'invisible institution' and black youth crime: The church as an agency of local social control. *Journal of Youth and Adolescence, 29,* 479–498.

Johnson, B. R., Larson, D. B., Jang, S. J., & Li, S. (2000). Who escapes the crime of inner-cities: Church attendance and religious salience among disadvantaged youth. *Justice Quarterly, 17,* 701–715.

Johnson, B. R., & Siegel, M. (2006). *The role African American churches in reducing crime among black youth.* Institute for Studies of Religion (ISR Research Report), Baylor University. Retrieved from http://www.BAYLORISR.org/publications/reports/.

Johnson, B. R., & Wubbenhorst, W. (2017). *Assessing the faith-based response to homelessness in America: Findings from eleven cities.* Program on Prosocial Behavior, Baylor University. Retrieved from http://www.BAYLORISR.org/publications/reports/.

Johnston, J. B. (2013). Religion and volunteering over the adult life course. *Journal for the Scientific Study of Religion, 52*(4): 733–752.

Kelly, P. E., Polanin, J. Johnson, B. R., & Jang, S. J. (2015). Religion, delinquency, and drug use: A meta-analysis. *Criminal Justice Review, 40,* 505–523.

Kidd, T. S. (2017). *Benjamin Franklin: The religious life of a founding father.* New Haven, CT: Yale University Press.

Koenig, H. G. (2015). Religion, spirituality, and health: A review and update. *Advances in Mind-Body Medicine, 29*(3): 19–26.

Krause, N. (2006a). Church-based Social Support And Mortality. *Journal of Gerontology: Social Sciences, 61*(3): S140–S146.

Krause, N. (2006b). Exploring the stress-buffering effects of church-based social support and secular social support on health in late life. *Journal of Gerontology: Social Sciences, 61*(1): S35–S43.

Krause, N. (2010). Church-based volunteering, providing informal support at church, and self-rated health in late life. *Journal of Aging and Health, 21*(1): 63–84.

Krohn, M. D., & Thornberry, T. P. (1993). Network theory: A model for understanding drug abuse among African-American and Hispanic youth. In M. R. De La Rosa & J. R. Adrados (Eds.), *Drug abuse among minority youth: Advances in research and methodology.* Rockville, MD: NIDA Research Monograph, U.S. Department of Health and Human Services. 130: 102–128.

Lam, P. (2002). As the flocks gather: How religion affects voluntary association participation. *Journal for the Scientific Study of Religion, 41,* 405–422.

Lam, P. (2006). Religion and civic culture: A cross-national study of voluntary association membership. *Journal for the Scientific Study of Religion, 45,* 177–193.

Lee, M. T., Johnson, B. R., Pagano, M. E., Post, S. G., & Leibowitz, G. S. (2017). From defiance to reliance: Spiritual virtue as a pathway towards desistence, humility, and recovery among juvenile offenders. *Spirituality in Clinical Practice, 4*(3), 161–175.

Levin, J. (2020). *Religion and medicine: A history of the encounter between humanity's two greatest institutions.* New York, NY: Oxford University Press.

Lim, C., & MacGregor, C. A. (2012). Religion and volunteering in context: Disentangling the contextual effects of religion on voluntary behavior. *American Sociological Review, 77*(5), 747–779.

Lim, C., & Putnam, R. D. (2009). Religion, social networks, and life satisfaction. *American Sociological Review, 75*(6), 914–933.

Mahoney, A., Pargament, K. I., Murray-Swank, A., & Murray-Swank, N. (2003). Religion and the sanctification of family relationships. *Review of Religious Research, 44*, 220–236.

Makridis, C. (2019). Human flourishing and religious liberty: Evidence from over 150 countries, 2006–2018. *SSRN*. Retrieved from https://papers.ssrn.com/sol3/papers.cfm?abstract_id=3472793.

Makridis, C., Johnson, B. R., & Koenig, H. G. (2020). Does religious affiliation protect people's well-being? Evidence from the great recession after correcting for selection effects. *SSRN*. Retrieved from http://booksandjournals.brillonline.com/content/books/10.1163/ej.9789004205970.i-277.7.

Maruna, S. (2001). *Making good: How ex-convicts reform and rebuild their lives.* Washington, DC: American Psychological Association. http://dx.doi.org/10.1037/10430-000.

Maruna, S., & LeBel, T. P. (2003). Welcome home? Examining the 'reentry court' concept from a strengths-based perspective. *Western Criminology Review, 4*, 91–107.

McClure, J. M. (2013). Sources of social support: examining congregational involvement, private devotional activities, and congregational context. *Journal for the Scientific Study of Religion, 52*(4), 698–712.

McCullough, M.E. (2008). *Beyond Revenge: The Evolution of the Forgiveness Instinct.* Jossey-Bass.

McCullough, M. E., Bono, G., & Root, L. M. (2005). Religion and forgiveness. In R. F. Paloutzian & C. L. Park (Eds.), *Handbook of the psychology of religion and spirituality* (pp. 394–411). New York, NY: The Guilford Press.

Merino, S. (2013). Religious social networks and volunteering: examining recruitment via close ties. *Review of Religious Research, 55*, 509–527.

Park, C. L. (2005). Religion as a meaning-making framework in coping with life stress. *Journal of Social Issues, 61*(4), 707–729.

Petts, R. (2009). Trajectories of religious participation from adolescence to young adulthood. *Journal for the Scientific Study of Religion, 48*, 552–571.

Productivity Commission. (2003). Social capital: Reviewing the concept and its policy implications. Research Paper. AusInfo, Canberra.

Putnam, R. D. (2000). *Bowling alone: The collapse and revival of American community.* New York, NY: Simon & Schuster.

Putnam, R. D., & Campbell, D. E. (2010). *American grace: How religion divides and unites us.* New York, NY: Simon & Schuster.

Putnam, R. D., & Feldstein, L. M. (2003). *Better together: Restoring the American community.* New York, NY: Simon & Schuster.

Regnerus, M. D. (2003). Linked lives, faith, and behavior: An intergenerational model of religious influence on adolescent delinquency. *Journal for the Scientific Study of Religion, 42*, 189–203.

Ronel, N., & Elisha, E. (2011). A different perspective: Introducing positive criminology. *International Journal of Offender Therapy and Comparative Criminology, 55*(2), 305–325. http://dx.doi.org/10.1177/0306624X09357772.

Ronel, N., & Segev, D. (eds). 2015. *Positive criminology.* New York, NY: Routledge.

Rosmarin, D. H., & Koenig, H. G. (2020). *Handbook of spirituality, religion, and mental health.* 2nd ed. London, UK: Academic Press.

Schuck, P. H., & Wilson, J. Q. (2008). *Understanding America: The Anatomy of an exceptional nation.* New York, NY: Public Affairs.

Stark, R. (1997). *The rise of Christianity: How the obscure, marginal Jesus movement became the dominant religious force in the western world in a few centuries.* Princeton, NJ: Princeton Press.

Stark, R. (2005). *The victory of reason: How Christianity led to freedom, capitalism, and western success.* New York, NY: Random House.

Stark, R. (2014). *How the west won: The neglected story of the triumph of modernity.* Wilmington, DE: ISI Books.

Thompson, G. J., & Jenkins, J. B. (1993). *Verbal judo: The gentle art of persuasion.* New York, NY: William Morrow and Company, Inc.

Tocqueville, A. D. (2003). *Democracy in America and two essays on America.* London, UK: Penguin Books.

VanderWeele, T. J. (2017). On the promotion of human flourishing. *Proceedings of the National Academy of Sciences, 114*(3): 8148–8156. doi:10.1073/pnas.01702996114.

VanderWeele, T. J., Yu, J., Cozier, Y. C., Wise, L., Argentieri, M. A., Rosenberg, L., … Shields, A. E. (2017). Attendance at religious services, prayer, religious coping, and religious/spiritual identity as predictors of all-cause mortality in the black women's health study. *American Journal of Epidemiology, 185,* 515–522.

2018 Volunteering in America. Washington, DC: Corporation for National and Community Service.

Wilken, R. L. (2019). *Liberty in the things of god: The Christian origins of religious freedom.* New Haven, CT: Yale University Press.

Wilson, J., & Musick, M. (1997). Who cares? Toward an integrated theory of volunteer work. *American Sociological Review, 62,* 694–713.

Wuthnow, R. (1991). *Acts of compassion: Caring for others and helping ourselves.* Princeton, NJ: Princeton University Press.

4

THE DISRUPTIVE POTENTIAL OF OFFENDER-LED PROGRAMS

"Lived Experience" and Inmate Ministry

Desistance moved from an Ivory Tower jargon word to a style of delivering justice-related interventions that foregrounded the strengths and expertise of ex-prisoners themselves to act as mentors, "wounded healers," and architects of their own rehabilitation....In the coming phase, I would argue that the "real action" in desistance will move away from both the universities and the criminal justice agencies and be centered around grassroots advocacy work from {non-profit organizations}.[1]

Lived Experience: Peer Mentoring, Wounded Healers, and Inmate Ministry

Dating back to the 1950s, criminologists have recognized the value of previously convicted citizens working as practitioners in helping offenders reform.[2] Faith-based and addiction-focused programs have been particularly active in utilizing peer-based "wounded healers" as valuable assets in rehabilitative programming.[3] It is widely recognized, for example, that former addicts are often viewed as the most effective drug treatment counselors—not because they have academic credentials in addiction therapy, but because they possess authentic "lived experience" that includes overcoming the challenges of addiction.[4] Perhaps the most enduring contribution of research on "peer mentoring" of this sort has been documentation of its *bi-directional salutary benefits*, both for those receiving help as well as for those offering it.[5] Shadd Maruna's work has been particularly useful in documenting how the generative impulses of stigmatized offenders may be harnessed for helping others "make good."[6] More importantly, as practitioners of 12-step therapies often attest, the act of "giving back to others" in fact becomes a key staple of their own rehabilitation.

Many citizens undertaking "self-help" agendas prefer interacting with peers over professionals, since peers empathize differently than outsiders regarding shared struggles and challenges—and can provide affirmation without stigma regarding what many inmates characterize as being "otherized" by the criminal justice system and/or "medicalized" by alienating professional schemas. While 12-step programs utilize *anonymity* to assure confidentiality—as in Alcoholics "Anonymous" —they more importantly also prioritize a *needs-focused egalitarianism* in delivering services. By trading primarily upon their status as mutually compromised equals, wounded healer's legitimacy is perversely enhanced, not reduced, in the eyes of those needing help. In that narrow space of access and trust, wounded healers are sometimes able to assist where outsiders cannot. Through serving in correctional settings by offering unique situational empathy

DOI: 10.4324/9781003171744-4

and sense of common purpose—wounded healers leverage their skills and lived experience toward charting a pathway through the stigmas and barriers that will confront offenders for the rest of their lives.

While no panacea to the challenges facing prisons, enhanced opportunities for what we call here "offender-led programming" can add much to the often limited menu of rehabilitative services provided to men and women in prison. Expanded use of peer mentoring is certainly today an increasingly recognized facet of correctional programming.[7] Receiving support from peers who face similar challenges and who have often confronted similar fears and setbacks, can lend inspiration and hope to men and women who not only perceive their situation to be hopeless, but who also often face debilitating shame and isolation. "Lived experience not only communicates that [peer mentors] understand the hardships of navigating the criminal justice system, but also signals their proven ability to transcend its challenges."[8]

This book explores the expanded use and potential of inmate-led programs, particularly in the aftermath of COVID-19, which has dramatically complicated budgetary efforts to introduce new rehabilitative programs into prisons. By specifically exploring a large set of privately funded and newly implemented "inmate ministry" programs, this book offers a unique perspective into a growing retinue of correctional programs now active in dozens of US maximum-security prisons. Efforts to cope with reduced taxpayer spending on corrections have featured prominent uses of peer mentoring, often developed through cooperation with penal voluntary sector (PVS) organizations—especially those involving "faith-based" groups emphasizing restorative methods for helping prisoners succeed.[9] While research documents that peer mentors have been deployed with "remarkable success" in working with addicts and those struggling during prisoner reentry,[10] what we consider to be the "disruptive potential" of peer mentoring *inside prisons* has received less attention. We believe authentic restoration and rehabilitation should become the predominant objective of all carceral regimes—and that indiscriminate punitivism has clearly failed as a social policy tool.[11] More importantly, we document how restorative methods and programming are expanding in many dozens of US maximum-security prisons, brought about through new public-private partnerships between religious volunteer educators and prison administrators working with inmates.

Transactional versus Transformational Corrections: Deterrence versus Desistance

Operating under the therapeutic rubric of "wounded healers," peer mentors are able to venture where others are not easily welcomed, offering a holistic and alternative touchstone for mentees that is informal, non-judgmental, confidential, and generally separate from the official record. As David Skarbeck notes, "inmates create extralegal governance institutions when official governance is insufficient."[12] Inside prisons facing deep crisis, peer mentors emphasize their ability to "cut through the bullshit"—by recognizing both the severity of challenges faced by their peers, but also, for example, by being present during periods of crisis when mentees may insist they are "doing just fine" but in actuality are self-isolating or in fear. As coiner of the term "wounded healer" Henri Nouwen describes the work involved: "When our wounds cease to be a source of shame and become a source of healing, we have become wounded healers" (1974, p. 3). These very challenges comprise pearls of great price earned by peer mentors who have successfully faced similar challenges. In such cases, a pivotal transformation has taken place: peer mentors no longer run from their stigma, but seek instead to use it for greater purpose. Successful peer mentors demonstrate that a productive life is possible after failure—and indeed, embody a journey of self-development that is prosocial based on transcending past failures.

While criminologists tend to emphasize the *mentoring* aspects of peer mentoring, mentors themselves highlight the centrality of their status as *peers*.[13] Peer mentors occupy a rarified status in correctional settings, holding dual credibility with nominally oppositional groups: prison officials and inmates themselves. As noted by numerous scholars, peer mentoring generates "carnivalesque," "Alice in Wonderland" types of inversions to correctional practices, hierarchies, and staff/inmate relations that we argue here are paradigm-shifting and highly effective.[14] Drawing from Skarbek (2016), we argue that both the "importation" and "pains of imprisonment" models of prison life are highly contingent upon both the "quality of official governance" and specific "inmate demographics" of particular prisons (2016, p. 847). Put simply, the "pains of imprisonment" vary greatly by prison and are experienced differently by individual inmates.[15] When conditions are considered to be "illegitimate," however—that is to be unduly and unjustly painful or arbitrary—inmates will establish alternative and informal authority structures for providing safety and scarce resources. Increasingly, as shown below, the unique authentic "lived experience" of inmates who succeed in prison and after is recognized as just such a resource. As Gill Buck puts it, inmate peer mentoring "challenges the established order and dominant definitions of expertise" in the context of corrections (2019, p. 352). In short, peer mentoring turns the traditional order of prison relations upside down (see also Albertson & Fox 2019; Cooper 2015; Sparks, Bottoms & Hay 1996).[16]

Inmates and ex-offenders often come to be distrustful of the criminal justice system. As a result of this mistrust, they often shy away from accessing official help—which they often perceive as likely to harm them as to help them.[17] Self-transformation therefore becomes a common preoccupation of peer mentors, especially given their oftentimes direct personal experience with the criminal justice system operating as a de facto *hindrance* toward achieving their success.[18] Peer mentors shine light on possibilities of positive change from a different vantage point, offering unique (and not always favorable) perspectives on all things "official" in the system, while also having a unique level of access to populations in need. More importantly, peer mentors focus by definition on desistance rather than deterrence, seeking ways to improve and best survive, rather than obsessing on past mistakes. In short, peer mentors can help create an alternative frame of reference that proves cathartic and healing for inmates both inside and as they exit prison. Their work involves an alternative to the leveraging of transactional threats from authorities, seeking instead to achieve a transformational process of self-reflection and agency not wholly dependent upon official definitions of success or authority.

Inmate Peer Ministry: New Practices, New Paradigm

As we argue here, the growing devolution of correctional responsibility to inmate peer mentors inside prisons presents opportunities for the introduction of important counter-narratives to punitive justice that carry with them paradigm-shifting implications for both prisoners and prisons.[19] Not only are at once stigmatized yet institutionally recognized peer mentors being "responsibilized" for providing offender treatment, but peer mentors themselves are increasingly recognized as valuable institutional commodities proffering access to charitable resources. As prisons become more dependent upon philanthropic resources for meeting even basic needs, and more comfortable with facilitating the penal devolution we describe here, is the extent to which *many transformations long the aspiration of prison reformers have in fact become reality*: increased community access and transparency, increased utilization of prosocial modeling and social capital, cultivation of new programming and resources amid cutbacks—and replacement of indiscriminate punitivism as the dominant experience of incarceration with the twin goals of authentic healing and rehabilitation.[20] Peer mentors' value in the penal marketplace derives not only from their unique ability to hold dual institutional legitimacy by virtue of an "expertise" only they possess, but more importantly for the paradigm-shifting agenda they invoke inside prisons: that of restoration instead of punishment.[21] And make no mistake—corrections officials, driven by both increasing need and growing recognition of programmatic success, are turning to inmates themselves as rehabilitative agents—particularly in "inmate peer ministry."[22] As Texas Department of Criminal Justice (TDCJ) recently characterized the value of inmate lived experience for rehabilitation, TDCJ Executive Director Brian Collier speaking at a recent inmate peer minister graduation ceremony stated:

> I don't have it, our chaplains don't have it, a lot of our volunteers don't have it. You've got credibility with your peers in the system, and that's what matters. You've walked in their shoes, you've been where they are, you know that path, and you've seen a different path.[23]

Collier concluded by assuring the new "field ministers" that their ministry work is valued:

> As you walk the path, I want you to hear this from me directly: I absolutely fully support your mission. At TDCJ we fully support what you're doing, our wardens fully support what you're doing, and we are on the same team. We're excited about the changes that your work is going to bring.[24]

The Expansion of Inmate Peer Ministry

This chapter describes utilization of inmate "lived experience" as a correctional resource deployed through inmate peer ministries in six US maximum-security prisons. Drawing upon data from a multi-institution, multi-year research agenda exploring the impact of inmate ministries supported by private charities in maximum-security prisons, this chapter considers inmate peer ministry using life-history interviews, prison site visits, and archival research.[25] The chapter documents how through strategic "insourcing" of inmate ministerial volunteers (using internal inmate labor instead of paid employees), prison work assignments once reserved for chaplains and professional counselors have been supplanted with privately trained and religiously responsibilized inmates. Each prison described was visited for program overviews while inmate interviews were conducted at the two largest sites, Angola and Darrington. Hundred and thirty-one life-history interviews of inmate peer ministers were conducted at Angola and 67 at Darrington.[26] Ongoing research is underway exploring inmate peer ministry throughout Texas.[27] An analysis of the funding mechanisms, training provided, and work assignments of inmate peer ministers comprise the focus of this chapter's analysis (Table 4.1).

TABLE 4.1 Prisons and Prison Seminaries Examined

Host Prison	PVS/Sponsoring Seminary
Louisiana State Penitentiary—Angola	New Orleans Baptist Theological Seminary
Mississippi State Penitentiary—Parchman	New Orleans Baptist Theological Seminary
Hardee Correctional Institution—Florida DOC	New Orleans Baptist Theological Seminary
Handlon Correctional Institution—Michigan DOC	Calvin College & Calvin Seminary
Sing Sing—NY Dept of Corrections & Community Supervision	New York Theological Seminary
Darrington Correctional Institution—Texas Department of Criminal Justice	Southwestern Baptist Theological Seminary

Paradigm Shift: Transforming Prisons with Faith-based Charity

With an explicit emphasis on expanding program resources and instilling into prisons a "personal and not bureaucratic" approach to rehabilitation, legislation for "faith-based" programming in the United States straightforwardly prioritized the monetary and human capital assets of religious volunteer organizations as a proxy resource for correctional budgeting.[28] In recognition of the challenges faced by prisons due to overcrowding, understaffing, and challenged budget scenarios, legislation for expanding faith-based involvement in prisons began as incarceration rates skyrocketed. The 2001 enabling legislation authorizing America's first and largest entirely "faith-based" correctional agenda, which took place in Florida, demonstrates how utilization of faith-based programming on behalf of prisons supplanted the state corrections budget—conscripting chaplains to the task of recruiting religious volunteers for program delivery, while also seeking to leverage the social capital of outside religious groups for assistance with prisoner reentry[29]:

> Whereas, faith-based organizations are "armies of compassion" devoted to changing individuals' hearts and lives and can offer cost-effective substance abuse treatment through the use of volunteers and other cost saving measures, and Whereas research has proven that *one-on-one private and faith-based programming is often more effective than government programs* in shaping and reclaiming lives because they are free to assert the essential connection between responsibility and human dignity; *their approach is personal, not bureaucratic*; their service is not primarily a function of professional background, but of individual commitment; and they inject an element of moral challenge and spiritual renewal *that government cannot duplicate* and Whereas, in an effort to transform lives and break the personally destructive and expensive recidivism cycle, Florida should increase the number of chaplains who strengthen volunteer participation and expand the pilot faith-based dormitory program that includes a voluntary faith component that supports inmates as they reenter communities. Be It Enacted by the Legislature of the State of Florida (*emphasis added*)[30]

While having faded from national prominence since the heyday of faith-based programming during the administration of President George W. Bush, prison administrators enduring sustained budget cuts have happily continued to accept resources from religious volunteers, including everything from musical instruments to ceiling fans to actual program delivery inside prisons.[31] That religious voluntarism has become a prominent staple of correctional budgeting is well documented, as correctional administrators and state legislatures utilize penal voluntary sector assets as a means of achieving disruptive innovation.[32]

New Stakeholders, New Worldviews

> Neoliberal austerity measures and welfare state retrenchment have meant that voluntary organizations around the globe are increasingly called upon to perform statutory social services. Despite a large and rising presence in criminal justice services delivery, volunteers and voluntary organizations have scarcely received scholarly analysis.[33]

Renewed penal optimism surrounding inmate peer mentoring highlights its tendency to privilege lay understandings over professional ones, an issue traceable back to Victorian-era religious penal voluntarism.[34] Writing about progressive reform in American corrections, historian

Lawrence Friedman credits the wave of 20th-century "professionalization" in prisons for expanding public access to institutions and fostering transparency for inmate families:

> When change did occur, it was partly because the system was becoming more professional—and more differentiated. There are maximum, medium, and minimum-security prisons, prisons for men, and prisons for women, and juvenile institutions of various sorts. The civil rights movement, an increased sensitivity toward minorities, and the general rights-consciousness of society itself: these forces and influences scaled the walls of the prison or whatever substituted for walls. The prison became more a microcosm of the outside world than an island, hermetically sealed.[35]

Today religious volunteer service organizations are once again becoming mainstay components of status quo corrections operations.[36] While the dominant correctional service model is still that of "professionalized" prisons utilizing paid staff—prisons are once again commonly resorting to unpaid volunteers, albeit, with prisons again being hermetically sealed-off and hardly transparent at all.[37] As prison officials become structurally dependent upon PVS partnerships to run programs, however, research "making visible the fine dynamics of penality" inside these prisons should expand.[38] As one inmate minister put it at Angola:

> Everyone in prison has PTSD: your crime, arrest, imprisonment, etc. are all traumas. The seminary acknowledges that and the seminary's teachings here healed me on many levels. There's a camaraderie in the midst of the preparing, the equipping, that I learned in seminary that you're just not going to get apart from that.[39]

As we argue here, while disruptive of traditional models of service delivery, increasing reliance upon PVS resources and personnel introduces into penal environments both new stakeholders and new worldviews that can be antithetical to traditional models of corrections—especially in ways that elevate the dignity of inmates.[40] As one inmate minister at Angola describes the personal elevation he receives from his work (Hallett et al. 2017, p. 47)[41]:

> In actuality you're like an inmate chaplain. You know, that's the responsibility you have. You deliver death messages, you do counseling, you set the schedules, you host outside ministries that come in. You make rounds. You know, there's a lot more to do than I thought. There's a lot of responsibilities. But I tell you I can't say anything bad about my religious responsibilities. I thank God for them. It's been a life changing experience for me.
>
> *(EW 1:54)*

Inmate peer ministry programs view the offending pasts of inmates as only one aspect of prisoners' entire life story. Cultivating holistic renderings of inmate biographies that highlight positive aspects of inmates' past lives introduces new opportunities for forming prosocial self-identity while mitigating the shame and isolation common to prison life.[42] Put simply, inmate peer ministry aspires to replace the pervading experience of incarceration as punitive with a new focus—"healing"—offering unique resources for emotional labor derived from the unique lived experience of inmates "in the same boat"—but who are also equipped with formal training in pastoral counseling.[43] As inmate peer minister Paul Will puts it: "Listen, I'm not here to convert anybody. I'm just trying to help someone self-identify."[44]

In contrast to the correctional norm in sometimes violent "warehouse" prisons, inmate peer ministry proffers opportunities for face-to-face catharsis minus the shame and discomfort of traditional encounters with "professionals."[45] Said one inmate peer minister:

> The seminary process has helped us, as a community of leaders, teach people how to identify where emotional wounds took place in inmates' lives, and with that we began a learning pattern. And it teaches them how to (1) accept that that happened; (2) to stop identifying themselves as a victim, which has been perpetuated by that wound; and (3) then teach them how to bring back the reasonable voice that was left as a casualty when emotional imbalance took over their life. So what happens is, we have learned how to identify and accept the wounds and rehabilitate one another through common love experiences outlined in the Gospel.[46]

The Angola Prison Seminary: Necessity, the Mother of (Re)Invention

> How can wounds become a source of healing? This is a question which requires careful consideration. For when we want to put our wounded selves in the service of others, we must consider the relationship between our professional and personal lives.[47]

So how did all of this come about? In largest part quite by accident. In the aftermath of the federal government's revocation of Pell Grant eligibility for convicted felons in 1994, then Louisiana State Penitentiary at Angola Warden Burl Cain feared elimination of this collegiate educational resource was uniquely harmful to his prison.[48] The prison had long been one of the most violent in America and still retains the distinction of being America's toughest prison in terms of sentencing. Collegiate education programs were among the few incentives for good behavior available to Angola's prisoners. Fearing an increase in violence, Cain reached out to New Orleans Baptist Theological Seminary (NOBTS) administrators to explore the possibility of their offering some collegiate-level courses as a gift to the prison.

Deeply embedded in its history, religious practice at Angola dates to its earliest days as a slave plantation. Recent interviews of Angola's oldest inmates and staff, a few of whom have spent the majority of their long lives at the prison after first arriving around 1950, explained inmate worship at the prison dates back to convict leasing and before. One inmate, who first arrived at Angola in 1957, and was still there in 2015, described "old timers worshiping and praying when I got here." Another long-serving warden, himself born and raised on "the farm," confirmed "religion has always been at Angola."[49]

As NOBTS administrators soon learned, Angola's informal inmate religious culture was expanded into formal congregations in the aftermath of a 1974 federal consent decree finding conditions at the prison infamously "shocked the conscience of any right-thinking person."[50] After the federal intervention, religious practice at Angola was identified as one of the few resources immediately available to inmates which they valued, with prisoners thereafter being granted permission to turn what had been described as "inmate-led religious clubs" into active "churches." And so they did, forming Baptist, Pentecostal, Catholic, Methodist, and other Christian worship communities—collectively referred to today as the "Angola Church." Several inmate-built churches and even two Catholic chapels exist today on the grounds of Angola.[51] Inmate-led churches provided unique opportunities for inmate leadership in the aftermath of a period of well-documented prison neglect.[52]

Overcoming initial reservations and after learning about Angola's inmate churches, NOBTS administrators concluded that providing courses to the prison could fall within their self-described mission: "to equip the local church." After first offering a few classes, NOBTS soon planted a fully functioning Christian seminary on the grounds of the prison—recruiting students from Angola's inmate population and matriculating trained ministers to serve its autonomously governed inmate-run churches of various denominations.[53] At its own cost, NOBTS has operated the program tuition-free for Angola inmates since 1995.

Priding themselves on the "direct overlap" between Angola's seminary program and that offered by NOBTS in the free world, graduates of Angola's prison seminary go on to lead active voluntary congregations at the prison just as NOBTS graduates do on the outside. With intensive training in grief counseling and conflict management, including a period of supervised apprenticeship, Angola's Inmate Ministers are deployed throughout the prison—serving not only as church leaders, but also as grief counselors, hospice orderlies, funeral directors at the prison cemetery, chaplain's assistants, and seminary tutors. Governed by a personalist ethic of what they call "Relationship Theology," Angola's Inmate Ministers strive to serve both staff and their fellow inmates through focused attention to interpersonal relationships.[54]

Getting to Scale: The Scope of US Inmate Peer Ministry

As with inmate peer ministry at each of the programs examined here, Angola's seminary graduates often find themselves to be among the most highly educated individuals at their prisons—something not hard to accomplish, since roughly 60% of Angola corrections staff have only a high school or GED equivalency (and some less than that). Put simply, deployed by wardens using a basic correctional "unit management" strategy, Angola's inmate peer ministry program is utilized to professionally staff the prison.[55] Over the past 25 years, approximately 40 graduates of Angola's Christian seminary have also been sent to other Louisiana prisons as well, serving as self-described "missionaries from Angola," leading inmate worship and serving as chaplain's orderlies.

Importantly, the position of "inmate minister" at Angola predates the NOBTS seminary, as it has long been practiced by correctional staff to rely upon the prison's unique religious culture for serving inmates in crisis. Inmate peer ministers are noted by staff to be particularly effective during specific times of distress for inmates: upon notification of death of a loved one outside the prison, upon first entry into the prison, after family visits, and during the "last rites" process for inmates on death row.[56]

At present 27 states have active inmate peer ministry programs in advanced development or in full operation (GPSF 2019; see Appendix I). These programs deploy privately funded religious educational institutions inside prisons for the purpose of training inmates to serve in an explicitly religious capacity in multiple types of inmate peer ministry, with matriculated graduates carrying out prison work assignments ranging from individual caseloads for process counseling, leading congregate religious worship and small group exercises, to passively acting as "agents of God" in all facets of their lives in prison.

While inmates are nominally provided the education they receive for free, both program sponsors and prison administrators frequently prioritize recruiting inmates with life sentences "for greater return on investment."[57] In return for their education, inmates are expected to "give back to the prison," in what many inmate peer ministers describe as a "24–7/365 assignment" (e.g., "Always on duty for Jesus"). In the nation's largest such program, inmate peer ministry in Texas has expanded not just to producing inmate peer ministers serving one host institution, but to sending out prison seminary graduates across the entire state prison system—so-called "field ministers," of whom there are 164 currently working in direct contact with inmates in 32 Texas prisons.[58] As the sponsoring religious education provider, Southwestern Baptist Theological Seminary, noted about their work in Texas:

> This is not just about putting a seminary in a prison. … We equip the men to go. And through the graciousness of the board and TDCJ, these men are allowed to actually go as field ministers and take this equipment to be able to preach and counsel and evangelize and just let someone cry on their shoulders.
>
> *(SWBTS Online, May 14, 2019)*

Reinscribing Reinvention: Penal Entrepreneurship and Inmate Peer Ministry

The starvation diet imposed upon many state prison systems is part of a larger funding crisis faced by corrections overall, driven in part by tax-conscious politicians who now rightly question the "return on investment" gained for taxpayers by prisons that offer so little programming and such high recidivism.[59] In numerous instances since the mid-1990s, sustained austerity and high staff turnover has resulted in a growing number of maximum-security prisons turning to religious volunteers to sustain programming for inmates.[60] Referring to criminal justice as the "last sacred cow of big government," conservative reform advocate Grover Norquist recently stated: "Spending more on education doesn't necessarily get you more education….It turns out it's also true about criminal justice and fighting crime."[61] "Once you believe that prisons are like any other agency, then it becomes natural to suspect that wardens and prison guards, like other suppliers of government services enjoy a monopoly, inflating costs and providing shoddy service."[62]

In further demonstration of Tomczak and Buck's (2019) notion that voluntary sector engagements in criminal justice are "hybridizing" the penal marketplace, 27 states, and over 70 maximum-security prisons nationwide now deploy privately trained inmate peer ministers for rehabilitative work assignments inside prisons.[63] This work includes but is not limited to making rounds for pastoral counseling through "tier walking," leading individual and group worship ceremonies, receiving private confessions, offering group or individual counseling, conducting hospice and death row visitation, and encouraging personal growth through active listening and conflict management—all work traditionally undertaken by chaplains and prison counselors.

Drawing upon Susie Scott's (2010) discussion of "reinventive institutions," Crewe and Ievins (2019) note that "whereas inmates of total institutions are committed against their will, members of reinventive institutions are voluntary participants, who believe that they need to change and that doing so is their personal responsibility."[64] In the outside world, reinventive institutions include monasteries, health clinics, spiritual retreat centers and the like. Unlike in total institutions such as prisons, here both enrollment and exit are voluntary. As Scott puts it, reinventive institutions provide their volunteers spaces for self-reinvention. Reinventive institutions are "places to which people retreat for periods of intense self-reflection, education, enrichment and reform, but under their own volition, in pursuit of 'self-improvement.'"[65] As Burnett and Maruna have observed, prisoner volunteerism allows for inmates to self-select rehabilitation agendas based on their personal strengths.[66] "Rather than coercing obedience, strengths-based practices are therefore thought to develop intrinsic motivations towards helping behaviors— what Mike Clark (2001) calls the difference between compliance and growth."[67]

We suggest that the introduction of religious penal voluntary sector (PVS) organizations into prisons for the purposes of training inmate peer ministers is "hybridizing" American prisons in prosocial ways by introducing a reinvigorated element of self-reinvention. As PVS stakeholders introduce supplemental programs featuring opportunities for religious self-reinvention, the experience of incarceration becomes more "reinventive" and less "totalizing." While noting there is always "a great deal of power flowing" inside prisons amid an ever present element of "latent coercion," there is also a "normative" measure of voluntarism available for most inmates.[68] Indeed, despite being available to literally thousands of inmates at Angola for almost 25 years, only some 350 volunteers availed themselves of the opportunity to complete Angola's prison seminary. Increasing opportunities for self-reinvention and strengths-based programming by "treating prisoners as positive resources and providing opportunities for them to develop prosocial self-concepts" both supplements rehabilitation and renders incarceration less punitive.[69]

In sum, today the 25 year educational vacuum produced by the 1994 Pell Grant revocation has produced a unique and growing element of religious penal voluntarism in maximum-security prisons, in an explicit example of what Malcolm Feeley calls "penal entrepreneurship."[70] In cooperation with amenable prison administrators, Christian educators sponsoring collegiate degree programs inside US prisons—all with private fundraising efforts, political co-sponsors, and adjunct nonprofit organizations—are "hybridizing" traditional maximum-security prisons.[71] While Angola warden Burl Cain personally sought out the help of religious volunteers for assistance at his prison, today Christian seminaries have reversed direction of "the ask," proffering their services in some 27 states and in over 70 maximum-security prisons nationwide. Echoing Malcolm Feeley's concept of "penal entrepreneurship,"[72] penal entrepreneurs "create demand for and then supply new forms of social control. Indeed, the history of modern criminal justice is to some extent the history of the success of entrepreneurs in generating new or significantly expanded forms of social control."[73]

Expanding Footprint of Prison Seminary Programs

As shown in Table 4.2, "Training and Work Assignments Undertaken by Inmate Peer Ministers," a broad array of work assignments and training comprise the activity of inmate peer ministers. First, each of the programs examined offers tuition-free collegiate level degree programs, ranging from Associate-level degrees (Handlon/Calvin College) to a Master of Arts (Angola/Sing Sing). One degree program includes an Associate's degree in passing to a bachelor's (Handlon), while that offered by Sing Sing is exclusively a Master of Professional Studies emphasizing religious training. The remaining four programs provide baccalaureate-level degrees. All of the programs are fully accredited by their respective regional accrediting bodies.

All six of the programs examined here center their training in Christian theology and pastoral counseling. All programs examined contain work expectations of graduates in return for the education, albeit in two of the six prisons no formal work assignment is made (Sing Sing and Handlon). Reluctance on the part of institutions for giving inmates religious work assignments involves strictures governing inmate relations inside prisons, perceived Constitutional conflicts, or having unionized chaplains and staff.[74] The most elaborate inmate religious work assignments are those at Angola and Darrington, which feature specific assigned caseloads for tiers and dorms, while the programs at Handlon and Sing Sing conceptualize their work as "ministries of presence," expected to offer an informal "ministry of presence" as chaplains wherever they are placed.[75] In total, the institutions examined have produced some 850 inmate peer ministers working with literally thousands of prisoners on a yearly basis. Texas alone has deployed 164 field ministers in 32 prisons.[76] Finally, at this juncture, only Angola pays inmate peer ministers a fiscal wage for their work, with the remaining institutions expressing reluctance to do so for reasons regarding "establishment of religion."[77]

TABLE 4.2 Training and Work Assignments Undertaken by Inmate Peer Ministers

	Degree Offered	Religious Work Assigned	Peer Ministry Training	Peer Minister Wage?	Funding Source, Eligibility	#Grads
LSP Angola	BA, MA Christian Ministry[78]	Lead Worship, Pastoral Counseling, Assigned caseload	Pastoral Counseling, Conflict Resolution, Crisis Intervention	Yes	NOBTS,[79] Judson Baptist Assoc; LA Bapt Assoc; Life sentence	352
Darrington Unit TDCJ	BA, Biblical Studies[80]	Lead Worship, Pastoral Counseling, Assigned caseload	Pastoral Counseling, Conflict Resolution. Discipleship/ Ministry Devel.	No	SWBTS,[81] Heart of Texas Foundation At least 10 years left on sent	162
Handlon CI	Calvin College, AA/BA Ministry Leadership[82]	*No formal ministry assignment, Religious Leadership, Personal Example	Foundations of pastoral care; Ministry Development	No	Calvin Prison Initiative[83]; 12+ years	15 AA (2018)
Sing Sing NYDCCS	MA, Prof Studies & Religious Leadership[84]	*No formal ministry assignment, Religious Leadership, Personal Example	General Religious Education, Min of Presence, "Leadership by Example"	No	NYTS,[85] Bard Prison Initiative; −10 year minimum	200
Parchman MSP	BA Christian Ministry[86]	Lead Worship, Pastoral Counseling, Assigned caseload	Pastoral Counseling, Conflict Resolution, Crisis Intervention	No	NOBTS[87]; Preference for lifers; 10 year minimum	85
Hardee CI FL DOC	BA Christian Ministry[88]	Lead Worship, Pastoral Counseling/ Caseload	Pastoral Counseling, Conflict Res, Caseload	No	NOBTS[89]; 10 year minimum, lifer preference	40

Austerity as Opportunity: "Mainstreaming" Public-Private Partnerships in Corrections

Within a criminal justice context there is mounting evidence that peer support and mentoring programmes do have a significant impact on reducing offending behavior as well as reducing the likelihood of high-risk behavior such as drug use and self-harm for offenders, both in and out of prison.[90]

Efforts to reduce taxpayer spending on corrections have featured expanded use of private for-profit corporations as well as increased use of voluntary sector organizations, particularly "faith-based" programs seeking offenders' self-transformation. In an effort to end the "government monopoly" on delivery of services in criminal justice, a new level of both "structural charity" and "market competition" is an increasingly commonplace feature of correctional budgeting.[91] The reality is that, today, nonprofit organizations and volunteer networks are utilized as de facto line items in state budgeting. In what criminologist Mary Corcoran describes as "mainstreaming," nonprofit organizations are now increasingly recognized assets deployed in criminal justice operations.[92] Under the auspices of "faith-based" programming, the strategic vesting of "faith-based" charitable resources for delivery of services in American prisons has been used to justify reduced spending.[93] An under-recognized facet of faith-based correctional programming in the United States, in fact, involves too little appreciation for how such legislation sought to supplant correctional budgets by using the resources of religious charities.[94]

In her work theorizing the penal voluntary sector, criminologist Mary Corcoran (2014, 2017) denotes the "assimilation" of penal voluntary sector organizations into expanded uses of penal charity by public sector correctional agencies.[95] Corcoran documents five specific effects of utilizing nonprofit organizations and volunteers as competing agents in delivery of criminal justice services that we believe mirror that of American faith-based programs:[96]

1   Governments have strategically mobilized and deployed the voluntary sector as a vehicle for installing market reforms in public services.
2   Legislation has created deregulated competitive markets which outsourced police, probation, resettlement (reentry), and prison-based public services to competing providers from the commercial, public, and voluntary sectors.
3   The state has made space for voluntary sector organizations to participate in penal services markets under managed conditions demanding charities meet specific performance targets.
4   The installation of market logics for voluntary and charitable work is coordinated with disciplinary paradigms such as audits and performance targets.
5   The creation of contract markets renders charitable organizations market competitors with former partners by incorporating their services into performance metrics for the awarding of "contracts."

Faith-based correctional programming in the United States achieves the equivalent of voluntary sector "mainstreaming" as described by Corcoran—wherein, "the devolution of welfare from provision by the centralized Keynesian state to nonprofit intermediaries" has in fact taken place.[97] Such efforts to incorporate religious volunteer organizations into service delivery formulae for prisons both supplements public budgets with private resources and alters the division of labor inside prisons. Put another way, while serving rationales of necessary humanistic innovation and managing costs, prison seminaries have become not just a means of providing supplemental resources, but a mechanism for disruption of the penal marketplace in terms of both program delivery and operating philosophy. In short, as religious stakeholders gain a foothold inside prisons, they become more humane, less punitive, and more genuinely rehabilitative.

Religion has long proved a valuable asset for inmates in prison, not least because it is highly accessible and protected by the US Constitution. In his book *Faith Based: Religious Neoliberalism and the Politics of Welfare in the United States*, Jason Hackworth documents how contemporary "faith-based" religious voluntarism aimed to supplement government expenditures, reflecting what he calls the fundamental "anti-statism" of "faith-based welfare."[98] With the rise of overcrowding in American prisons, rehabilitation programs have become far less prominent. In this worldview, faith-based charities were "crowded out by the rise of the welfare state but would grow again to overcome their capacity constraints and represent an improved replacement, if the government were to reduce its profile or remove itself entirely from the sector."[99] As such, "religious neoliberalism" facilitates an agenda for expanding rehabilitative opportunities for inmates led by stakeholders outside of the traditional regime of punitive incarceration.[100]

In part because so much of religious programming in prisons is provided at no cost by religious volunteers, correctional officials have been uncharacteristically open to allowing outside stakeholders access to prisons for the purpose of interacting with inmates. As Winnifred Sullivan explains in her book *Prison Religion: Faith-Based Reform and the Constitution,* not only is religious programming ubiquitous in US prisons, but correctional administrators find it useful for reasons of cost, accessibility, and appeal to inmates:

> An enormous variety of religion is everywhere in US prisons, religion facilitated by prison chaplains, various external organizations, and groups attached to large conglomerates of the world religious traditions, as well as every form of small-scale and new religious movement.[101]

By bringing in outside resources, stakeholders, and perspectives, religious volunteers operating in prisons provide unique opportunities for new types of programming that challenge the traditional punitive ethos of corrections.[102]

An under-recognized facet of faith-based correctional programming in the United States involves too little appreciation for how such legislation sought first to supplement correctional budgets by using the resources of religious charities.[103] Today, however, faith-based programming in a growing number of US prisons involves a further hybridization of correctional practice—incorporating the private resources of religious charities into the actual division of labor inside prisons using inmates and structural charity. Such "outsourcing" of rehabilitative training to privately funded religious groups (e.g., Christian seminaries, Prison Fellowship Academy, etc.), combined with the simultaneous "insourcing" of inmate peer ministers trained in externally funded but "immersive" programs inside US prisons, represents a new and advanced iteration of faith-based programming that further accomplishes its original aims: expanding assets for rehabilitation inside prisons, humanizing the inhumane environment of prison, and shifting control for rehabilitation away from the sole purview of correctional administrators to community-based partnerships who work with and assist corrections officials.

By relying upon and celebrating the "Lived Experience" of inmate peer ministers as a criterion of employment, a unique transformation of the penal marketplace is accomplished: rehabilitation training is supplemented by charitable providers and the work of offender treatment itself inside prisons is "insourced" to carefully selected inmate volunteers at no cost. This assignment of rehabilitative training to externally funded personnel, fundamentally alters the penal marketplace and represents a "next level" iteration of faith-based programming.

Conclusion: Making Prisons More "Reinventive," Less Totalizing and Punitive

> The tendency to present neoliberal penal reforms as inexorable and to produce grimly pessimistic accounts of the criminal justice state risks reinforcing the very situation that commentators purport to expose. Determinedly pessimistic scholarship creates its own set of problems, as emphasizing dystopic visions of crime control leads scholars to overlook trends that point in a different direction.[104]

This chapter argues that innovations established by the "religious neoliberalism" of emerging "inmate peer ministry" programs is disrupting the penal marketplace through "mainstreaming" of "fully-immersed" but privately funded Christian seminaries under the auspices of "faith-based" programming. This utilization of offenders' lived experience toward rehabilitative ends corresponds with larger tectonic shifts in both correctional practice and correctional budgeting. While "austerity" regimes have certainly produced deleterious effects in many prisons, in cases where programmatic need has created opportunities for new players to enter prisons from the outside, multitudinous and sometimes robust program agendas have emerged to fill the gap. As we argue here, increasing reliance upon penal voluntary sector assets and third-party organizations for the private training and deployment of inmate peer ministers introduces new stakeholders with worldviews that can be antithetical to punitive corrections. In a system facing dramatic employee turnover and dangerous levels of understaffing, Texas Department of Criminal Justice has fully embraced inmate peer mentoring (see McCullough, 2019).[105]

Of course, we've seen some of this before in American corrections. Jennifer Graber meticulously documents the dashed hopes of religious volunteers working in multiple American prisons—finding themselves repeatedly marginalized by prison administrators and beset by their own internal doctrinal bickering.[106] Clearly, the religious penal voluntary sector should not be viewed as a panacea.[107] By introducing market logics into the political economy of punishment, newly present religious stakeholders often brazenly privilege sectarian framings of rehabilitation while being openly dismissive of proven "secular" treatment modalities such as Cognitive Behavioral Therapy, suggesting that "only Jesus saves."[108]

While we have extensive but resolvable concerns about the need for external monitoring and issues of Constitutionality and have written elsewhere about these concerns,[109] they are not the topic of this chapter. In cases such as documented by Sullivan (2009), wherein religious volunteers operate immersive programs that become so "pervasively sectarian" as to frame rehabilitation exclusively as a function of religion, concerns about state religious establishment and coercive indoctrination must be highlighted.[110]

But arguably the larger threat is the opposite of that noted by Hackworth regarding faith-based groups being "crowded out." Without programming offered by religious volunteers, increasingly many prisoners will have *no access to programming at all*. Religious programs will not solve all problems in prisons. Religious programs are not suitable for every prison nor every prisoner. Above all, religious programs must always remain entirely voluntary, non-coercive, and closely monitored.[111] But if a "desistance movement" of the sort invoked by Maruna in our opening epigraph is to truly emerge—who is going to lead it? Who is it that has access, cooperation, resources, and desire to immerse themselves in prison environments? What private citizens are actually going to endure the risks, costs, and discomforts associated with going inside prisons to work with inmates? We submit that—in the United States at least—it is largely religiously motivated volunteers. Moreover, evidence suggests that such a movement requires treating prisoners with the dignity of elevating them into positions of trust. The programs we describe achieve that elevation and are transforming correctional practice. As Maruna puts it:

> Perhaps the most interesting implication of the research so far has been for the potential role of former prisoners as "wounded healers," drawing on their experiences to help others avoid their mistakes and benefit from the inspiration of their achievements....After all, if the core message of desistance research is that there was much to learn from "success stories" who move away from crime, then surely the same thing could be said about the criminal justice environment.[112]

TABLE 4.3 US Inmate Peer Ministry Programs

State	Prison	Religious Partner
Alabama	Bibb County Correctional Facility	Birmingham Theological Seminary
Arkansas	Varner Unit Correctional Institution	Mid-America Baptist Theological Seminary
Arizona	Arizona State Prison Complex	The Cell Church
California (2,3)	San Quentin; statewide	Gateway Seminary in Prison, World Impact Ministries; Prison Fellowship/TUMI (30 CA prisons)
Colorado	Federal Prison Complex Florence; Arrowhead CC, Buena Vista CF, Cheyenne Mountain Reentry Center, Delta CC, Crowley CF, Arkansas Valley CF, Kit Carson CC, Sterling CF, Limon CF, Colorado Territorial CF	Denver Seminary, The Cell Church (ten prisons)
Florida	Hardee County CI	New Orleans Baptist Theological Seminary
Georgia (2)	Philips State Prison; Walker State Prison	New Orleans Baptist Theological Seminary; Covington Theological Seminary;
Illinois (2)	Danville CC; Stateville CC	Divine Hope Reformed Bible Seminary; School of Restorative Arts North Park Theological Seminary
Indiana	Indiana State Prison	Divine Hope Seminary
Louisiana	LSP Angola + 4	New Orleans Baptist Theological Seminary
Michigan	Handlon Correctional Institution	Calvin College
Minnesota	Minnesota Correctional Facility—Shakopee	Prison Fellowship Academy
Mississippi (2)	MSP Parchman; Central Mississippi CF	New Orleans Baptist Theological Seminary
Missouri	Potosi CC	Hannibal-LaGrange University
Montana[a]	Montana State Prison	The Cell Church
New Mexico	Lea County CF	University of the Southwest Prison Seminary Program
New York	Sing Sing CF	New York Theological Seminary
North Carolina	Nash Correctional Institution	Southeastern Baptist Theological Seminary; Game Plan for Life
Ohio	Marion Correctional Institution	Winebrenner Theological Seminary
Oklahoma[a]	Oklahoma Department of Corrections	(To Be Determined)
Oregon	Oregon State Correctional Institution	Paid In Full Ministries
South Carolina	Lee Correctional Institution	Pilgrim Theological Seminary
South Dakota	South Dakota State Penitentiary	Prison Lighthouse Fellowship
Tennessee[a]	Tennessee Prison for Women	Lipscomb University
Texas	Darrington + 31 statewide	Southwestern Baptist Theological Seminary; Heart of Texas Foundation
West Virginia	Mt Olive Correctional Center	Appalachian Bible College, Catalyst Ministries; Mt Olive Bible College
Wisconsin	New Lisbon Correctional Institution	The Cell Church

a Program in development.

In closing, at a time when prison administrators and politicians express concerns about program effectiveness and cost—and express an eagerness to work with religious volunteers whom they believe bring value and salience to the prison environment—these new programs constitute an important development. Just as Neil Barsky, founder of the American Marshall Project, recently put it in a *New York Times* Editorial he titled: "Let Us In! How to fix our prisons? Let the public inside":

> The public should see firsthand the conditions within the walls, to meet the men and women who reside in our prisons, to look them in the eye, shake their hands...What I'm talking about is a thorough effort to bring down the wall separating the incarcerated and the free. Let Us In could change the relationship between the public and the imprisoned.[113]

(Barsky, 2019)

While religious penal entrepreneurs are changing the penal marketplace, feedback and recommendations from outside the prison environment are in fact "getting through"—and amid a season of cutbacks, new programs for inmates where few existed before are in fact being created. While more research is necessary to explore and document the ethnographic and programmatic dynamics of these programs, this chapter offers a glimpse into a novel and growing set of programs transforming maximum-security prison environments. As a means of helping prisons become more reinventive and less totalizing for inmates, inmate prison ministries have begun the work. A more comprehensive listing of inmate ministry programs nationwide (at the time of this writing) is presented in Table 4.3.

Notes

1 Maruna (2016).
2 Cressey (1965), Eglash (1958–59), Einat (2017), White (2000).
3 LeBel et al. (2015), Maruna (2001), Maruna et al (2006), Heidemann et al (2016), Shapiro (2004), Corcoran and Carr (2019), Reiner (2012), Cooper (2015).
4 LeBel (2007), LeBel, Richie, and Maruna (2015).
5 Maruna (2001, 2017), Hinde and White (2019), Lebel et al (2015).
6 Nouwen (1974).
7 Nouwen (1974), Maruna (2001), Hallett, Hays, Johnson, Jang, and Duwe (2017), Maruna (2017).
8 Quinn (2019).
9 Hallett et al. (2017), Jang et al. (2017, 2019), Hallett (2006).
10 Hinde and White (2019).
11 Cullen et al. (2014).
12 Skarbek (2016, p. 845).
13 LeBel et al. (2015), Hallett et al. (2017).
14 Maguire, William, and Corcoran (2019), Buck (2019), Quinn (2019), Kaufman (2015).
15 Sykes (1958), Irwin and Cressey (1962), see also Crewe (2020).
16 Sparks et al. (1996).
17 Miller (2014).
18 Maruna (2017), Petersilia (2001).
19 Maruna (2016, 2017).
20 Hallett et al. (2017), Hallett, Hays, Johnson, Jang, and Duwe (2015).
21 Nouwen (1974), Maruna (2017).
22 Peer-based programming in correctional settings has increased dramatically over the past 20 years, in areas including basic literacy, health and hygiene, and religious education. Bagnall, A.M., South, J., Hulme, C. et al. (2015). A systematic review of the effectiveness and cost-effectiveness of peer education and peer support in prisons. *BMC Public Health*, *15*, 290. The Implementation of Inmate Mentor Programs in the Correctional Treatment System as an Innovative Approach. Jana Cook, Scott McClure, Igor Koutsenok & Scot Lord.
23 Sibley (2019).

24 Sibley (2019).
25 Hallett et al. (2015, 2017), Hallett, Johnson, Hays, Jang, and Duwe (2019), Jang et al (2019), Duwe, Hallett, Hays, Jang, and Johnson (2015).
26 Hallett et al. (2017), Duwe et al. (2015).
27 Jang, Johnson, Hays, Hallett, and Duwe (2017, 2019).
28 Hallett (2006), Cooperman (2004), Dagan and Teles (2012).
29 Garland (1990), Hallett (2006).
30 Preamble (2001).
31 Hallett and McCoy (2014), Hallett et al. (2017), Cooperman (2004).
32 Corcoran (2011, 2014, 2017, 2019), Hinde and White (2019), Dagan and Teles (2012), Cooperman (2004).
33 Kaitlyn Quinn (2019).
34 Rowbotham (2009), Buck (2019), Friedman (1994), Green (2013).
35 Friedman (1994).
36 Erzen (2017), Willison, Brazzell, and Kim (2010), Sullivan (2009).
37 Thompson (2017).
38 Crewe and Ievins (2019), Buck (2018), Tomczak (2017).
39 Hallett (2019).
40 Portions of this research involving human subjects were approved by Institutional Review Boards at the Texas Department of Criminal Justice, Louisiana Department of Corrections, University of North Florida, and Baylor University, IRB Project # 49899.
41 Hallett et al. (2017).
42 Trained in process counseling and pastoral care through the private assets of NOBTS, Angola's "offender ministers" carry state-issued identification cards granting them access to the prison's various compounds for completion of their religious work assignments (Hallett et al. 2015, 2017).
43 Capps (2015), Nouwen (1974).
44 Hallett (2019).
45 Buck (2019, 2020), Hallett et al. (2015), Gilligan and Lee (2004), LeBel et al. (2015), Hallett (2019), Helminen and Mills (2019).
46 Hallett et al. (2017).
47 Nouwen (1974).
48 Global Prison Seminary Foundation (2019).
49 Hallett et al (2017).
50 Hallett et al. (2017).
51 Hallett et al. (2017).
52 Rideau and Sinclair (1985).
53 Hallett et al. (2017).
54 Hallett et al. (2015, 2017).
55 Hallett et al. (2017).
56 Hallett et al. (2017).
57 Shimron (2018).
58 Jang et al. (2017, 2019).
59 Silver (2016).
60 Erzen (2017).
61 Norquist in Dagan and Teles (2012).
62 Norquist in Dagan and Teles (2012).
63 Tomczak and Buck (2019).
64 Crewe and Ievins (2019).
65 Scott (2010).
66 Burnett and Maruna (2006).
67 Burnett and Maruna (2006).
68 Crewe and Ievins (2019).
69 Burnett and Maruna (2006).
70 Feeley (2002).
71 Hallett et al. (2019).
72 Feeley (2002).
73 Feeley (2002).
74 Hallett et al. (2019). See also Corban University (2019). Don't let this man rest: The story behind Paid in Full Oregon. (2019). Retrieved from https://www.corban.edu/dont-let-this-man-rest-the-story-behind-paid-in-full-oregon/.
75 See especially Sullivan (2009, 2014).

76 Numbers may vary due to "rolling admission" and graduation policies in some of the programs examined. While inmate peer ministry students work in cohorts, circumstances often make "on time" graduation difficult. Angola, for example, took to holding a formal graduation only every three years, while students were allowed and encouraged to "work at their own pace."
77 Hallett et al. (2019)
78 https://baptistmessage.com/nobts-graduation-jesus-changes-everything/.
79 https://baptistmessage.com/nobts-graduation-jesus-changes-everything/.
80 https://swbts.edu/news/releases/darrington-graduates-challenged-be-fearless-ministry/.
81 https://www.tdcj.texas.gov/connections/-articles/20190600_darrington.html.
82 https://calvin.edu/news/archive/high-expectations-for-handlon.
83 https://calvin.edu/prison-initiative/.
84 https://www.nyts.edu/academic-programs/master-of-professional-studies/.
85 https://www.nyts.edu/academic-programs/master-of-professional-studies/
86 https://www.nobts.edu/extensions/lams-centers/default.html.
87 https://www.nobts.edu/extensions/lams-centers/default.html.
88 https://www.nobts.edu/news/articles/2018/May2018Commencement.html.
89 https://www.nobts.edu/extensions/lams-centers/default.html.
90 Hinde and White (2019).
91 see Corcoran (2017), Hannah-Moffat (2000).
92 Corcoran (2017).
93 Cooperman (2004).
94 Hallett (2006).
95 Corcoran (2014, 2017).
96 Corcoran (2017, p. 288).
97 Hackworth (2012, pp. 8–9).
98 Hackworth (2012, p. 17, 19).
99 Hackworth (2012, pp. 8–9).
100 Hallett et al. (2017).
101 Sullivan (2009, p. 14).
102 See also Corcoran (2014, 2017, 2019).
103 Hallett (2006).
104 Tomczak (2014).
105 See McCullough (2019).
106 See Graber (2008, 2012, 2013).
107 Hallett et al. (2019), Hallett (2019).
108 Hallett et al. (2019).
109 Hallett et al. (2019), Hallett (2019).
110 Sullivan (2009, p. 144), Hallett et al. (2019).
111 Hallett et al. (2019).
112 Maruna (2017, p. 9).
113 Barsky (2019).

References

Albertson, K., & Fox, C. (2019). The marketization of rehabilitation: Some economic considerations. *Probation Journal, 66*(1), 25–42.

Barsky, N. (2019, December 17). How to fix our prisons? Let the public inside. *The New York Times.*

Buck, G. (2019). Politicization or professionalization? Exploring divergent aims within UK voluntary sector peer mentoring. *The Howard Journal of Crime and Justice, 58*(3), 349–365.

Buck, G. (2020). Peer mentoring in criminal justice. *Probation Quarterly*, (18), 41–43.

Burnett, R., & Maruna, S. (2006). The kindness of prisoners: Strengths-based resettlement In theory and in action. *Criminology & Criminal Justice, 6*(1), 83–106.

Capps, D. (2015). Deliverance to the captives: Karl Barth's prison sermons. *Pastoral Psychology, 64*, 417–435. doi:10.1007/s11089-014-0627-z.

Clark, M. (2001). Influencing positive behavior change: Increasing the therapeutic approach of juvenile courts. *Federal Probation, 65*(1), 18–27.

Cooper, M. (2015). The theology of emergency: Welfare reform, US foreign aid and the faith-based initiative. *Theory, Culture & Society, 32*, 53–77. doi:10.1177/ 0263276413508448

Cooperman, A. (2004, April 25). An infusion of religious funds in Florida prisons. *The Washington Post*. Retrieved from https://www.washingtonpost.com/archive/politics/2004/04/25/an-infusion-of-religious-funds-in-fla-prisons/.

Corban University. (2019). *Don't let this man rest: The story behind Paid in Full Oregon*. Retrieved from https://www.corban.edu/dont-let-this-man-rest-the-story-behind-paid-in-full-oregon/.

Corcoran, M. (2011). Dilemmas of institutionalisation in the penal voluntary sector. *Critical Social Policy, 31*(1), 30–52. https://doi.org/10.1177/0261018310385438

Corcoran, M. (2014). The trajectory of penal markets in an age of austerity: The case of England and Wales. *Sociology of Crime, Law and Deviance, 19*, 53–74. https://doi.org/10.1108/</ds> S1521-613620140000019002.

Corcoran, M. (2017). Resilient hearts: Making affective citizens for neoliberal times. *Justice Power and Resistance, 1*(2), 283–299.

Corcoran, M. (2019). Alice in Wonderland: Voluntary sector organizations' experiences of transforming rehabilitation. *Probation Journal, 66*(1), 96–112. https://doi.org/10.1177/0264550518820118.

Corcoran, M., & Carr, N. (2019). Five years of transforming rehabilitation: Markets, management and values. *Probation Journal, 66*(1), 3–7. https://doi.org/10.1177/0264550519825958

Cressey, D. R. (1965). Social psychological foundations for using criminals in the rehabilitation of criminals. *Journal of Research in Crime & Delinquency, 2*, 49–59. doi:10.1177/ 002242786500200201.

Crewe, B. (2020). The depth of imprisonment. *Punishment & Society*. https://doi.org/10.1177/1462474520952153.

Crewe, B., & Ievins, A. (2019). The prison as a reinventive institution. *Theoretical Criminology*. https://doi.org/10.1177/1362480619841900.

Cullen, Francis, Cheryl Lero Jonson, Mary Stohr. Editors. (2014). *The American Prison: Imagining a different future*. Los Angeles: Sage Publishing.

Dagan, D., & Teles, S. (2012, November/December). The conservative war on prisons. *Washington Monthly*. Retrieved from https://washingtonmonthly.com/magazine/novdec-2012/the-conservative-war-on-prisons/.

Duwe, G., Hallett, M., Hays, J., Jang, S. J., & Johnson, B. R. (2015). Bible college participation and prison misconduct: A preliminary analysis. *Journal of Offender Rehabilitation, 54*, 371–390. https://doi.org/10.1080/10509674.2015.1043481.

Eglash, A. (1958–59). Adults anonymous: A mutual help program for inmates and ex-inmates. *Journal of Criminal Law and Criminology, 49*, 237–245.

Einat, T. (2017). The wounded healer: Self-rehabilitation of prisoners through providing care and support to physically and mentally challenged inmates. *Journal of Crime and Justice, 40*(2), 204–221. https://doi.org/10.1080/0735648X.2015.1095647.

Erzen, T. (2017). *God in captivity: The rise of faith-based prison ministries in the age of Mass incarceration*. Boston, MA: Beacon Press.

Feeley, M. (2002). Entrepreneurs of punishment: The legacy of privatization. *Punishment & Society, 4*(3), 321–344. https://doi.org/10.1177/146247402400426770

Friedman, L. (1994). *Crime and punishment in American history*. New York: Basic Books.

Garland, D. (1990). *Punishment and modern society: A study in social theory*. Chicago, IL: University of Chicago Press.

Global Prison Seminary Foundation. (2019). Baton Rouge, LA.

Gilligan, James & Bandi Lee (2004). Beyond the prison paradigm: from provoking violence to preventing it by creating "anti-prisons" (residential colleges and therapeutic communities). *Annual Review of the New York Academy of Science Journal, 1036*, 300–324.

Graber, J. (2008). "When friends had the management it was entirely different": Quakers and Calvinists in the making of New York prison discipline. *Quaker History, 97*(2), 19–40.

Graber, J. (2012). Engaging the trope of redemptive suffering: Inmate voices in the antebellum prison debates. *Pennsylvania History: A Journal of Mid-Atlantic Studies, 79*(2), 209–233.

Graber, J. (2013). *The furnace of the affliction: Prisons and religion in antebellum America*. Chapel Hill, NC: University of North Carolina Press.

Green, D. (2013). Penal optimism and second chances: The legacies of American Protestantism and the prospects for penal reform. *Punishment & Society, 15*(2), 123–146. https://doi.org/10.1177/1462474513477789.

Hackworth, J. (2012). *Faith based: Religious neoliberalism and the politics of welfare in the United States.* Atlanta, Georgia: University of Georgia Press.

Hallett, M. (2006). *Private prisons in America: A critical race perspective.* Chicago, IL: University of Illinois Press.

Hallett, M. (2019). Confronting christian penal charity: Neoliberalism and the rebirth of religious penitentiaries. *Social Justice, 45*(1), 103–123.

Hallett, M., Hays, J., Johnson, B. R., Jang, S. J., & Duwe, G. (2015). First stop dying: Angola's Christian seminary as positive criminology. *International Journal of Offender Rehabilitation and Comparative Criminology, 61*(4), 445–463. doi:10.1177/ 0306624X15598179.

Hallett, M., Hays, J., Johnson, B. R., Jang, S. J., & Duwe, G. (2017). *The Angola prison seminary: Effects of faith-based ministry on identity transformation, desistance, and rehabilitation.* New York, NY: Routledge.

Hallett, M., Johnson, B., Hays, J., Jang, S. J., & Duwe, G. (2019). US prison seminaries: Structural charity, religious establishment, and neoliberal corrections. *The Prison Journal, 99*(2), 150–171.

Hallett, M., & McCoy, J. S. (2014). Religiously-motivated desistance: An exploratory study. *International Journal of Offender Therapy and Comparative Criminology, 59*(8), 855–872.

Hannah-Moffat, K. (2000). Prisons that empower: Neo-liberal governance in Canadian women's prisons. *The British Journal of Criminology, 40*, 510–531.

Heidemann, G., Cederbaum, J. A., Martinez, S., & LeBel, T. P. (2016). Wounded healers: How formerly incarcerated women help themselves by helping others. *Punishment & Society, 18*(1), 18–26. https://doi.org/10.1177/1462474515623101.

Helminen, M., & Mills, A. (2019). Exploring autonomy in the Finnish and New Zealand penal voluntary sectors: The relevance of marketisation and criminal justice policy environments in two penal voluntary sector organizations. *The Howard Journal, 58*(3), 404–429. https://doi.org/10.1111/hojo.12319.

Hinde, K., & White, R. (2019). Peer support, desistance and the role of the third sector. *The Howard Journal, 58*(3), 329–348. https://doi.org/10.1111/hojo.12333.

Irwin, J., & Cressey, D. (1962). Thieves, convicts and the inmate culture. *Social Problems, 10*(2): 142–155.

Jang, S. J., Johnson, B. R., Hays, J., Hallett, M., & Duwe, G. (2017). Religion and misconduct in "Angola" prison: Conversion, congregational participation, religiosity, and self-identities. *Justice Quarterly, 35*, 412–442. doi:10.1080/07418825.2017.1309057.

Jang, S. J., Johnson, B. R., Hays, J., Hallett, M., & Duwe, G. (2019). Prisoners helping prisoners change: A study of inmate field ministers within Texas prisons. *International Journal of Offender Therapy and Comparative Criminology.* doi:10.1177/0306624X19872966.

Kaufman, N. (2015). Prisoner incorporation: The work of the state and non-governmental organizations. *Theoretical Criminology, 19*(4), 534–553. https://doi.org/10.1177/1362480614567172.

LeBel, T. P. (2007). An examination of the impact of formerly incarcerated persons helping others. *Journal of Offender Rehabilitation, 46*(1–2), 1–24. https://doi.org/10.1080/10509670802071485.

LeBel, T. P., Richie, M., & Maruna, S. (2015). Helping others as a response to reconcile a criminal past: The role of the wounded healer in prisoner reentry programs. *Criminal Justice and Behavior, 42*(1), 108–120. doi:10.1177/0093854814550029.

Maguire, M., William, K., & Corcoran, M. (2019). 'Penal drift' and the voluntary sector. *The Howard Journal of Crime and Justice, 58*(3), 430–449.

Maruna, S. (2001). *Making good: How ex-convicts reform and rebuild their lives.* Washington, D.C.: American Psychological Association Books.

Maruna, S. (2016). Desistance and restorative justice: It's now or never. *Restorative Justice: An International Journal, 4*(3), 289–301.

Maruna, S. (2017, October). Desistance as a social movement. *Irish Probation Journal, 14*, 5–20.

Maruna, S., Wilson, L., & Curran, K. (2006). Why God is often found behind bars: Prison conversions and the crisis of self-narrative. *Research in Human Development, 3*, 161–84. https://doi.org/10.1080/15427609.2006.9683367.

McCullough, J. (2019, June 18). Texas prison guards to get a small raise, but some doubt it will help with chronic understaffing. *The Texas Tribune.* Retrieved from https://www.texastribune.org/2019/06/18/texas-prisons-understaffing-raise/.

Miller, R. J. (2014). Devolving the carceral state: Race, prisoner reentry, and the micropolitics of urban poverty management. *Punishment & Society, 16*(3), 305–335. https://doi.org/10.1177/1462474514527487.

Nouwen, H. (1974). *Wounded healers: Ministry in contemporary society.* New York, NY: Doubleday.

Petersilia, J. (2001). Prisoner reentry: Public safety and reintegration challenges. *The Prison Journal, 81*(3), 360–375.

Preamble. 2001. Florida Criminal Rehabilitation Act 2001 Fl. ALS 110; 2001 Fla. Laws ch. 110; 2001 Fla. SB 912.

Quinn, K. (2019, July 29). Inside the penal voluntary sector: Divided discourses of "helping" criminalized women. *Punishment & Society.* https://doi.org/10.1177/1462474519863461

Reiner, R. (2012). Political economy, crime, and criminal justice. In M. Maguire, R. Morgan, & R. Reiner (Eds.), *The Oxford handbook of criminology* (pp. 301–336). Oxford, UK: Oxford University Press.

Rideau, W., & Sinclair, B. (1985). Prisoner litigation: How it began in Louisiana. *Louisiana Law Review, 45*(5), 1061–1076.

Rowbotham, J. (2009). Turning away from criminal intent: Reflecting on the Victorian and Edwardian strategies for promoting desistance among petty offenders. *Theoretical Criminology, 13*(1), 105.

Scott, S. (2010). Revisiting the total institution: Performative regulation in the reinventive institution. *Sociology, 44*(2), 213–231. https://doi.org/10.1177/0038038509357198

Shapiro, S. (2004, April 15). Jails for Jesus. *Prison Legal News.* https://www.prisonlegalnews.org/news/2004/apr/15/jails-for-jesus/.

Shimron, Y. (2018, November 14). Seminaries partner with prisons to offer inmates new life as ministers. *Religion News Service.* https://religionnews.com/2018/11/14/seminaries-partner-with-prisons-to-offer-inmates-new-life-as-ministers/.

Sibley, A. (2019, May 14). Darrington graduates commissioned to share truth that sets men free. *Southwestern Baptist Theological Seminary News Release.* Retrieved from https://swbts.edu/news/releases/darrington-graduates-commissioned-share-truth-sets-men-free/

Silver, J. (2016, August 3). Texas prisons ponder cutting $250 million. *Texas Tribune.* Retrieved from https://www.texastribune.org/2016/08/03/prisons-agency-could-see-250-million-budget-cuts/.

Skarbek, D. (2016). Covenants without the sword? Comparing prison self-governance globally. *American Political Science Review, 110*(4), 845–862.

Sparks, R., Bottoms, A., & Hay, W. (1996). *Prisons and the problem of order.* New York, NY: Oxford University Press.

Sullivan, W. F. (2009). *Prison religion: Faith-based reform and the constitution.* Princeton, NJ: Princeton University Press.

Sullivan, W. F. (2014). *A ministry of presence: Chaplaincy, spiritual care, and the Law.* Chicago, IL: University of Chicago Press.

Sykes, G. (1958). *The society of captives: A study of a maximum security prison.* Princeton, NJ: Princeton University Press.

Thompson, H. A. (2017, April). What's hidden behind the walls of America's prisons? *The Conversation.* Retrieved from https://theconversation.com/whats-hidden-behind-the-walls-of-americas-prisons-77282.

Tomczak, P. (2014). The penal voluntary sector in England and Wales: Beyond neoliberalism? *Criminology & Criminal Justice, 14*(4), 470–486. https://doi.org/10.1177/1748895813505235.

Tomczak, P. (2017). *The penal voluntary sector.* New York, NY: Routledge.

Tomczak, P., & Buck, G. (2019, July). The penal voluntary sector: A hybrid sociology. *The British Journal of Criminology, 59*(4), 898–918. https://doi.org/10.1093/bjc/azy070.

White, W. (2000). *Toward a new recovery movement: Historical reflections on recovery, treatment and advocacy.* Talk presented at the Center for Substance Abuse Treatment, Recovery Community Support Program conference, Alexandria, VI.

Willison, B., Brazzell, D., & Kim, K. (2010). Faith-based corrections and reentry programs: Advancing a conceptual framework for research and evaluation. Washington, DC: Urban Institute.

APPENDIX I

US INMATE PEER MINISTRY PROGRAMS

29 US Inmate Peer Ministry Programs	Texas Inmate Peer Ministry Programs[b]
Alabama	Allred
Arkansas	Beto
Arizona	Byrd
California[a]	Clemens
Colorado[a]	Clements
Florida	Coffield
Georgia	Connally
Illinois	Daniel
Louisiana	Darrington[a]
Michigan	Eastham
Minnesota	Estelle
Mississippi	Ferguson
Missouri	Hughes
Montana[a]	Jester III
New Hampshire	Jordan
New Mexico	Lewis
New York	Lynaugh
North Carolina	McConnell
North Dakota[a]	Michael
Ohio[a]	Neal
Oklahoma[a]	Pack
Oregon	Ramsey
South Carolina	Roach
Tennessee[a]	Robertson
Texas	Smith
West Virginia	Stiles
Wisconsin	Stringfellow
Vermont	Telford
Virginia	Torres
	Wallace-Ware
	Wynne

a   Program approved but in development.
b   164 "Inmate Field Ministers" placed in 31 Texas prisons.

5

OFFENDER-LED RELIGIOUS MOVEMENTS AND RETHINKING INCARCERATION[1]

Recent scholarship from a host of disciplines falls within the broad categories of "social well-being" or "human flourishing." This research improves our understanding of how people experience happiness, find purpose, meaning, or hope, to mention just a few. Life experiences that lead to contentment, optimism, resiliency and thriving in the midst of difficult circumstances are additional markers of human flourishing. Moreover, scholars are also examining the ways in which religion may be consequential for flourishing and well-being.[2]

For example, a great deal of empirical evidence documents the ways in which religious involvement is linked to many different types of physical and mental health outcomes.[3] A growing subset of this research demonstrates how religious involvement may help to decrease crime,[4] as well as protect individuals residing in disadvantaged communities from engaging in illegal behavior.[5] In addition, there is a developing literature indicating religion can help to foster sobriety,[6] or even promote prosocial behavior among offenders.[7] Published studies have even confirmed the effectiveness of certain faith-based programs in reducing recidivism among former prisoners as well as the economic benefit to society of crime desistance.[8]

Although the evidence is still quite preliminary, there is a growing research literature confirming that faith-based interventions can be significant in addressing other contemporary social problems (e.g., drug treatment, prisoner rehabilitation, homelessness, etc.).[9] In sum, there is empirical evidence documenting that measures of religiosity (i.e., levels of participation or commitment) may help change an offender's identity, and be linked to other important prosocial outcomes (e.g., generosity, service to others, or civic engagement).[10] To state the obvious, the influence of religion is far more complicated and consequential than simply the typical focus on attendance at religious services or the acknowledgment that many regularly pray.

Religion Behind Bars: Moving from Jailhouse Religion to Faith-Based Prisons

It is easy to understand how and why people may view prisons as the antithesis of human flourishing. Prisons are known for many things, but far less understood is the fact that correctional facilities tend to be intensely religious places. Jailhouse religion is like most stereotypes—you can find examples of individuals who fake religion, but the examples tend to be outweighed by those who take faith seriously. This is reflected in recent scholarship suggesting religion can

DOI: 10.4324/9781003171744-5

engender human flourishing even within a prison.[11] Moreover, a mounting body of research documents the beneficial impact of religion on crime, delinquency, and prisoner reentry. In fact, there is an emerging "positive criminology" literature that provides preliminary evidence that may inform how scholars, professionals, and volunteers think about contemporary approaches to offender treatment and justice system reform more generally.[12]

A series of multivariate studies examining the effectiveness of Prison Fellowship (PF) programs tend to support the notion that PF participants fare significantly better. In the first study, Young and his coauthors investigated long-term recidivism among a group of federal inmates trained as volunteer prison ministers and found that the PF group had a significantly lower rate of recidivism than the matched group.[13] In the second study, Johnson and colleagues examined the impact of PF religious programs on institutional adjustment and recidivism rates in two matched groups of inmates from four adult male prisons in New York State. After controlling for level of involvement in PF-sponsored programs, inmates who were most active in Bible studies were significantly less likely to be rearrested during the year-long follow-up period.[14] In a follow-up to this study, Johnson extended the New York research on former inmates by increasing the length of study from one to eight years and found that frequent Bible study participants were less likely to be rearrested two and three years after their release.[15]

In one of the more anticipated studies of a faith-based intervention, Johnson published a six-year evaluation of Prison Fellowship's (PF) expressly Christian, faith-based prerelease prison program known as the InnerChange Freedom Initiative (IFI).[16] Launched in 1997 in Houston, Texas, Johnson and Larson evaluated the InnerChange Freedom Initiative, an 18- to 24-month-long faith-based prison program operated by Prison Fellowship (a Christian prison ministry). They found program participants were significantly less likely to be arrested than a matched group of prisoners not receiving this religious intervention (8%–20% respectively) during a two-year post-release period.[17] Johnson and Larson also found that the presence of a faith-motivated mentor was critical in helping ex-prisoners remain crime free following release from prison.[18]

A separate outcome evaluation reported similar results from Minnesota's InnerChange Freedom Initiative, a faith-based prisoner reentry program that has operated within Minnesota's prison system since 2002 (modeled after the InnerChange Freedom Initiative in Texas). Duwe and King (2013) examined recidivism outcomes among a total of 732 offenders released from Minnesota prisons between 2003 and 2009. A series of regression analyses document that participation in IFI significantly reduced the likelihood of rearrest (26%), reconviction (35%), and re-incarceration (40%) of former prisoners.[19] A new study extends the research on IFI by conducting a cost-benefit analysis of the program. Because IFI relies heavily on volunteers and program costs that are privately funded, the program involves no additional expense for the State of Minnesota. This study focused on estimating the program's benefits by examining recidivism and post-release employment. The findings showed that during its first six years of operation in Minnesota, IFI produced an estimated benefit of $3 million, which amounts to approximately $8,300 per participant.[20]

In yet another study of Prison Fellowship, Kerley and associates explored the relationship between participation in Operation Starting Line (OSL), a faith-based prison event, and the subsequent experience of negative emotions and incidence of negative behaviors.[21] OSL participants were less likely to experience negative emotions and to engage in fights and arguments with other inmates or prison staff. The results from this study are consistent with previous research and were supported in a second study where Kerley surveyed prisoners in order to determine whether levels of reported religiosity were associated with reduced levels of arguing and fighting. The study found religiosity directly reduces the likelihood of arguing and indirectly reduces the likelihood of fighting.[22]

These positive criminology approaches can draw upon secular as well as faith-based models. In the Minnesota Department of Corrections, mentors who visit offenders in prison are associated not only with faith-based programs such as the InnerChange but also with community service agencies that are not necessarily faith-based. For example, in the Twin Cities (i.e., Minneapolis and St. Paul) metropolitan area, organizations like Amicus—which recently merged with Volunteers of America-Minnesota—have provided volunteers with opportunities to mentor offenders in prison since the 1960s.[23] Programs like InnerChange, Amicus, and the Salvation Army, are doing important "positive criminology"-style work, some of which is faith-based and some of which is not. Decision-makers interested in cost-effective approaches to crime desistance among offender populations should pay attention to these promising approaches.

America's Bloodiest Prison Establishes a Seminary

The Louisiana State Penitentiary (aka Angola) is located in Angola, Louisiana, and is America's largest maximum-security prison, housing over 6,300 inmates in five separate complexes spread over 18,000 acres of a working prison farm. Cellblock and dormitory units are still called "camps" at Angola, a remnant of the traditional assignment of slaves to "work camps" across various locations of the property, a former slave plantation.[24] The property first became known as "Angola" because it was this region of Africa that supplied its slaves. Roughly 75% of inmates currently serving time at Angola are serving life sentences.[25] A "life sentence" in Louisiana means "natural life," expiring only upon the inmate's death.[26] The average sentence for "non-lifers" at Angola in 2012 was 92.7 years.

For many decades, most guards at Angola were convicts themselves. Armed with rifles and shotguns, these "trusties" guarded the periphery of the camps, under orders to shoot anyone attempting to escape. While the use of convict guards saved money, it also contributed in large measure to the brutality and low morale of prisoners at Angola over the years. By the 1960s, rampant violence surfaced in headlines featuring a sinister partnership between inmates and state corrections staff operating prostitution rings and illicit drug markets at the prison. Such common place corruption and violence led to Angola's reputation for being the "Bloodiest Prison in America."[27]

In 1995, Burl Cain was appointed the new warden at Angola. Knowing the dismal history and challenge of this under-resourced and notorious prison, Cain knew it was necessary to do something dramatically different to put Angola on a more humane and prosocial trajectory. His idea was a novel one: establish a Bible College as a means of providing educational programs for prisoners, and to give them another chance to make something positive out of their life. Cain was optimistic a prison-based seminary could successfully train prisoners to become ministers who over time would become effective change agents in the prison; ultimately replacing a culture of violence and corruption with a culture that was redemptive, hopeful, and personally transformative.

Later that year, Warden Cain was able to convince leaders of the New Orleans Baptist Theological Seminary to open a satellite campus within the walls of the Louisiana State Penitentiary. The building housing the Angola seminary was paid for with private donations. While legal doctrine has long rejected the notion that inmates have anything positive to contribute to the management of prisons, the Angola prison seminary and its unique inmate minister program operation challenge this notion (Figure 5.1).

FIGURE 5.1 The New Orleans Theological Baptist Seminary at Angola.

The Role of Religion in Identity Transformation and Offender Rehabilitation

In 2012, we led a research team in launching a major five-year study of prisoners at Angola, especially those participating in the Bible College. Previous research on religion within prisons had focused largely on faith-based programs administered by faith-motivated volunteers and generally confirms that these programs can increase prosocial behavior inside of prison and even reduce recidivism following release from prison.[28] However, very little was known about what happens when inmates form and lead their own religious groups, interpret theology from inside of prison and practice their faith communally inside the cellblocks. Our research culminated in a book entitled *The Angola Prison Seminary: Effects of Faith-Based Ministry on Identity Transformation, Desistence and Rehabilitation* (Hallett et al., 2016).

Over a period of five years, our research team analyzed survey data from 2,200 inmates at the Louisiana State Penitentiary (aka Angola), and conducted more than 100 life-history interviews of inmates and staff at this maximum security prison formerly known as one of the most violent and corrupt prisons in America. We examined the role of religious education and involvement in inmate-led religious congregations that was central to transforming prisoners and the housing units where they reside.

Utilizing a mixed-methods approach, a series of studies were produced that document the process of identity transformation, and the catalytic role that religion plays in this process. We also found significant linkages between participation in the prison seminary and inmate-led churches on crime desistance, rehabilitation, and prosocial behavior within the prison environment. Most importantly, the research points to the central role of inmate-led efforts to bring about these salutary findings.[29] Inmate ministers lead most of Angola's roughly two-dozen autonomous churches, but their ministry transcends these formal gatherings. Their unique status also grants them a relative freedom of movement to minister among their peers on a daily basis. As one Inmate Minister described it, we have "the opportunity to actually practice what we preach. It gives us the opportunity to actually *be* the church instead of just *having* church." This sense of service is the hallmark of an authentic faith that is common among inmate ministers we observed.

Ethnographic accounts of inmate graduates of Angola's unique prison seminary program suggest that inmate ministers assume a number of pastoral service roles throughout the prison. Inmate ministers establish their own churches and serve in lay-ministry capacities in hospice, cellblock visitation, tier ministry, officiating inmate funerals, and through tithing with "care packages" for indigent prisoners. Despite the fact they are serving life sentences without the possibility of parole, inmate ministers are able to find meaning and purpose for their lives. The inmate ministers assist others in finding that meaning, thereby providing them with the human grace and dignity they may have thought they lost or perhaps never had (Figures 5.2 and 5.3).

By embracing religion and being afforded the opportunity to choose a better self, inmates transform their lives, come to care about others, and display their humanity on a daily basis. Several themes of positive criminology emerge from inmate narratives: (a) the importance of respectful treatment of inmates by correctional administrations, (b) the value of building trusting relationships for prosocial modeling and improved self-perception, (c) repairing harm through faith-based intervention, and (d) spiritual practice as a blueprint for positive self-identity and social integration among prisoners.[30]

Though research on how incarcerated offenders can help other prisoners change is rare, the Field Ministry program within the Texas Department of Criminal Justice is a current example. The program enlists inmates who have graduated from a prison-based seminary to work as "Field Ministers," serving other inmates in various capacities.[31] Scholars have recently examined whether inmate exposure to Field Ministers is inversely related to antisocial factors and

FIGURE 5.2 Bible College students in the seminary library.

FIGURE 5.3 An inmate minister preaching at one of Angola's 29 inmate-led and autonomous congregations.

positively to prosocial ones at three maximum-security prisons where the Field Ministry program operates. Preliminary results indicate inmates exposed to Field Ministers more frequently and for a longer period tended to report lower levels of criminological risk factors (e.g., legal cynicism) and aggressiveness, and higher levels of virtues (e.g., humility), predictors of human agency (e.g., a sense of meaning and purpose in life), religiosity, and spirituality. We find that prisoners who are the beneficiaries of the inmate-led field ministry help other prisoners make positive and prosocial changes. We conclude that inmate ministers play an important role in fostering virtuous behavior,[32] and achieving the goal of offender rehabilitation.[33] Moreover, we find that some offenders in prison should be viewed as potential assets waiting to be reformed with the help of other offenders.[34]

A 2017 book and documentary film, both titled *If I Give My Soul: Faith Behind Bars in Rio de Janeiro,* argues that inmate-led Pentecostalism thrives inside of prison because it offers prisoners—mostly poor, darker-skinned young men—a platform to live moral and dignified lives in a social context that treats them as less than human, or "killable."[35] And a recent study conducted in El Salvador by scholars at Florida International University, concludes that the only realistic hope for incarcerated MS-13 gang members to desist from a life of crime and violence is by means of a conversion to Christianity and subsequent involvement in Evangelical or Pentecostal churches.[36,37] This initial study is intriguing, but more rigorous and systematic research is necessary to understand how, if at all, inmate-led religious interventions may be linked to positive and consequential outcomes.

Research on Offender-Led Religious Movements

In the book *The Wounded Healer* (1979) Henri Nouwen states, "the great illusion of leadership is to think that man can be led out of the desert by someone who has never been there."[38] This line of reasoning would seem to suggest that prisoners may well be the most appropriate people to aid other inmates in the process of being reformed. Who is more equipped to challenge, affirm, or relate to a prisoner than another prisoner? Similarly, offenders participating in 12-step programs are essentially working from a similar "wounded healer" paradigm—where addicts help other addicts stay sober through various social support and acts of service.

A new line of research is necessary that will focus specifically on religious groups indigenous to the cellblocks—what can be called Offender-Led Religious Movements (ORMs). ORMs have the capacity to provide participants a strong identity, an alternative moral framework and a set of embodied practices that emphasize virtue and character development. Though there are significant roadblocks to the proliferation of ORMs, this innovative approach to rehabilitation and reform holds significant potential to transform the character of not only individual prisoners, but particular cellblocks or housing units, and possibly entire correctional facilities. Though nearly invisible to scholars and co-religionists on the outside, studying ORMs may provide rich insight on how virtues like forgiveness and accountability, as well as how constructs like character and other-mindedness are developed inside of correctional facilities through inmate-led religious groups. This kind of research will help scholars and practitioners understand if ORMs can provide a path for prisoners to experience an identity transformation that is consistent with the need to rehabilitate offenders. Moreover, this line of research will shed light on how ORMs emphasize or facilitate prosocial behavior, spiritual awakening, service to others, prayer, perseverance, and forgiveness. This new line of research should address questions such as these:

- How and why do ORMs emerge?
- What character traits and virtues are promoted by ORMs?
- How are these values and behaviors developed by prisoners participating in ORMs?
- What impact do ORMs have on the broader prison environment?
- How can social scientists accurately measure the impact of ORMs on individual offenders, housing units, and the prison environment more generally?

Answering questions like these could go a long way in helping practitioners, correctional leaders, volunteers, and scholars think more effectively, more constructively, and more optimistically about incarceration and the goal of restorative corrections. If we are to genuinely rethink our current approaches to incarceration, it is going to require a willingness to rely upon empirical evidence for what is working and what is not. In spite of all the rhetoric and endorsements for embracing evidence-based decision-making in government, the field of corrections has not done a good job of relying upon empirical evidence for making policy decisions, especially regarding the role of prison-based programs or the overarching correctional goal of rehabilitation. As we have demonstrated in the chapters of this book, there is ample research documenting that our present correctional system is not working effectively. Considering all the problems currently plaguing prisons (e.g., post-traumatic stress disorders, suicide, mental illness, overcrowding, a paucity of educational, vocational, and rehabilitative prison programs, under-resourced prisoner reentry programs), it is time for leaders in criminal justice and policy experts to truly rely upon data-driven solutions in order to reimagine the field of corrections. This will be difficult because it will require decision-makers to exercise humility when it comes to admitting what works and what does not. Data suggest that faith-motivated volunteers and faith-based prison programs can help prisoners experience an authentic identity transformation that helps them develop a "new self" that is prosocial. Admitting that faith-based programs can help some prisoners as well as reduce crime, violence, and suicide in prisons, will be hard for some to admit. Second, it is going to take a new boldness to insure that such efforts are not hindered, or merely tolerated, but embraced. This kind of boldness could usher in a dramatic shift in correctional policy toward the restorative prison.

Rethinking incarceration is going to require humility because it is going to be a difficult transformation for many correctional leaders and policy-makers to be willing to admit. The fact that volunteers and prisoners themselves can help reform our prisons may be a pill too difficult to swallow; but swallow it we must, if we are going to make the necessary steps to reform our current system of incarceration. Faith-based correctional programs raise new concerns about the efficacy of harsh prison sentences for offender rehabilitation. Religious volunteers working with inmates inside some of America's worst prisons often conclude that their punitivism is counter-productive (see Chapter 6). More importantly, the very methods and resources that seem to help faith-based programs succeed—holistic approaches that treat prisoners with respect while helping them revisit positive aspects of their lives beyond their criminal offense while setting a new direction—may hold deeper lessons for both corrections policy and society itself. Perhaps the central activity of faith-based programming lies in assisting prisoners in reauthoring their self-narrative with emphasis on positive aspects of their lives that offer hope for the future. Just as the "Good Lives Model" described in Chapter 1 emphasizes the importance of first meeting physical and social needs, faith-based volunteers working in prisons highlight many of the same priorities. But without sentencing reform and genuine changes to community-based supervision and the collateral consequences of imprisonment, even the best faith-based efforts inside prisons may be doomed to fail.

As Robert L. Woodson, Sr., a former civil rights activist, has argued for decades, the answer to inner-city problems like crime, gang violence, and drug abuse, can be found within those same communities. What these communities need more than outside "experts" is simply resources. Referred to by many as the "godfather" of the neighborhood empowerment movement, Woodson argues that low-income citizens in the worst of circumstances—long after government and the free market have failed them—are able to come up with their own solutions to their own problems. "Whether it's a storefront church, or a boxing club, or a twelve-step group, they gather in community to meet their needs according to their values."[39]

A growing body of research points to the restorative power of faith-based programs in prisons for lowering recidivism and comprehensively achieving the goals of prison reform. The programs described here document an emerging shift in focus found in a growing number of maximum security prisons. While some may be uncomfortable with religious volunteers working in prisons—and with religion itself in prisons (in the same way that some are uncomfortable with school prayer, for example), American prisons today find themselves in a state of genuine crisis and neglect. If prison reformers object to religious volunteers offering voluntary programs in prisons or to inmates praying in prisons, who then we ask is going to help achieve prison reform? We find that state authorities have demonstrated a profound neglect of prison institutions, almost from the inception of the prison itself. After such an extensive record of programmatic failure, and the imposition of great human suffering upon countless citizens who have found themselves incarcerated over many decades, what is it going to take to transform the prison to become truly "restorative"? Who specifically is going to help bring about the desistance-focused programming of the sort Shadd Maruna and others describe as vital for turning prisons around? While we are unconvinced by abstract calls for "prison abolition," we are compelled by efforts to end prison as we know it—starting with these direct efforts to use prison differently than before. In the next chapter, we show how former inmates themselves can play a vital role in this important transformational work—offering new hope for both employment and a pathway toward restoration.

Notes

1 This chapter is based on the following paper, "Offender-Led Religious Movements: Identity Transformation, Rehabilitation, and Justice System Reform," In Cohen, A. (ed.) (2020). *Religion and flourishing*. Waco, TX: Baylor University Press.
2 VanderWeele (2017a, 2017b, 2018).
3 Koenig, King, and Carson (2012).
4 Johnson (2011), Johnson and Jang (2012).
5 Johnson, Larson, Jang, and Li (2000a, 2000b), Jang and Johnson (2001), Johnson, Jang, Larson, and Li (2001), Ellison, Trinitapoli, Anderson, and Johnson (2007), Ulmer, Ulmer, Desmond, Jang, and Johnson (2010, 2012), Jang and Johnson (2011).
6 Lee, Pagano, Johnson, and Post (2016), Lee, Pagano, Johnson, Post, and Leibowitz (2017).
7 Johnson (2004, 2006, 2018a, 2018b).
8 Johnson (2011), Johnson and Jang (2012), Johnson (2012), Duwe and Johnson (2013).
9 Johnson, Thompkins, and Webb (2006), Johnson and Wubbenhorst (2017), Wydick, Glewwe, and Rutledge (2013, 2017), Glewwe, Ross, and Wydick (2017).
10 Brooks (2007), Pagano, Wang, Rowles, Lee, and Johnson (2015), Johnson, Lee, Pagano, and Post (2015), Stark (2015).
11 Hallett, Hays, Johnson, Jang, and Duwe (2016).
12 Johnson, Lee, Pagano, and Post et al. (2016), Johnson et al. (2017), Jang and Johnson (2017).
13 Young, Gartner, O'Conner, Larson, and Wright (1995).
14 Johnson et al. (1997).
15 Johnson (2004).
16 The InnerChange Freedom Initiative (IFI) is a reentry program for prisoners based on the life and teachings of Jesus Christ. Inmates begin the program 18–24 months before their release date and continue for an additional 12 months once they have returned to the community. Prison Fellowship would later change the name of IFI to the Prison Fellowship Academy.
17 Johnson and Larson (2006).
18 Johnson (2011).
19 Duwe and King (2013).
20 Duwe and Johnson (2013).
21 Kerley et al. (2005a).
22 Kerley et al. (2005b).
23 Duwe and Johnson (2016).
24 Carleton (1971).
25 Louisiana Department of Corrections (2015).
26 Nellis (2010).
27 Rideau (1985).
28 Johnson (2011).
29 Hallett et al. (2016).
30 Hallett, Hays, Johnson, Jang, and Duwe (2017).
31 Duwe, Hallett, Hays, Jang, and Johnson (2015).
32 Jang, Johnson, Hays, Hallett, and Duwe (2018).
33 Jang, Johnson, Hays, Hallett, and Duwe (2017).
34 Hallett et al. (2016).
35 Johnson (2017).
36 Cruz, Rosen, Amaya, and Vorobyeva (2018).
37 Maslin (2018).
38 Nouwen (1979).
39 Woodson, R. L. (2020). *Lessons from the least of these: The Woodson principles*. New York, NY: Bombardier Books.

References

Brooks, A. C. (2007). *Who really cares: The surprising truth about compassionate conservatism*. New York, NY: Basic Books.
Carleton, M. T. (1971). *Politics and punishment: The history of the Louisiana state penal system* (p. 89). Baton Rouge, LA: Louisiana State University Press.

Cruz, J. M., Rosen, J. D., Amaya, L. E., & Vorobyeva, Y. (2018). *The new face of street gangs: The gang phenomenon in El Salvador.* Miami, FL: Florida International University.

Duwe, G., & King, M. (2013). Can faith-based correctional programs work? An outcome evaluation of the InnerChange Freedom Initiative in Minnesota. *International Journal of Offender Therapy and Comparative Criminology, 57*(7), 813–841.Duwe, G., Hallett, M., Hays, J., Jang, S. J., & Johnson, B. R. (2015). Bible college participation and prison misconduct: A preliminary analysis. *Journal of Offender Rehabilitation, 54*, 371–390.

Duwe, G., & Johnson, B. R. (2013). Estimating the benefits of a faith-based correctional program. *International Journal of Criminology and Sociology, 2*, 227–239.

Duwe, G., & Johnson, B. R. (2016). The effects of prison visits from community volunteers on offender recidivism. *The Prison Journal, 96*, 279–303.

Ellison, C. G., Trinitapoli, J. A., Anderson, K. L., & Johnson, B. R. (2007). Religion and domestic violence: An examination of variations by race and ethnicity. *Violence Against Women, 13*, 1094–1112.

Glewwe, P., Ross, P. H., & Wydick, B. (2017). Developing hope among impoverished children: Using child self-portraits to measure poverty program impacts. *Journal of Human Resources.* doi:10.3368/jhr.53.2.0816–8112R1.

Hallett, M., Hays, J., Johnson, B. R., Jang, S. J., & Duwe, G. (2016). *The Angola prison seminary: Effects of faith-based ministry on identity transformation, desistence and rehabilitation.* New York, NY: Routledge Press.

Hallett, M., Hays, J., Johnson, B. R., Jang, S. J., & Duwe, G. (2017). First stop dying: Angola's christian seminary as positive criminology. *International Journal of Offender Therapy and Comparative Criminology, 61*(4), 445–463.

Jang, S. J., & Johnson, B. R. (2011). The effects of childhood exposure to drug users and religion on drug use in adolescence and young adulthood. *Youth and Society, 43*, 1220–1245.

Jang, S. J., & Johnson, B. R. (2017). Religion, spirituality, and desistance from crime: Toward a theory of existential identity transformation. In A. Blokland & V. van der Geest (Eds.), *International handbook of criminal careers and life-course criminology* (pp. 74–86). London, UK: Routledge.

Jang, S. J., Johnson, B. R., Hays, J., Hallett, M., & Duwe, G. (2017). Religion and misconduct in 'Angola' prison: Conversion, congregational participation, religiosity, and self-identities. *Justice Quarterly, 35*(3), 412–442.

Jang, S. J., Johnson, B. R., Hays, J., Hallett, M., & Duwe, G. (2018). Existential and virtuous effects of religiosity on mental health and aggressiveness among offenders. *Religions, 9*, 182. doi:10.3390/rel9060182.

Johnson, A. (2017). *If I give my soul: Faith behind bars in Rio de Janeiro.* New York, NY: Oxford University Press.

Johnson, B. R. (2004).Religious programs and recidivism among former inmates in prison fellowship programs: A long-term follow-up study. *Justice Quarterly, 21*(2), 329–354.

Johnson, B. R., & Larson, D. B. (2006). *The innerChange freedom initiative: A preliminary evaluation of a faith-based prison program.* Institute for Studies of Religion (ISR Research Report), Baylor University (2003/2006). Retrieved from http://www.BAYLORISR.org/publications/reports/.

Johnson, B. R. (2011). *More God, less crime: Why faith matters and how it could matter more.* Conshohocken, PA: Templeton Press.

Johnson, B. R. (2012). Can a faith-based prison reduce recidivism? *Corrections Today, 73*, 60–62.

Johnson, B. R. (2018a). The role of religion in advancing the field of criminology. In J. Levin (Ed.), *Religion and the social sciences: Basic and applied research perspectives* (pp. 181–207). Conshohocken, PA: Templeton Press.

Johnson, B. R. (2018b). Why religious freedom is good for inmates, prisons, and society. In W. Jeynes (Ed.), *The Wiley handbook of christianity & education* (pp. 119–140). New York, NY: Wiley/Blackwell.

Johnson, B. R., & Jang, S. J. (2012). Religion and crime: Assessing the role of the faith factor. In R. Rosenfeld, K. Quinet, and C. Garcia (Eds.), *Contemporary issues in criminological theory and research: The role of social institutions* (pp. 117–150), Collected Papers from the American Society of Criminology 2010 Conference.

Johnson, B. R., Duwe, G., Hallett, M., Hays, J., Jang, S. J., Lee, M. T., Pagano, M. E., & Post, S. G. (2017). Faith and service: Pathways to identity transformation and correctional reform. In K. Kerley (Ed.), *Finding Freedom in Confinement: The Role of Religion in Prison Life*, Santa Barbara, CA: Praeger.

Johnson, B. R., Jang, S. J., Larson, D. B., & Li, S. D. (2001). Does adolescent religious commitment matter?: A reexamination of the effects of religiosity on delinquency. *Journal of Research in Crime and Delinquency, 38*, 22–44.

Johnson, B. R., Larson, D. B., Jang, S. J., & Li, S. D. (2000a). The 'invisible institution' and black youth crime: The church as an agency of local social control. *Journal of Youth and Adolescence, 29*, 479–498.

Johnson, B. R., Larson, D. B., Jang, S. J., & Li, S. D. (2000b). Who escapes the crime of inner-cities: Church attendance and religious salience among disadvantaged youth. *Justice Quarterly, 17*, 701–715.

Johnson, B. R., Lee, M. T., Pagano, M. E., & Post, S. G. (2015). Alone on the inside: The impact of social isolation and helping others on AOD use and criminal activity. *Youth and Society.* doi:10.1177/0044118X15617400.

Johnson, B. R., Lee, M. T., Pagano, M. E., & Post, S. G. (2016). Positive criminology and rethinking the response to adolescent addiction: Evidence on the role of social support, religiosity, and service to others. *International Journal of Criminology and Sociology, 5*, 75–85.

Johnson, B. R., Thompkins, B., & Webb, D. (2006). *Objective hope – Assessing the effectiveness of religion and faith-based organizations: A systematic review of the literature.* Waco, TX: Institute for Studies of Religion (Research Report), Baylor University. Retrieved from www.BAYLORISR.org/publications/reports/.

Johnson, B. R., & Wubbenhorst, W. (2017). *Assessing the faith-based response to homelessness in America: Findings from eleven cities.* Waco, TX: Program on Prosocial Behavior, Baylor University.

Kerley, K. R., Matthew, T. L., & Schultz, J. T. (2005a). Participation in Operation Starting Line, experience of negative emotions, and incidence of negative behavior. *International Journal of Offender Therapy and Comparative Criminology, 49*(4), 410–426.

Kerley, K. R., Matthews, T. L., & Blanchard, T. C. (2005b). Religiosity, religious participation, and negative prison behaviors. *Journal for the Scientific Study of Religion, 44*(4), 443–457.

Koenig, H., King, G., Dane, E., & Carson, V. B. (2012). *Handbook of religion and health.* 2nd ed. New York, NY: Oxford University Press.

Lee, M. T., Pagano, M. E., Johnson, B. R., & Post, S. G. (2016). Love and service in adolescent addiction recovery. *Alcohol Treatment Quarterly, 34*(2), 197–222.

Lee, M. T., Pagano, M. E., Johnson, B. R., Post, S. G. & Leibowitz, G. S. (2017). From defiance to reliance: Spiritual virtue as a pathway towards desistance, humility, and recovery among juvenile offenders. *Spirituality in Clinical Practice, 4*(3), 161–175.

Louisiana Department of Corrections. (2015). Briefing book. Baton Rouge, LA: Author. Retrieved from http://www.doc.la.gov/wp-content/uploads/2009/10/Jan2015bb.pdf.

Maslin, S. E. (2018, April/May). Can religion solve El Salvador's gang problem? *The Economist.*

Nellis, A. (2010). *Throwing away the key: The expansion of life without parole sentences in the United States* (p. 28). Washington, DC: The Federal Sentencing Reporter. Retrieved from http://sentencingproject.org/doc/publications/inc_federalsentencingreporter.pdf.

Nouwen, H. J. M. (1979). *The wounded healer.* New York, NY: Random House.

Pagano, M. E., Wang, A. R., Rowles, B. M., Lee, M. T., & Johnson, B. R. (2015). Social anxiety and peer-helping in adolescent addiction treatment. *Alcoholism: Clinical and Experimental Research, 39*(5), 887–895.

Rideau, W. (1985). *The Angolite.* Angola, LA: Louisiana State Penitentiary.

Stark, R. (2015). *The triumph of faith: Why the World is more religious than ever.* New York, NY: Intercollegiate Studies Institute.

Ulmer, J. T., Desmond, S., Jang, S. J., & Johnson, B. R. (2010). Teenage religiosity and changes in marijuana use during the transition to adulthood. *Interdisciplinary Journal of Research on Religion, 6*, 1–19.

Ulmer, J. T., Desmond, S., Jang, S. J., & Johnson, B. R. (2012). Religiosity and dynamics of marijuana use: Initiation, persistence, and desistence. *Deviant Behavior, 33*, 448–468.

VanderWeele, T. J. (2017a). Religious communities and human flourishing. *Current Directions in Psychological Science, 26*, 476–481.

VanderWeele, T. J. (2017b). On the promotion of human flourishing. *Proceedings of the National Academy of Sciences, 31*, 8148–8156.

VanderWeele, T. J. (2018). Is forgiveness a public health issue? *American Journal of Public Health, 108*, 189–190.

Wydick, B., Glewwe, P., & Rutledge, L. (2013). Does international child sponsorship work? A six-county study of impacts on adult life outcomes. *Journal of Political Economy*, *121*, 393–436.

Wydick, B., Glewwe, P., & Rutledge, L. (2017). Does child sponsorship pay off in adulthood? An international study of impacts on income and wealth. *The World Bank Economic Review*, *31*, 434–458.

Young, M., Gartner, J., O'Conner, T., Larson, D. B., & Wright, K. (1995). Long-term recidivism among federal inmates trained as volunteer prison ministers. *Journal of Offender Rehabilitation*, *22*, 97–118.

6

WOUNDED HEALERS IN "FAILED STATE" PRISONS

A Case Study of Mississippi State Penitentiary at Parchman

In short, the moment has never been better for a redemption-based justice model that can counter the othering and demonizing forces of the "just us" movement facing the world. I sincerely hope that restorative justice and desistance are up to this immense task. If they are not, then it is time to "change lenses" once again and abandon them both to the graveyard of former revolutionary ideas that deteriorated into careerist claptrap and academic jargon.[1]

Somewhere along the way America lost focus on the rehabilitative ideals of its earliest prisons. While never intended to be comfortable, the original ambition of incarceration was not simply to be punitive, but also to be "correctional"—to leave prisoners better off than we found them, for the good of inmates and the country. Philadelphia's Walnut Street Jail (1773–1838), America's first briefly "correctional" regime, experimented with opportunities for self-betterment including a school for carpentry, fair wages for shoe making and stone cutting, family visitation, visitor-led religious services, and early release for good behavior.[2] The goal was to prepare *citizens* for the new mercantile economy, not to keep them relentlessly warehoused as *inmates*.[3]

Early models of correctional practice were more collaborative than prisons of today, combining state resources with philanthropic, religious, and civic assets to better manage offenders.[4] The main goal was to incentivize future good behaviors, not simply punish previous bad ones. But in a legacy that has defined the entire history of American corrections, Walnut Street Jail quickly became a nondescript human dumping ground—so overcrowded and rampant with violence and disease that betterment of its prisoners was soon abandoned.[5]

Today's prisons feature severe overcrowding, widespread mental illness, high levels of post-traumatic stress disorder, almost nonexistent levels of programming, extreme violence, unforgiving sentences, corrosive employee turnover, and costly recidivism. National data reveal that the longer someone spends in prison, the *more likely* they are to reoffend. Because of these toxic burdens, coupled with shrinking resources, today's prisons not only fail to "correct," they often make things worse. At great expense to taxpayers.

But a new model of corrections is quietly taking hold in the United States—built in part on the ideals of old, but also putting into place newer practices gleaned from the painful experience of mass incarceration. By necessity, these new approaches are being developed in some

DOI: 10.4324/9781003171744-6

of America's largest maximum-security prisons, and yet largely remain hidden in plain sight. However, in order to fully appreciate the accomplishments of these innovations, it requires a willingness to rethink many current practices both inside and outside of prisons.

Drawing from work inside some of America's largest and most extreme prison environments, this book promotes an alternative model of penal help—what we call "restorative corrections"—that strategically deploys the lived experience of carefully selected "wounded healers" toward redesigning incarceration with the goal of improving the prospects and wellbeing of citizens sent into their custody. Lois Presser defines the Restorative Prison as one that seeks to implement a "culture of care" over punitivism and "that embraces respect and rehabilitative programming toward the goal of a good life once one leaves prison" (2014, p. 20).[6] Combined with the larger goal of dramatically reduced use of incarceration overall, prisons may certainly become more restorative than they are today. We believe inmate ministry as described here constitutes one important example of some very real steps being taken in the direction of changing prisons to become more restorative.

Research documents the overwhelming desire of citizens serving time in prison to achieve redemption and a genuine willingness to follow a path toward earned social acceptance—only to encounter a profound lack of opportunities for achieving these goals.[7] In part due to a prison system that has become an irrationally punitive and unimaginative human dumping ground, many prisons today offer services to fewer than 10% of their inmates. American corrections is quite simply out of ideas, bankrupt in its results, and failing both society and American taxpayers. Inmates emerge from America's prisons only to reoffend at higher rates than before, with the majority being reincarcerated within five years. Put simply, America's prison system not only fails to be "correctional"—it is criminogenic.[8]

In this book, we describe a transformative agenda taking hold in American maximum-security prisons fast becoming a disruptive alternative to mainstream corrections. At a time when criminal justice reform is at the forefront of American politics, this book offers a specific agenda for redeeming America's prisons and offering hope for a positive future. Combined with proposals to dramatically reduce incarceration through sentencing reform, prisons must become the restorative institutions they were once envisioned to be. We agree with Lydia Pellot-Hobbs' view, however, that "reform" and "abolition" are neither antithetical nor impossible to achieve. In fact they must and always do occur together:

> Prison abolition's ethos of transformative change follows in lineage of W.E.B. Du Bois' conceptualization of Radical Reconstruction as an experiment in abolition democracy where ambition meant not only the abolition of slavery but the creation of a new type of society where slavery would be unthinkable. Thus prison abolitionist reforms include both those that build up new institutions, ideologies, and cultural norms and those that work to dismantle criminalizing regimes and end state violence. While it might seem difficult to imagine a reform that moves in the direction of abolition, in practice, examples abound.[9]

Parchman Farm: How Incremental Change Matters in Prison

Perhaps no better example of the multi-dimensional failure of America's prison system exists than Mississippi State Penitentiary (MSP)—the former plantation known as Parchman Farm, America's second-largest maximum-security prison (Louisiana State Penitentiary at Angola is the largest). Prisons are deeply contested spaces of public policy, resistant to change from the outside and unlikely to be "abolished" anytime soon.[10] Meanwhile, millions of citizens endure and suffer maltreatment inside prisons, in no small part due to a longstanding "hands off" sentiment in both law and American culture.

As an institution where "no one is safe, not even the guards," Parchman was struggling to retain staff while staving off federal intervention, even before the onset of COVID-19. After losing nearly half its correctional officers, Mississippi Department of Corrections has also lost roughly one-third of its education staff and 20% of its probation officers since 2014.[11] Numerous beatings, rapes, and literal burnings of inmates have been documented recently in Mississippi state prisons.[12] Sentencing reform legislation aimed at lessening overcrowding while diverting savings to rehabilitation was briefly successful—only to have these monies clawed back by the legislature to help pay for corporate tax cuts.[13] Meanwhile, Mississippi's inmate population has crept back up to near record levels.

But Mississippi is by no means unique. The severe budgetary constraints imposed upon many state prison systems is part of a longstanding funding crisis faced by corrections overall, dramatically impacting prison operations.[14] In Florida's prison system, for example (the nation's third-largest), only 6% of inmates receive any type of programming.[15] Florida's current Secretary of Corrections describes Florida's system as in a "death spiral," while chair of the state senate's criminal justice appropriations committee noted: "This is not a prison system that anybody can look you in the eye and tell you a person… will be safe in the state's care."[16]

God Help Us: New Partners for Changing "Failed State" Prisons

News that retired warden Burl Cain of Louisiana State Penitentiary (LSP) at Angola had been confirmed as Secretary of Mississippi Department of Corrections (MDC) came as good news to our ears. Southern plantation prisons play a unique role in American corrections and they face unique challenges. Mississippi State Penitentiary, the state's largest prison, is second only to Angola in size. Recent accounts show Parchman's physical plant to be decrepit, septic, unheated, and dangerous. Conditions have deteriorated to the point where inmates openly attack staff *for the purpose of* being sent to solitary confinement. Such conditions comprise what Cambridge University prisons scholar Alison Liebling calls "failed state" prisons.[17] In "failed state" prisons, even the most basic level of care and safety cannot be provided by authorities. Such institutions cause more disorder than they prevent. Steeped in dynamics of race relations that date to America's founding, Angola and Parchman are America's largest and most notorious plantation prisons. The large majority of inmates in both institutions have always been black.

On a team of five criminologists, we spent five years at Angola evaluating the impact of the prison's unique Christian seminary, established in 1995 after Congress revoked Pell Grant eligibility for convicted felons as part of the 1994 Crime Bill. Fearing an increase in violence and facing continuous budget cuts, then Warden Burl Cain described himself as desperate for his job. Through friends at church he reached out to New Orleans Baptist Theological Seminary (NOBTS) to inquire about the school's offering a few courses as a gift to the prison. As Cain hopefully put it, he wanted NOBTS faculty to come "*on campus*" at Angola.

During LSP's own federal takeover of 1974, religious practice was identified by inmates as one of the few program options prisoners actually valued, thereafter requesting permission to turn what they described as informal "religious clubs" into prison-approved programs. Inmates had long gathered on Angola's yards to sing Gospel music and preserve a semblance of community. With the state's permission, inmates were allowed to form their own Baptist, Pentecostal, Catholic, Methodist, Episcopal, and other worship communities as new programs of the prison. Several inmate-built interdenominational chapels and two Catholic churches exist on the grounds of Angola today. A small population of Muslim inmates also openly worships at the prison.

After initial reluctance, NOBTS faculty surprisingly decided that instruction at Angola not only fell within its mission—it affirmed their mission. Moved by the isolation of Angola and its active religious life, NOBTS Dean Dr. Jimmy Dukes described encountering inmates "in threadbare clothing articulating themselves about King David's moral failings and comparing the violence of illicit drug markets to that found in [the Old Testament book of] 1 Kings." No pushover, Dukes stayed cool to the overtures of inmates. But Dukes soon learned by attending services and walking the prison—that few ever actually left Angola alive. Ninety percent in fact died on site, with many quietly buried in the prison cemetery after serving a life sentence with no family members present.

As Dukes absorbed the desolation of Angola, he concluded there was literally no earthly gain to inmates' moral curiosity about the Bible. Dukes also confesses to altering his own viewpoint regarding what he now considers to be "throw-away prisons." At the conclusion of these early visits, he and others felt something was not right—and that something should be done. In its decision to plant a fully functioning Christian seminary on the grounds of Angola, NOBTS single-handedly salvaged collegiate education for convicted felons at a time when virtually no other prison was able to do so.

Once established, the seminary immediately opened enrollment to inmates from across Angola's five prison complexes. The school hired an outside Director to work fulltime *on campus* at Angola and four years later graduated its first small cohort of what they called "trained ministers." But in addition to bringing collegiate education back to the prison, NOBTS accomplished something more novel: they had pierced the hermetically sealed environment of America's largest maximum-security prison. By introducing a host of outside stakeholders with a newly vested interest in positively impacting the prison, the inmates soon found their environment unalterably changed.

In what is fast-becoming a new nationwide model in public-private partnerships, the programs we describe here are being adopted by prison wardens all over the United States and are now collaborating with religious educators and nonprofit organizations working inside over 50 US maximum-security prisons in 29 states. Paid for with private external funding and endorsed by powerful legislative advocates, a prison reform movement not dissimilar to that initiated by the Religious Society of Friends is now well underway. Motivated by concerns about prison conditions and America's failing prisons, religious volunteers are stepping up to deliver what they call a new "purpose-driven" ministry. Griffith notes the higher level of engagement and commitment to prison reform held by evangelicals who have direct experience with the prison system (2020). Just before the onset of COVID-19, religious educators were dramatically expanding their presence in many dozens of US maximum-security prisons.

Paradigm Shift: "Nothing Disciplinary" * Inmate Peer Ministry

Because space limitations constrained worship on Sunday mornings at Angola, religious services were scheduled each weekday evening—with many inmates thereafter attending open services seven days per week. With this denominational cross-fertilization, Angola's congregations congealed around a shared sense of purpose, collectively "tithing" to indigent prisoners with gifts including everything from soap, toothpaste and socks, to spare sweatshirts. Put another way, after a season of prolonged violence and prison neglect, Angola's inmate churches became organizing venues not just for religious programming, but for all kinds of enrichment programs including remedial education, 12-step meetings, individual outreach to the cell blocks, and workshops of all kinds.[18]

Since religious leaders must be confirmed by the faithful, Angola's churches bolstered inmate voice and leadership through nominating their own "pastors." Priding itself on the functional equivalence of their "prison seminary" to any on the outside, Angola also began to attract free world attention. Evangelists and preachers soon visited Angola's churches by invitation—opening a vibrant new channel of philanthropy to the prison. Visitors brought precious items in short supply: boxes of winter clothing, personal hygiene items, socks, blankets, work boots, stationery and postage, and reading materials. In organizing to distribute these goods, Angola's inmate churches suddenly took on a unique caretaking role for the entire prison. A sense of community developed, with inmates organizing a service in response to the tragic death of a correctional officer's young child and frequently sharing food and worship with staff. While no panacea to the many challenges of life in a maximum-security prison, the Angola prison seminary bolstered the prison with outside resources at a time when governmental support for inmates waned.

With most correctional officers holding only a high school diploma or less, Inmate Ministers soon found themselves to be among the most educated individuals on site. Trained in process counseling and conflict management, and having unique access to fellow inmates, new seminary grads immediately found their greatest workload not in prison chapels but in dorms and cell blocks. Security warden Davy Kellone witnessed seminary students consoling an inmate in distress. In crisis situations, after a suicide or upon notification of the death of a loved one at home, "the seminary students *were far more effective* than sending over a chaplain or security," Kellone stated. "There's an access level there that I don't have—because it's those men helping each other as equals." Starting in 1999, Kellone implemented Angola's unique "Inmate Minister" program—sending seminary grads across the prison to "check on inmates and just talk to them. That's it. Nothing disciplinary."[19]

Together Cain, Kellone and head chaplain Robert Toney placed seminary graduates who had earned trustee status into the role "offender minister," assigning them formal caseloads in dorms and cell blocks for counseling and wellness checks. Said Cain:

> Their only job is to try to make sure people are ok and see what they need. That's it. No interrogation. If we can give them what they need, we will. If they want to be mean, we can do that too. It's like Burger King: have it your way.[20]

Multiple independent data sources show violence and self-harm at Angola fell for 20 straight years after implementation of the prison seminary. While not the only program active at the prison, both staff and inmates independently stress the importance of Angola's unique religious culture as the central organizing venue for community life. Cain explains he took chances on inmates because he didn't have a choice—and that occasionally he got burned. But to his surprise, most of the time he did not. This proved most transformational for Cain himself: he'd asked for inmates' help and received it.

Angola's administrative security staff first resisted Cain's decision to allow Inmate Ministers free movement across the prison. But amid continuous budget cuts and few program options, Cain pressed forward. The old model was failing. "The only time we ever have enough money to run this prison safely is after we lose a lawsuit. It's no way to live," Cain told us. Angola's seminary grads were now doing work once reserved for prison chaplains and professional counselors no longer on the payroll—and seemingly doing a better job of it. Violence and self-harm continued to fall. Cain realized the culture that had to change was not just the inmate culture—it was his own culture, that of what he characterizes as "so-called professional corrections." That bold conclusion imbued a paradigm shift that is since taking hold all over the nation.

Finally, in an ironic twist, the model of staffing prisons with inmate trustees due to inadequate funding of prisons by states—a model that had been "relegated to the museums" due to successful inmate litigation—has increasingly become necessary once again.[21] Unlike in the past, however, volunteer organizations funding programs inside prisons bring a new measure of outside transparency to institutions still desperately underfunded and in need of support.[22] As Sriharan notes, the 1995 Prison Litigation Reform Act dramatically curtailed prisoners' ability to sue states over prison conditions. Left increasingly isolated, inmate litigation over prison conditions has fallen dramatically.[23] Religious volunteers working inside prisons, however, bring with them both needed resources and a new measure of transparency previously unheard of in maximum-security prison settings. As stated repeatedly by religious volunteers sponsoring the programs we describe here, moreover, resources for programs of all kinds for prisons must be expanded not contracted—with less use of incarceration overall being the primary goal.[24]

THE A-Team: "Only they have the Real Credentials"

Parchman Head Chaplain Ron Olivier graduated from Angola's prison seminary in 2005. Paroled in 2018 from Angola and subsequently recruited by now Commissioner Burl Cain to work as Head Chaplain at Parchman, after graduating from seminary Olivier pastored an inmate church at Angola's Camp C for 15 years. A remote outcamp of the prison challenged by few resources and even fewer visitors, Camp C often became a desperate place. In order to hire Olivier, Cain boldly changed state rules to allow convicted felons to work in Mississippi prisons. "But who better?" Cain asks. "These men have literally saved people's lives. This is the A-team."

Just as former drug addicts often make the best addictions counselors, Angola's former Inmate Ministers possess what Cain calls "the real credentials"—actual lived experience in successfully facing the challenges of prison. Inmate Ministers are model inmates by definition, earning trustee status as a condition of application to the seminary—and then rising to the top of a competitive application process. The most important credential of Cain's A-Team, however, is having successfully faced incarceration with a long sentence while growing personally in the process. And such experience is increasingly recognized by correctional authorities as a valuable, commodifiable resource. In a growing number of prisons all across the United States, religious educators are partnering with correctional leaders to deliver tuition-free religious education programs to inmates-who are then put to work in maximum-security facilities helping their peers. Sponsored by evangelical volunteers and educational institutions concerned about prison conditions and often motivated by their own experiences volunteering inside maximum-security prisons, privately sponsored religious degree programs for inmates in US prisons are expanding rapidly.

Wounded Healers: "We Came Out of the Hog Pen"

In recruiting released Angola seminary grads as staff chaplains at Parchman and other state prisons, new Mississippi Department of Corrections Commissioner Burl Cain is drawing on experience from his worst days at Angola. Cain references "Angola's bad old days" as a key resource for moving forward. "Inmate Ministers are just here to instill some hope and help build a sense of community, if they can." NOBTS now has a functional seminary at Parchman modeled off of Angola's and donations from outside churches have already begun helping the prison. Pending concerns regarding COVID-19, a new privately funded inmate chapel—currently under construction—is slated to open at Parchman on Easter Sunday, 2021. Undaunted by the violence and conditions at Parchman, A-team members remain hopeful. "See, everybody sees Parchman right now probably differently than we see it," explains former Angola church leader and new MSP Prison Chaplain Sydney Deloch. Referencing the parable of the Prodigal Son, Deloch says "But we came out of the hog pen":

> We're not as challenged by the environment as an outsider would be. See this is kind of like home for us. It's normal for us. But what we've got here now assembled is a strong team of leaders to let men in this prison know what we already know: that it can get better. I did 41 years at Angola. I think you'll agree that's hard time. Our mission is to bring back respect and love to this place, a hopeless place. I was *saved in prison*—you understand? There's no going back from that. All of us came out of this very same hog pen, you get it? So I'm here to say to each and every man you are still a man. And I'm going to treat you like a man. Like a human being—first by exhibiting kindness but then by listening. Nothing they tell me is going to make me flinch. I'm back in prison because I love God and I'm a witness. And it's simple -if you put love at the center of your life you will be free no matter where you are. No enemies. No agendas. Just God's love. So see I left prison a long time ago, even when I was still incarcerated. And that's why I'm here. You get it? That's why we're all here. To tell these men what we already know.[25]

Moving Forward: Counter-Narratives, Post-Traumatic Growth, and Forgiveness

Academic critics of religious immersion programs in prison argue they reinforce hierarchies of economic and social relations that may violate inmates' Constitutional rights, while ignoring larger conditions regarding race and social inequality.[26] Religion in prison helps the state paper over the destructiveness of social conditions that cause mass incarceration in the first place, they argue, tautologically scapegoating blame for crime on "sinners" in prison while ignoring social injustices that cause crime. Interjecting sectarian understandings of crime into prisons is inappropriate, moreover, even as preaching to a captive audience of prisoners is coercive since they have no means of resisting it.[27] In short, religious interventions in prison are in fact distractions away from the real issues facing American corrections, critics say—while ignoring and reproducing the very power imbalances that cause so much crime in the first place. Religion becomes co-opted by state authorities and thereby "sanctifies" incarceration, helping authorities mask rather than address the very real social injustices that create mass incarceration.[28] At best, the good but misguided intentions of religiously motivated prison volunteers who "cannot resist capture" by state authorities[29] or who in the end "risk obscuring deep problems and delaying much needed change" only stymie aggressive efforts at prison reform.[30]

But the fact is that in contemporary American corrections religious programs and volunteers have often been the genesis of reform—not the hindrance of it. Only after the federal government revoked Pell Grant eligibility for convicted felons was NOBTS invited to Angola. Nationwide expansion of the programs described here, moreover, has been predicated on the widespread continuation of the Pell Grant *exclusion* of convicted felons. Even under the renewed Second Chance Pell (SCP) Grant program, which partially reinstated eligibility for convicted felons starting in 2015, fewer than half of SCP grants were utilized by prisoners because inmates remained "ineligible anyway."[31]

A demonstrable pattern of reflexive blindness regarding religious practice and religious volunteers engaged in prison reform pervades criminology, especially regarding the desistance process. Perhaps no better indication of criminological blindness toward religion lies in Travis

Hirschi's initial decision to omit religion as a social bond in his original theory of social control. While Hirschi and Stark (1969) walked that back somewhat in their delineation of "hellfire" as a deterrent, overall the pattern has held.[32] Daniel Mears puts it this way:

> The neglect by researchers of the faith-reentry nexus might reflect a potential bias. Whether true or not, the inattention is striking. Maruna's (2001) otherwise excellent account of the "reformation" process during reentry is illustrative. Despite an extensive focus on how, as his books subtitle states, "ex-convicts reform and rebuild their lives," the text makes little to no mention of the potential role of faith in the reentry process, even though reformation of the self is a concept central to many faiths and certainly to faith-based programs.[33]

Finally, concerns about the societal racial injustice of mass incarceration are of course not lost upon inmates themselves. To suggest otherwise reflects an unspoken conceit that inmates' own critical faculties are somehow lesser than academics' or that personal agency somehow disappears for those in prison, particularly when it comes to religion. In fact, however, Angola inmates are acutely aware of the prison's history as a slave plantation and deeply concerned about racial injustice.[34] But what emerges upon closer examination is a more nuanced and complex history than often acknowledged in academic research.[35]

Inmates' decision to participate in religious programming while serving time in prisons that otherwise offer them very little may not only be entirely rational—doing so may also be quite evidently freely chosen since the majority of inmates generally still do not participate. While it is certainly true that *failed state* prisons often provide opportunities for religious volunteers, these "opportunities" are proffered out of larger recognition of the prison's failures—not a celebration of American corrections. The same may historically be said for hospitals, schools, orphanages, and asylums. *Religious programs in prisons offer a type of sanctuary away from the sea of turmoil that is normal prison life.*[36] While religious programs sponsored by volunteers are commonplace, programs remain overall quite limited when compared to need and actual levels of participation.[37] In short, to suggest that volunteer-based activities in prisons are automatically subject to "reductionist capture" is more academic conjecture than proven fact. Scholars who have spent extended periods immersed in prison environments generally tell a very different story.[38]

Put simply, we did not find religion playing handmaiden to racial oppression in the prisons we've examined—to the contrary. Amid a highly racialized punishment regime existing in America's most punitive state (Louisiana), we found religion playing the role we hoped it would play: that of healing the wounded, of caretaking for the poor, and uplifting the down in spirit. We found religion at Angola enhanced inmate wellness and assisted in the reduction of violence and self-harm, especially by offering unique personalist attention to inmates' needs and private pains—often expressed for the very first time to Inmate Ministers working with peers sorting through difficult emotions and struggles. In short, in the cases examined here religion is stepping in where the state has clearly failed, working to make prisons more transparent while also bringing real and immediate resources that are changing common practice in maximum-security prison environments. We believe this religious programming in prisons enhances what Cambridge University prisons scholar Alison Liebling calls the "moral performance" of the prison: "By moral performance we mean those aspects of a prisoner's mainly interpersonal and material treatment that render a term of imprisonment more or less dehumanizing and/or painful."[39]

In sum, religion in prisons interjects into forbidding environments powerful counternarratives to punitive justice that many inmates find to be both cathartic and restorative.[40] With an emphasis on forgiveness and the ability to achieve new pathways forward, religious practice offers inmates what they often describe as a "precious resource" for rebuilding their lives, both in and out of prison.[41] Indeed, narrative self-reconstruction is a key part of the desistance process often deeply enriched by religious practice.[42] Religious programs in prisons offer key tools for self-reflection and refuge from state-imposed definitions of prisoners as "convicts" or "thugs."[43] Through adoption of self-definitions as "redeemed children of God," for example, inmates successfully use religion to cross-examine state definitions of them as irredeemable and recon-struct positive prosocial identities. Moreover, insofar as "redemption scripts" (self-narratives that fundamentally alter and help inmates to resolve negative self-identities) often become keys to successful desistance. Religious programs and practices offer much of value for achieving both desistance and rehabilitation.[44] As sociologist Peggy Giordano and her colleagues write:

> Thus, in addition to its relative accessibility, religion seems to have potential as a mech-anism for desistance because many core concerns within religious communities and the Bible relate directly to offenders' problem areas (e.g., temptation and forgiveness). Even more importantly, religious teachings can provide a clear blueprint for how to proceed as a changed individual.[45]

Religion as a Resource for Post-Traumatic Growth: Wounded Healing

Thus, like Dubler and Lloyd (2020) and a small but growing number of scholars (e.g., Peggy Giordano and colleagues), we believe the actual evidence shows that religion and religious resources have at least as much potential for helping prisons reform as they do for reifying the social relations that created them. Indeed, a few scholars go so far as to suggest that lasting and deep-level prison reform cannot be achieved without religious engagement:

> Only by getting religion can the movement against prisons sufficiently empower itself to break the prison's stranglehold on "justice" in America, making it possible for us to imag-ine and build an alternative justice—a real justice—worthy of that name.[46]

More importantly, the character of these programs is generally so antithetical to the predom-inant ethos of punitivism in American corrections that they represent what prison psychol-ogist James Gilligan calls "anti-prison" programs—programs that are the exact opposite of mainstream corrections wherein they seek to educate, support, and lift up prisoners through providing education and by incentivizing and rewarding good behavior not simply by punish-ing bad behavior.[47] Religious volunteers in prison environments become new stakeholders in corrections, expanding transparency and transforming daily operations. Deep level histories of such programs, in fact, often demonstrate that they first faced stiff resistance from correctional authorities even historically.[48]

In short, religious volunteers are among those most acutely aware of the inhumanity of prison conditions and those citizens most willing to take personal responsibility for improving prisons by volunteering their time and personal resources. It is often the case, however, that while researchers abstractly support the goals of prison reform, they also often reflexively ob-ject to such programs because they are "religious." But the record is more nuanced than often portrayed in academic research and scholars must renew their commitment to deep level and ethnographic research inside prisons. The salutary benefits of religious practice for citizens facing all kinds of personal struggles have largely been ignored by criminology, especially re-garding incarceration. Religious practice is frequently associated with post-traumatic growth, for example, especially when associated with periods of acute personal trauma and life crisis.[49] Tedeschi and Calhoun characterize post-traumatic growth as a prosocial byproduct of religious practice that assists in the overcoming of trauma through multiple stages—those very similar to those experienced during incarceration: (1) incomprehension and disabling paralysis; (2) deep rumination; (3) development of new schemas for understanding; (4) improved self-efficacy through revised self-narrative; and ultimately (5) wisdom.[50] In cases where traumatizing events must become formative elements of an individual's revised personal identity—such as in being sent to prison—"growth occurs when the trauma assumes a central place in the life story."[51] Such personal growth can be facilitated by the very re-biographing offered through religious practice in prison.[52]

Conclusion: The Central Place of Forgiveness for Changing Prisons

In sum, on top of punitive sentences and harsh conditions inside prisons, released inmates emerge from American prisons often damaged by the experience. It is past time for an aggressive agenda to fix America's prisons. This book describes just such a development taking place in dozens of American prisons working to disrupt traditional corrections and reinforce a measure of humane treatment of prisoners. Given that austerity-driven realities of state budget cuts are likely to continue amid the aftermath of COVID-19, volunteer-based resources will become all the more important for state prisons and prisoners in the years ahead. And equipping inmates to care for themselves and one another through innovative public private partnerships is proving to be a uniquely powerful resource. "Will this solve all our problems? No." says Burl Cain. "Is it for every prison? No. For every inmate? No. But can these programs improve the lives of many in our care while bringing resources we desperately need but do not currently have? Absolutely."

Building upon recognition of the need to change the culture of American corrections, we recommend an aggressive return to desistance-focused programming that incentivizes good behavior and helps equip citizens in prison with the skills and emotional resources to succeed upon release. This book shows how inmates often use religious faith as a resource for meeting the challenges associated with long-term incarceration in what can only be described as *traumatic environments*. Too often in criminal justice discourse, however, "rehabilitation" is characterized as the unproblematic transition of "responsibilized" offenders who finally "take full responsibility" for their past behavior back into the community. But in cases where actual success after prison is achieved and offenders stop offending, too often former offenders never gain full acceptance and resocialization back into society. Why? Because society generally fails to forgive ex-offenders. Aside from changing the "corrections culture," deeper level public education regarding the failures of harsh sentencing needs to take place.

All facets of peer-based prison ministry and religious life described here are voluntary and privately funded. No taxpayer money is used to sustain these programs and students may withdraw at any time. Ecumenical openness characterizes religious worship in prison, for simple lack of an alternative. As former Angola inmate and current Parchman Chaplain George King puts it:

> Most people think using the Bible means quoting scriptures or preaching sermons. But I think the greatest effect about using the Bible in prison is with your own life. A message is preached every day—whether we're behind the pulpit or not. It's about how you treat people.

This statement uttered by a former inmate now working as a prison chaplain in maximum security seems to us to be both a perfect demonstration of genuine rehabilitation and the value of reconceptualizing the goals and methods of American incarceration. Building upon these impulses, the nonprofit Mississippi Prison Chapel fund is sponsoring construction of an inter-denominational chapel for use by prisoners at Parchman. "It gives us inmates hope, something to look forward to," said inmate Henry Dennis, who has been behind bars for 17 years.

> A lot of us come in here thinking all of us has been forgotten, that everybody did away with us. So this is hope for us, new life for us, and this is a symbol of that. With the church being here, it brings that.[53]

Notes

1 Maruna (2016, p. 289).
2 Skidmore, R. (1948). Penological pioneering in the Walnut Street Jail, 1789–1799. https://scholarlycommons.law.northwestern.edu/cgi/viewcontent.cgi?article=3569&context=jclc.
3 Takagi, P. (1975). *The Walnut Street Jail: A penal reform to centralize the powers of the state.* Berkeley, CA: Social Justice.
4 Rowbotham, J. (2009). Turning away from criminal intent: Reflecting on the Victorian and Edwardian strategies for promoting desistance among petty offenders. *Theoretical Criminology, 13*(1), 105.
5 See François-Alexandre- Frédéric de la Rochefoucauld-Liancourt, D. (1796). *On the prisons of Philadelphia, by an European* (pp. 6–7). Philadelphia, PA: Moreau de Saint-Mery; see also: Johnston, N. (ed.) (1994). *Eastern state penitentiary: Crucible of good intentions.* Philadelphia, PA: University of Pennsylvania Press.
6 Presser (2014, p. 20).
7 Stansfield and Mowen (2019).
8 Cullen, Jonson and Stohr (2014).
9 Pelot-Hobbs (2018); also Skarbek (2016), Hallett (2019), Hallett et al (2019).
10 Innocence Project (2020), Sullivan (2009).
11 Neff, J., & Santo, A. (2020). Mississippi prisons: "No one is safe, not even the guards": Too many prisoners, too few guards leads to violence. The Marshall Project Feature Essay. Retrieved January 17, 2021, from https://www.themarshallproject.org/2020/02/20/mississippi-prisons-no-one-s-safe-not-even-the-guards.
12 Mitchell (2019).
13 Mitchell (2019).
14 Silver (2016).
15 Mahoney, E. (2019, September 19). Florida corrections secretary seeks help from lawmakers to curb prison violence. *Tampa Bay Times.*
16 Mahoney (2019).
17 Liebling (2017).
18 Hallett, Hays, Johnson, Jang, and Duwe (2017).
19 Personal Interviews, Hallett et al. (2017).
20 Personal Interviews, Hallett et al. (2017).
21 Feeley and Swearingen (2004).
22 Sriharan (2020).
23 Sriharan (2020).
24 Hallett et al. (2017, pp. 14–16).
25 Hallett, M., Johnson, B., & Jang, S. J. (2021). *Religious freedom in action: Disrupting America's prisons through religious partnerships* (pp. 1–9). Cornerstone Forum. Washington DC: Religious Freedom Institute, No. 291.
26 Sullivan (2009, 2014), Erzen (2017).
27 Sullivan (2009).
28 Guzman (2020), Graber (2013).
29 Buck (2019, 2020, p. 43).
30 Tomczak and Bennett (2020, p. 637).

31 Tahamont et al. (2020).
32 Mill and Pollack (2015).
33 Mears (2007).
34 Rideau (1985).
35 Mears, Roman, Wolff, and Buck (2006).
36 Dubler (2013).
37 Johnson (2011).
38 Dubler (2013), Becci and Dubler (2017), Dubler and Lloyd (2019), Hallett et al. (2017), Kewley, Lar-kin, Harkins, and Beech (2017).
39 Liebling (2004, 2011, p. 530).
40 Ellis (2020), Dubler (2013), Becci and Dubler (2017), Flores (2018).
41 Hallett et al. (2017, p. 53)
42 Dubler (2013), Becci and Dubler (2017), Flores (2018).
43 Maruna, Wilson, and Curran (2006), Burnett and Maruna (2006).
44 Maruna et al. (2006).
45 Giordano, Longmore, Schroeder, and Seffrin (2008, p. 116).
46 Dubler and Lloyd (2020, p. 126)
47 Gilligan and Lee (2004).
48 Graber (2013).
49 Rambo and Farhadian (2014).
50 Tedeschi and Calhoun (1996), Pargament (1997).
51 Tedeschi and Calhoun (1996, p. 85).
52 Gilligan & Lee (1996); Maruna (2001, 2006).
53 WTOK Staff. (2021, January 26). Prisoners at parchman to build privately-funded church. Retrieved from https://www.wtok.com/2021/01/27/prisoners-at-parchman-to-build-privately-funded-church/.

References

Becci, I., & Dubler, J. (2017). Religion and religions in prisons: Observations from the United States and Europe. *Journal for the Scientific Study of Religion, 56*(2), 241–247.

Buck, G. (2019). Politicization or professionalization? Exploring divergent aims within UK voluntary sector peer mentoring. *The Howard Journal of Crime and Justice, 58*(3), 349–365.

Buck, G. (2020). Peer mentoring in criminal justice. *Probation Quarterly,* (18), 41–43.

Burnett, R., & Maruna, S. (2006). The kindness of prisoners: Strengths-based resettlement in theory and in action. *Criminology & Criminal Justice, 6*(1), 83–106.

Cullen, F., Jonson, C. L., & Stohr, M. K. (eds.) (2014). *The American prison: Imagining a different future.* Los Angeles, CA: Sage Publishing.

Dubler, J. (2013). *Down in the chapel: Religious life in an American prison.* New York, NY: Farrar, Straus and Giroux.

Dubler, J., & Lloyd, V. (2019). *Break every yoke: Religion, Justice and the Abolition of Prisons.* New York, NY: Oxford University Press.

Ellis, R. (2020). Redemption and reproach: Religion and carceral control in action among women in prison. *Criminology, 58*(4), 747–772.

Erzen, T. (2017). *God in captivity: Prison ministries in the age of mass incarceration.* Boston, MA: Beacon Press.

Feeley, M., & Swearingen, V. (2004). The prison conditions cases and the bureaucratization of American corrections: Influences, impacts, and implications. *Pace Law Review, 24,* 433–475.

Flores, E. O. (2018). *Jesus saved an ex-con: Political activism and redemption after incarceration.* New York, NY: New York University Press.

Gilligan, J., & Lee, B. (2004). Beyond the prison paradigm: From provoking violence to preventing it by creating "anti-prisons" (residential colleges and therapeutic communities). *Annual Review of the New York Academy of Science Journal, 1036,* 300–324.

Giordano, P. C., Longmore, M. A., Schroeder, R., & Seffrin, P. (2008). A life-course perspective on spirituality and desistance from crime. *Criminology, 46*(1), 99–132.

Graber, J. (2013). *The furnace of the affliction: Prisons and religion in antebellum America.* Chapel Hill, NC: University of North Carolina Press.

Griffith, A. (2020). *God's law and order: The politics of punishment in Evangelical America*. Cambridge, MA: Harvard University Press.

Guzman, M. (2020). Sanctifying the expansion of carceral control: Spiritual supervision in the religious lives of criminalized Latinas. *Punishment & Society, 22*(5), 681–702.

Hallett, M., Johnson, B., & Jang, S. J. (2021). *Religious freedom in action: Disrupting America's prisons through religious partnerships* (pp. 1–9). Cornerstone Forum. Washington DC: Religious Freedom Institute, No. 291.

Hallett, M. (2019). Confronting Christian penal charity: Neoliberalism and the rebirth of religious penitentiaries. In M. Hallett (Guest ed.), *Emancipatory justice: Confronting the Carceral state*. Berkeley, CA. Social Justice.

Hallett, M., Hays, J., Johnson, B. R., Jang, S. J., & Duwe, G. (2017). *The Angola prison seminary: Effects of faith-based ministry on identity transformation, desistance, and rehabilitation*. New York, NY: Routledge.

Hallett, M., Johnson, B. R., Hays, J., Jang, S. J., & Duwe, G. (2019). US prison seminaries: Structural charity, religious establishment, and neoliberal corrections. *The Prison Journal, 99*(2), 150–171.

Hirschi, T., & Stark, R. (1969). Hellfire and delinquency. *Social Problems, 17*(2), 201–213.

Innocence Project Staff. (2020). The last legacy of Parchman Farm: The prison modeled after a slave plantation. Retrieved November 2020, from https://innocenceproject.org/parchman-farm-prison-mississippi-history/.

Johnson, B. R. (2011). *More God, less crime: Why faith matters and how it could matter more*. West Conshohocken, PA: Templeton Press.

Kewley, S., Larkin, M., Harkins, L., & Beech, A. (2017). Restoring identity: The use of religion as a mechanism to transition between an identity of sexual offending to a non-offending identity. *Criminology & Criminal Justice, 17*(1), 79–96.

Liebling, A. (2004). *Prisons and their moral performance: A study of values, quality, and prison life*. New York, NY: Oxford University Press.

Liebling, A. (2011). Moral performance, inhuman and degrading treatment and prison pain. *Punishment and Society, 13*(5), 530–550.

Liebling, A. (2017). Appreciative inquiry, generative theory, and the "failed state" prison. In J. Miller & W. Palacios (Eds.), *Qualitative Research in Criminology* (pp. 251–269). London, UK: Routledge.

Maruna, S. (2001). *Making Good: How Ex-Convicts Reform and Rebuild Their Lives*. Washington, D.C.: American Psychological Association Books.

Maruna, S. (2016). Desistance and restorative justice: It's now or never. *Restorative Justice: An International Journal, 4*(3), 289–301.

Maruna, S., Wilson, L., & Curran, K. (2006). Why God is often found behind bars: Prison conversions and the crisis of self-narrative. *Research in Human Development, 3*, 161–84. https://doi.org/10.1080/15427609.2006.9683367.

Mears, D. P. (2007). Faith-based reentry programs: Cause for concern or showing promise? *Corrections Today, 69*, 2.

Mears, D. P., Roman, C., Wolff, A., & Buck, J. (2006). Faith-based efforts to improve prisoner reentry: Assessing the logic and the evidence. *Journal of Criminal Justice, 34*, 351–367.

Mill, M., & Pollack, W. (2015). Was Hirschi right? A national level longitudinal examination of religion as a social bond. *Deviant Behavior, 36*(10), 783–806.

Pargament, K. I. (1997). *The psychology of religion and coping: Theory, practice and research*. New York, NY: Guilford.

Pelot-Hobbs, L. (2018). Scaling up or scaling back? The pitfalls and possibilities of leveraging federal interventions for abolition. *Critical Criminology, 26*, 423–441.

Presser, L. (2014). The restorative prison. Chapter 2. In F. Cullen, C. L. Jonson, & M. Stohr (Eds.), *The American prison: Imagining a different future* (pp. 20–32). Los Angeles, CA: Sage Publishing.

Rambo, L. R. & Farhadian, C. (2014). *The Oxford Handbook of Religious Conversion*. Oxford, UK: Oxford University Press.

Rideau, W. (1985). Prisoner litigation: How it began in Louisiana. *Louisiana Law Review, 45*(5), 1069.

Silver, J. (2016, August 3). Texas prisons ponder cutting $250 million. *Texas Tribune*. Retrieved from https://www.texastribune.org/2016/08/03/prisons-agency-could-see-250-million-budget-cuts/.

Skarbek, D. (2016). Covenants without the sword? Comparing prison self-governments globally. *American Political Science Review, 110*(4), 845–862.

Sriharan, D. (2020). Death by virus: Why the prison litigation reform act should be suspended. CHLB Scholarship. 77. Retrieved from https://digital.sandiego.edu/law_chlb_research_scholarship/77.

Stansfield, R., & Mowen, T. (2019). Religious involvement, moral community and social ecology: New considerations in the study of religion and reentry. *Journal of Quantitative Criminology, 35*, 493–516.

Sullivan, W. F. (2009). *Prison religion: Faith-based reform and the Constitution.* Princeton, NJ: Princeton University Press.

Sullivan, W. F. (2014). *A ministry of presence: Chaplaincy, spiritual care, and the Law.* Chicago, IL: University of Chicago Press.

Tahamont, S., Hyatt, J., Pheasant, B., Lafferty, J., Bell, N., & Sheets, M. (2020). Ineligible anyway: Evidence on the barriers to Pell eligibility for prisoners in the second chance Pell pilot program in Pennsylvania prisons. *Justice Quarterly.* doi:10.1080/07418825.2020.1853798.

Tedeschi, R., & Calhoun, L. (1996). The posttraumatic growth inventory: Measuring the positive legacy of trauma. *Journal of Traumatic Stress, 9*, 455–471.

Tomczak, P., & Bennett, C. (2020). Evaluating voluntary sector involvement in mass incarceration: The case of Samaritan prisoner volunteers. *Punishment & Society, 22*(5), 637–657.

7

LESSONS WE CAN LEARN FROM PRISONERS

Background

Scholars have produced a number of studies of prisoners over the last three decades and have written about the role of religion and faith-based programs in enhancing prisoner adjustment and offender rehabilitation[1] lowering recidivism,[2] and the fostering of prosocial behavior among prisoners.[3] In this chapter we discuss how religious involvement and practices have helped prisoners redeem their lives and rewrite their life narratives as they seek to reconcile their past and "former self" with a new and "future self" that is both prosocial and hopeful. Drawing on diverse studies of faith-based interventions in offenders inside and outside the United States, we integrate data from surveys, in-depth face-to-face interviews, as well as observational research, to highlight evidence-based lessons learned by inmates that have important implications not only for prisoners, but for all people.

Most people would likely be surprised to learn there are thousands of peer-reviewed publications linking something as simple as church attendance to various aspects of mental and physical health, as well as a host of other salutary outcomes. For example, attendance or participation in religious communities and activities is associated with greater life-expectancy, less depression, less suicide, less smoking, less substance abuse, better cancer and cardiovascular disease survival, less divorce, greater social support, more meaning and purpose in life, greater life satisfaction, higher rates of charitable giving, more volunteering, greater civic engagement, and higher levels of human flourishing.[4]

In addition to all of these important outcomes, how well people are able to cope with a variety of difficult circumstances is also affected by church attendance.[5] For example, though it is well established within the field of economics that personal well-being tends to be highly correlated with up or down turns in the economy, regular church-goers are significantly less likely to be emotionally affected by either the boom or bust of business cycles.[6] Moreover, scholars have also examined how religious congregations enhance social capital and provide important networks of social support that may foster well-being or human flourishing.[7] In sum, there is a mounting body of evidence documenting that regular attendance at religious services is a powerful predictor of many important and beneficial outcomes.

However, almost all of the religion and health literature is based on studies of individuals residing outside of correctional institutions, or "free world" people. But one can reasonably

DOI: 10.4324/9781003171744-7

argue that "free world" people represent a far less difficult test when it comes to gauging the influence of attendance at religious services or participation in religious activities. A more difficult proposition is to determine if attending or participating in religious service activities carries the same benefits for prisoners as it does in the general population. By definition, inmates are rule-violators who have been sentenced to prison and most of whom have extensive track-records for not obeying laws or abiding by moral teachings, much less exhibiting virtuous behavior espoused in most religious traditions.

In this chapter we review the relevant research literature that assesses the role of religion in the lives of prisoners. In particular, we highlight the ways in which religious involvement and practices are linked to inmate adjustment, decision-making, recidivism reduction, the development of virtues, and the experience of identity transformation. We explore not only how religion can help offenders redeem a dark past, but also adopt a new and positive life that is other-minded and prosocial. Citing multiple studies of prisoners in different states and different countries, and incorporating diverse research methodologies, we draw a number of conclusions about faith-based programs and interventions. We highlight evidence-based lessons learned by inmates that not only have important implications for the field of corrections and prisoners, but for all people and society at large.

Hope and Opportunity for Self Change

According to Nouwen, faith offers offenders many things including knowledge, resources, and creative problem-solving.[8] But even more importantly, Nouwen claims what offenders need most is the spiritual and psychological experience of hope. Moreover, Nouwen argues that hope may be the greatest need people have as we struggle to live in an increasingly troubled world. Without hope, there is little motivation to face wounds, to heal, and to make changes. As noted throughout this book, many inmates will dramatically transform their lives if given an opportunity they believe to be authentic. Indeed, we believe the power of offender-led programs lies in just that authenticity—offered by the "lived experience" men and women who themselves have changed.

A number of criminological theories have long held that people without a stake in society are no longer bonded by conventional norms and are thus free to deviate or break the law since they have nothing to lose.[9] Decades of research confirms that people without family support, lack of employment, and little to no money are more likely to turn to drugs and crime (Johnson, 2018). The loss of hope in finding a better life through conventional or legitimate means can ultimately lead to despair and criminal activity. Clearly, the social isolation and family breakdown associated with life in many of our most blighted and crime-ridden neighborhoods testify to the hopelessness faced by many American citizens.

But how can lives be instilled with hope? What are the sources of determination to overcome setbacks, to persevere against challenges, and to commit to trying to achieve a "good life"? What distinguishes a person with hope from one without hope? According to Robert Emmons, people who have purpose or feel their life has meaning are more likely to exhibit hope.[10] Experiencing fulfillment or contentment can also be viewed as a natural byproduct of hope.[11] Conversely, what are manifestations of despair? Shanahan and colleagues suggest that despair is a multifaceted construct with manifestations in different, interrelated domains including depression, anxiety, irritability, hopelessness, and interpersonal difficulties.[12] Moreover, they found evidence that despair is linked to premature mortality from suicides, drug poisoning, and alcohol-induced liver disease. In order to determine if religious involvement increases the hope of offenders, or mitigates a sense of despair, it is necessary to examine how participation in religious activities is (or is not) related to factors often attributed to prisoners—anger, resentment, violence, and depression.

Jang et al., examined whether religiosity is inversely related to negative emotions and aggressiveness among prison inmates.[13] They examined whether the relationships were attributable to an inmate's sense of meaning and purpose in life and/or their virtues. Specifically, they hypothesized that religiosity is inversely related to feelings of depression and anxiety and the intention of engaging in interpersonal aggression. They also hypothesized that these relationships were mediated by an offender's existential belief in life's meaning and purpose and various virtues (compassion, forgiveness, gratitude, purpose of God, and gratitude to God).

By drawing upon survey data collected from a random sample of male inmates from three prisons in Texas, Jang and associates found that existential belief explained the effect of religiosity on negative emotional states and intended aggression. In addition, forgiveness and gratitude mediated the effect on anxiety, whereas purpose in God and gratitude to God mediated the effect on depression.[14] Thus, they found increasing religiosity counters or is protective against harmful emotions and aggression. Perhaps the greatest strength of religious practice is that religiosity instills in someone a sense of connectedness with and deeper-seated belonging to a community more powerful than the vicissitudes of life. Stated differently, religiosity is linked to finding purpose as well as the expression of gratitude, both of which lessen despair, and by extension the harmful factors associated with it. Excerpts from interviews with inmate and correctional staff regarding faith-based interventions give additional insights that support these conclusions[15]:

> I'd say that 80 percent of correctional officers would say that this program is legitimate... You know prisons often times help create monsters—this faith-based program gives prisoners hope.
>
> *(Correctional Officer)*

> I'm a stronger believer in God, I have grown in patience, I have a peace of mind that I never had in the world. I have joy. I stopped asking God for parole. Whenever He wants me out is okay, I'm willing to stay in prison another year. My father passed while I was here, but this program has helped me deal with his death.[16]
>
> *(Phil)*

When interviewed, program participants consistently verbalized themes indicating they are thankful to have the opportunity to start their life over again. One of the common statements expressed by participants was that "I'm not who I used to be."[17] Their newfound faith or the rediscovery of a lost faith from their childhood made it possible to begin a new life. They felt they had been given a second chance. Their current self-accounts represent a dramatic departure from their negative and often painful past. According to Shadd Maruna, this process of "willful, cognitive distortion" helps offenders desist from crime and to "make good" with their lives. Many would come to say they had developed a sense of meaning and purpose they had not known before.[18] For many, there was a Christian conversion experience that marked a turning point in their life—a spiritual awakening or reawakening that was foundational for them in this spiritual transformation.

Although Jang and colleagues did not include hope as a variable in this study, the salutary effect of religiosity was likely attributable, in part, to hope generated by a faith-based sense of meaning and purpose in life. Based on extensive prison surveys, observational work at many different prisons, and face-to-face interviews we have conducted with both inmates as well as correctional staff, there is empirical evidence that participation in faith-based programs, as well as attendance at religious services and activities, can reduce despair and bring hope to prisoners.

In a world full of uncertainty, where anxiety, depression, suicide, and addictions abound, there is a great need for hope. We know from our research on prisoners that religious involvement is key to bringing hope to the incarcerated. A new hope found in religion appears to motivate many prisoners who want to change their life and start a begin a new and positive or prosocial life, that often is accompanied by the experience of rehabilitation. Religious programs in prisons are about second chances. A by-product of many faith-based programs is that participants develop a new found meaning and purpose—a reason for being. Such programs allow many to start a new life; rewriting their life narrative. In this new narrative they are able to finally articulate the experience of reconciliation between their old self—often times a painful and troubled past—with a much more hopeful and positive future self. As one former prisoner stated after being out of prison for several years:

> I'm not proud of the things I have done in the past, but I'm thankful of what I've become in Christ. Going to prison was good for me. If I hadn't gone to prison, I'd be dead.

> Lesson 1: Religion Can Replace the Despair of Everyday Life with Hope and Opportunity for Self Change

Forgiveness

Forgiveness has been identified as important for human social functioning within and across cultures. According to Meninger, forgiveness is a five-step process.[19] The first step in beginning to deal with our wounds is by denying or minimizing them. When we are finally able to face them and recognize the ones who inflicted them, we are only then able to begin the process of achieving forgiveness. This usually involves trying to excuse the perpetrator and blaming ourselves for causing the original harm. When we are able to stop the self-blame, we begin to feel sorry for ourselves and to experience self-pity and resentment. The next step is the determination to do something about what happened to us and move forward with our lives and we actively seek healing.[20] This leads us to the final stage: wholeness. Similarly, Enright, Freedman, and Rique define forgiveness as "… a willingness to abandon one's right to resentment, negative judgment, and indifferent behavior toward one who unjustly injured us, while fostering the undeserved qualities of compassion, generosity, and even love toward him or her" (pp. 46–47).[21]

Empirical findings from the last four decades point to the role of forgiveness in improving physical, mental, and spiritual health.[22] Empirical studies demonstrate that learning to forgive improves physiological wellness and offers protection against future problems.[23] As a result, forgiveness practices have been extended into the fields of counseling, psychology, education, and peace-making. Indeed, the literature on forgiveness is wide-ranging and a good deal of this work has been conducted outside the context of religion.[24] Even so, forgiveness is an integral part of virtually every major faith tradition.[25] As research in the field has progressed, researchers have also begun to study forgiveness by God, forgiveness from others, and self-forgiveness. Studies suggest that religious involvement increases a person's likelihood to forgive and practicing forgiveness mediates the effect of religion on health.[26]

However, until recently, there has been little empirical research on the role of forgiveness among prisoners, and especially on the connection, if any, between the religious practices of prisoners and the likelihood of experiencing forgiveness. In the study of Prison Fellowship's InnerChange Freedom Initiative (InnerChange), at the Carol Vance Unit (near Houston, TX),

Johnson conducted interviews with members of the correctional staff to see if they thought attendance in the faith-based program generated authentic change among participants.[27] The interviews took place over a six-year period and confirmed that correctional staff believed inmates participating in InnerChange were not only showing signs of rehabilitation, but that the program seemed to be influencing the broader prison environment.

> I have been here since InnerChange started. Some people have it and some don't. You can see the difference. Some of them just come here to get close to home. Instead they get close to God... I would say that 85 to 90 percent of those who are gone, have left out of here with a completely different perspective. I have noticed that they are even trying to change their families... They learn to take blame for themselves; to face reality. I have heard them say "I brought myself here and I need to accept responsibility." That's not typical.
>
> *(Correctional Officer with 5 years of experience)*

> The difference between InnerChange and for example, the drug treatment programs I have observed over the years, is the family and community emphasis of InnerChange. There's a lot of involvement from the outside. And the free-world people are seeing what we're seeing—change. It's intensive. I expect them to do a lot better than general population inmates when they are released.
>
> *(Correctional Officer with 18 years of experience)*

> Before entering this faith-based program, I was kind of at a fork in the road, not knowing which way to go. I had a bad attitude and a hard time getting along with people. I used to get in fights all the time. I remember telling myself I didn't want to live like this anymore and I prayed for God to take control and I gave my heart to the Lord. I'm beginning to control my thoughts and my anger. I'm beginning to find peace for the first time. Something that used to get me into a fight, I will now laugh at. I don't curse anymore. Instead I try to share God with people. It's nice to hear positive things being said about me for the first time in my life. When someone tried to help me before, I would deny it. I didn't think anyone cared—I see now they really do.
>
> *(Len)*

> For the first time I have respect for others. I even try to encourage others and pray for them. The books we use here and the Bible have really helped. Praying has helped. When I stumble, now I repent. When I get out of here, the church is going to be a big part of my life.
>
> *(Juan)*

> The program has awakened me. It has birthed a new me. I'm learning to get along with others and to understand why people do what they do. I am learning more by listening. This program has made me feel like I am somebody and that I have potential. I have a whole lot more discipline and self-control than before. Being able to be obedient to not just authority, but to everyone. And I'm learning to control my anger. Things out of my control have always bothered me. I struggled with this every day. Change is not overnight and it's not easy to change, but God is changing me. God has shown me what I used to be about and what I'm about now.
>
> *(Gale)*

Jang et al., examined an offender's beliefs concerning God's forgiveness, engagement, and judgment in relation to prison misconduct.[28] Analyzing survey data of inmates in a maximum-security prison, Jang and colleagues found religiously involved inmate's belief in God's level of engagement in their lives and their willingness to forgive, were inversely associated with disciplinary convictions.

In sum, there is evidence that volunteers and religious programs introduce prosocial models into the prison environment.[29] These models of "loving thy neighbor" and serving others are powerful tools for healing and enhancing trust of others.[30] At the same time, faith-motivated prosocial behavior mitigates and often replaces the punitive nature of correctional environments and can act as a powerful positive behavioral change agent.

Lesson 2: Religion Can Lead to Forgiveness and Positive Change and Prosocial Modeling

Accountability as the Key to Freedom

A robust literature suggests that religious practices and beliefs have implications for mental health, with many studies reporting salutary effects.[31] Research in this area has examined multiple aspects of religious life, including denominational affiliation and various belief systems, attendance at religious services, prayer, and even social identities that are formed in religious settings.[32] Even though rarely examined, it seems reasonable to assume that the mental health consequences of most aspects of religion are grounded in some form of accountability to God or to people.[33] Accountability facilitates personal growth, self-awareness, and social reintegration. As Giordano et al. (2002) summarize the issue:

> Thus, in addition to its relative accessibility, religion seems to have potential as a mechanism for desistance because many core concerns within religious communities and the Bible relate directly to offenders' problem areas. Even more importantly, religious teachings can provide a clear blueprint for how to proceed as a changed individual
>
> *(Giordano et al., 2008, p. 116)*

For example, religious organizations expose individuals to health-related beliefs and behaviors that members are expected to endorse and follow (e.g., dietary practices, substance use and abuse, an emphasis on spiritual matters over material ones, prayer, coping, etc.), while service attendance may reinforce these teachings and provide sanctions for violations.[34] Research on social control is grounded in the assumption that people are bonded (or accountable) to society and conventional norms as a result of various commitments, involvements, beliefs, and practices.[35] Moreover, work on social identities argues that religious participation leads to an identity that guides and shapes behavior and holds individuals personally accountable.[36]

Most people view accountability as the expectation that one will have to justify their behavior to someone that likely has the ability to dispense rewards for proper behavior and punishments for inappropriate actions.[37] Understood in this way, accountability is ubiquitous in human life.[38] In many instances, accountability has a negative connotation, and to "hold someone accountable" often means to simply mitigate problems or punish wrongdoers.[39] It is therefore not surprising that accountability is often viewed as something undesirable that people seek to avoid due to its involuntary and authoritarian nature.

However, accountability may also be viewed as a virtuous and voluntary part of life.[40] A person who embodies accountability as a virtue welcomes being accountable and views it as desirable and beneficial when certain conditions are met—that is, when the one to whom they are accountable has the requisite authority, there is a worthy goal at hand, the authority cares about them, and the authority is competent and provides worthwhile feedback.[41] In many ways, religious practice can become the occasion for personal accountability when opportunities for self-examination or confession help lead individuals to freedom from the self-woundings of our transgressions. As Henri Nouwen put it: "When our wounds cease to be a source of shame, and become a source of healing, we have become "wounded healers." New levels of achievement, interpersonal connection, or self-satisfaction are only attainable through a process of accountability. Indeed, a key part of the salience of inmate ministry is that the mutually compromised status of fellow peer inmates facilitates a process of confession and self-disclosure that becomes cathartic. As one inmate peer minister at Angola described his role: "Listen, I'm not here to convert anybody. I'm just trying to help someone self-identify" (Hallett, 2019, p. 21).

To date, however, little research has specifically conceptualized or measured if accountability to God/religion may be linked to crime desistance or offender rehabilitation. If religion has been found to be linked to offender rehabilitation and recidivism reduction, might religious practices and beliefs often function as mechanisms of accountability in a manner that promotes prosocial and/or virtuous behavior? Several studies shed light on this overlooked construct of accountability and how it may ultimately influence the rehabilitation of prisoners. In an evaluation of a faith-based prison program, Johnson (2006) conducted interviews of participants and found evidence that accountability was a central component of inmate reform.[42]

> God is pulling everything back together. I know God's in control. I have to deal with the inmate mentality here, where guys don't want to be confronted about sinful behavior... I now value accountability. I think this is where Christians blow it. They don't want to correct someone else even though they know they're in sin.
>
> *(Ricky)*

> The prison system says that you must play tough. But that's not real. Confession is good for you according to the Bible. I've come to realize that the inmate code is really nothing but a facade. I can be myself now.
>
> *(Neal)*

Some might confuse these examples of accountability as simply the act of assuming responsibility (as in being a responsible person), but that term (a) seems more consistent with being "held" responsible in an involuntary and coercive manner and (b) is often understood as a purely individual property.[43] In contrast, if one thinks of accountability as a virtue, then it makes sense that it has a relational nature that involves others.[44] It is not a condition where one is held accountable in a negative manner, but a responsive, forward-looking trait that is welcomed and viewed as an asset. People who possess this virtue are answerable, transparent, and honest about their behavior, adjust their efforts based on feedback, want to be pushed to do their best, internalize the accountability, and recognize that they improve by being accountable.[45]

Can attendance at religious gatherings in prison play a role in helping offenders make better decisions, such as desisting from criminal activity? A series of studies examining the effectiveness of Prison Fellowship (a Christian prison ministry) programs support the notion that faith-based participants fare significantly better than a comparison group of inmates not receiving Prison Fellowship programs. Young and his coauthors investigated long-term recidivism among a group of federal inmates trained as volunteer prison ministers and found that the Prison Fellowship group had a significantly lower rate of post-release recidivism than the matched group not receiving the faith-based intervention.[46]

Johnson, Larson, and Pitts (1997) examined the impact of volunteer-led religious programs sponsored by Prison Fellowship on institutional adjustment and recidivism rates in two matched groups of inmates from four adult male prisons in New York State. After controlling for the level of involvement in PF-sponsored programs, inmates who were most active in Bible studies were significantly less likely to be rearrested during a year-long, post-release period. In a follow-up to this study, Johnson (2004) extended the New York research on former inmates by increasing the length of study from one to eight years and found that frequent Bible study participants were significantly less likely to be rearrested two and three years after their release from prison.

Johnson completed an evaluation of the Prison Fellowship's InnerChange Freedom Initiative (InnerChange), an 18- to 24-month faith-based prison program.[47] The study found that program participants were significantly less likely to be arrested than a matched group of prisoners not receiving this religious intervention (8–20% respectively) during a two-year post-release period.[48] Johnson also found that continued contact with a mentor after release was associated with reduced recidivism.

An evaluation of the InnerChange Freedom Initiative in the state of Minnesota, reported similar results to those found in Texas. Duwe and King examined recidivism outcomes among a total of 732 offenders released from Minnesota prisons between 2003 and 2009.[49] They found that participation in the faith-based program significantly reduced the likelihood of rearrest (26%), reconviction (35%), and reincarceration (40%) of former prisoners.

In a study of prisoners at the Louisiana State Penitentiary (aka Angola), Jang and colleagues found that inmates' religious conversion and, to a lesser extent, religiosity itself were positively related to existential and cognitive transformations, which were, in turn, associated with positive emotional transformation.[50] This process was linked to a lower likelihood of disciplinary convictions. Similarly, Johnson found that the presence of a faith-motivated mentor was critical in helping ex-prisoners understand the need and desire for accountability.[51]

> You know I was so disappointed to get a serve-all (instead of early parole) because it was going to put me back an extra six months, but all-in-all I really do think it has been worth it. During that time my confidence has really been boosted-up and it has forced me to get up in front of people—it's been great. The extra time here has helped me to learn to lean on God, because I know I can't make it by myself.
>
> *(Gene)*

> You're more into God type activities here. Instead of a little religion here or there—you're surrounded by it. The program builds your knowledge and hopes. One can never quit growing and I know I have a long way to go. Church will be a very important part of my life when I get out. My mentor will be a help to me too.
>
> *(Dan)*

Based on the evidence from a number of peer-reviewed publications drawing from diverse samples and methodologies, church attendance and/or participation in religious services or activities helps prisoners to be more self-controlled and to make better decisions, as well as better cope with difficult circumstances. In this way increasing religiosity helps offenders refrain from violating institutional rules, and enables them to desist from crime. But desistance from illegal behavior in prison rarely happens in in isolation. Indeed, prisons have long been labeled as crime laboratories. Instead of rehabilitating offenders, many are able to learn how to be better criminals. On the other hand, most religious traditions are based on adherents being accountable to God as well as accountable to other people. This is especially true in prison environments. Prisoners participating in religious programs, activities, and services, become part of close-knit social networks. In addition to providing social support, these networks prisoners accountable to each other. In this way, religious programs in prisons—often led by volunteers—are able to enhance the social capital of inmates through the use of volunteer resources and the introduction of outside stakeholders into the prison environment. The combination of accountability to one's neighbor as well as being accountable to God, help prisoners to not only desist from deviant behavior, but to engage in prosocial behavior that is other-minded.

Lesson 3: Religious Participation Enhances Living Accountably and Experiencing Freedom

Identity Transformation

Prior research has long confirmed that religion has a salutary effect on mental health as well as a preventive effect on crime.[52] However, similar research examining the effect of religion on prisoners has only emerged in the last several decades. For example, Johnson found that completing an 18–24-month faith-based prison program was linked not only to lower post-release recidivism, but to the notion that participants felt a need to give back to society by serving others.[53]

Hallett and colleagues found that inmates enrolled in the Angola prison seminary were less likely to break institutional rules.[54] Likewise, inmates attending one of the 29 inmate-led congregations were less likely to have committed prison infractions. Prisoners who participated in the seminary as well as attended one of the inmate-led churches were even less likely to break prison rules. Based on one of the largest surveys ever conducted within a prison that particularly focused on religion, Hallett et al. found that participation in the prison seminary and participation in inmate-led congregations were both independently linked to conversion narratives, increased religiosity, and the identity transformation of prisoners.[55] The research team spent a great deal of time at the prison during the five-year study. In addition to collecting survey data and conducting in-depth interviews, the research team observed these prisoners (many of whom are serving life sentences) over a significant period of time and saw first-hand how they dealt with the difficulties associated with prison life. Repeatedly they observed inmates not only desisting from crime but being involved in prosocial activities and acts of service to others. Virtuous behaviors like gratitude and forgiveness were commonplace. Prisoners do not typically seek to emulate transparency or humility, but this research found that these virtues were indeed modeled by inmates experiencing an identity transformation.

In a recent study, Jang and colleagues examined whether religiosity is inversely related to negative emotions and aggressiveness among prison inmates.[56] Additionally, they sought to assess whether these potential relationships were attributable to an inmate's sense of meaning and purpose in life and/or their virtues. The data used for this study came from a survey conducted at three maximum-security all-male prisons in Texas in 2017. The Texas Department of Criminal Justice (TDCJ) provided a random sample from of each of the three prison populations. Jang et al found prisoners' religiosity was positively related to a sense of meaning and purpose in life as well as a number of virtuous characteristics—compassion, forgiveness, gratitude, purpose of God, and gratitude to God—which were inversely associated with the offenders' negative emotional states and intended aggression. The study also confirmed that more religious offenders were less likely to report feelings of depression and anxiety and interpersonal aggression, because they were more likely to have a sense of meaning and purpose in life versus less or non-religious prisoners. This finding is consistent with previous research showing the psychologically detrimental impact of prisoners reporting an absence of meaning or purpose in their life.[57] In conclusion, this study shows that religion tends to have a prosocial effect on mental health and behaviors among offenders in prison, as their involvement in religion is likely to help them find meaning and purpose in life and become more virtuous.

Research on prisoners helping prisoners change is rare because programs that equip inmates with practical capacities for helping others rehabilitate in prison hardly exist. An exception is the Field Ministry program in Texas, which enlists inmates who have graduated from a prison-based seminary to work as "Field Ministers" and serve other inmates in various capacities. Jang et al. tested if exposure to Field Ministers would be inversely related to antisocial factors and positively to prosocial ones.[58] Jang et al. applied manifest-variable structural equation modeling to analyze data from a survey of a random sample of 244 male inmates at three maximum-security prisons where the Field Ministry program operated. They found that inmates exposed more frequently to the Field Ministry and for a longer time period, reported lower levels of criminological risk factors and aggressiveness as well as higher levels of virtues and predictors of human agency as well as religiosity and spirituality.[59]

Jang et al. studied male and female inmates in South African prisons in order to determine whether the relationship between religiosity and negative emotions (anger, frustration, depression, and anxiety) among prisoners is attributable to inmates' sense of meaning and purpose in life as well as personal virtues.[60] They also sought to determine whether religious involvement is linked with finding meaning in life as well as the virtues of forgiveness, gratitude, and self-control among female and male prisoners. To examine these relationships, they analyzed survey data from a sample of prisoners in South African correctional centers. Findings showed that more religiously active inmates, whether male or female, reported lower levels of negative emotions (anger, frustration, depression, and anxiety) to the extent that their religiosity enhanced a sense of meaning and purpose in life and increased levels of self-control as compared to less or non-religious prisoners.

One of the things we have consistently observed among prisoners participating in religious programs and services is a concern for others. Acts of humility, selflessness, and service to others is something that does not come easily for most people, let alone offenders. Yet, recent research of offenders who have attended religious services and activities consistently report a desire to participate in acts of service to others. For example, Johnson found that completing a faith-based prison program was linked not only to lower post-release recidivism, but to the notion that participants felt a need to give back to society by serving others.[61] Johnson also found that the presence of a faith-motivated mentor was critical in helping ex-prisoners remain crime-free following release from prison. These findings are consistent with those from recent longitudinal studies of court-referred addicts ($n = 195$) into a 12-step drug treatment program.[62] These studies confirm that religiosity or God-conscientiousness and acts of service were linked to success rehabilitation.[63]

It has been argued that nobody escapes being wounded. Indeed, whether emotionally, mentally, physically, or spiritually, we are all wounded people. The question is not "How can we hide from our wounds?" so we don't have to be embarrassed, but "How can we put our woundedness in the service of others?" When a person's wounds cease to be a source of shame, and become a source of healing, that person becomes a wounded healer.[64] Wounded healers have faced their deepest wounds and are able to provide service to others that is authentic becomes it come from a heart that was wounded by the suffering about which they now speak.

Over the last two decades in a number of mixed-method studies of offenders and prisoners, we have observed firsthand accounts of other-mindedness among inmates who have experienced an identity transformation. These selfless acts of service to others by offenders are manifestations of intentional decisions to learn from their own journeys of woundedness, and to share that learning with others. The following interview quotes with prisoners capture some of these observations.

> I didn't trust anyone before I came here. I thought I knew everything, that I had all the answers. Now I know I don't have anything figured out. And at the same time I'm at peace today with myself. It's changed how I view the world. I'm learning to have more patience. I have found that when I humble myself, I get closer to these guys.
>
> *(Lowell)*

> I have learned what life is about since being here. I have learned that life is about helping others to grow like I'm growing. I have found peace for the first time. The change came over me when I saw that other people loved me. Then I wanted to do the same to others. That's when my whole life began turning around.
>
> *(Lawrence)*

> I've always believed in God. But I got away from God as I got into my teens. This program has brought me back to my Christian roots. My feeling and thinking is different from when I got here. I see a big change in myself, I don't see things the way I used to. I used to be a loner, and didn't care about much else. I'm finding myself being more sociable and trying to help others. That wasn't true of me before I got into this program. Helping others find purpose in their life through God, has been a real blessing.
>
> *(Lou)*

> I wish everybody could go through this program. I came to the program to learn about the Bible. It has taught me that prayer is important. I wish my dad could go through IFI. He's serving 25 years in prison… I didn't come up in a spiritual life, but God has done a real work in my life since coming here. Sharing my faith with my family is important to me. Now I have a better relationship with my family too.
>
> *(Kerry)*

Hallett and associates, conducted more than 100 life-history interviews of prisoners, and conducted surveys of 2,200 inmates at the Louisiana State Penitentiary, in the most extensive study of religion within a prison.[65] Researchers examined the role of religious education and involvement in inmate-led religious congregations that was central to transforming prisoners and the housing units where they reside. They found that participation in the prison seminary and inmate-led churches not only linked to crime desistance and rehabilitation, but to prosocial behavior within the prison environment. In a series of studies, researchers point to the central role of inmate-led efforts to bring about a number of salutary findings.[66] Inmate ministers have the opportunity and relative freedom of movement to minister among their peers on a daily basis.

It is this healing power that a wounded healer models for others.

> I know I never would have healed myself. I'd tried that, but it didn't work. I needed that infusion of grace as well as an introduction to a roomful of wounded healers who, by their sharing, helped me find and maintain the hope that I, too, could heal.[67]

Therefore, religious programs in prison expand the transparency of prisons through the use of volunteers, chaplains, and other religious inmates that minister to other prisoners.

Lesson 4: Active Participation in Religious Activities can be Transformative for Individuals Looking for Positive Change

Conclusion

In sum, the studies reviewed in this chapter provide both qualitative and quantitative evidence that religious participation and involvement is linked not only to crime desistance, but to the identity transformation of prisoners. Although rehabilitation has long been a goal that more often than not has vexed correctional administrators, we now have data which documents that participation in religious interventions can enhance rehabilitation, and lead to an authentic identity transformation of prisoners.

The news that attendance and participation in religious activities is connected to salutary findings even among prisoners is certainly good news for prison administrators and correctional leaders. Regular attendance is associated with fewer infractions and better adjustment within prison, it is linked to reform and the adoption of a new self or what scholars call an identity transformation. Finally, religious involvement helps offenders become prosocial and other-minded; caring for the well-being of others and exhibiting this prosocial behavior through selfless acts of service. These compelling findings are relevant not only for prisoners but for people everywhere.

Notes

1 Johnson, Larson, and Pitts (1997), Johnson (2011), Kerley, Copes, and Tewksbury (2011), Jang, Johnson, Hallett, Duwe, and Hays (2017), Hallett, Hays, Johnson, Jang, and Duwe (2015).
2 Johnson (2004), Johnson (2008), Johnson (2011).
3 Hallett, Hays, Johnson, Jang, and Duwe (2016).
4 Koenig, King, and Carson (2012), Levin (2020), VanderWeele (2017a, 2017b).
5 Koenig (2015).
6 Makridis, Johnson, and Koenig (2019).
7 Cnaan and Boddie (2001), Krause and Hayward (2013, 2014a, 2014b), Krause, Hayward, Bruce, and Woolever (2014), Putnam and Feldstein (2003), Putnam and Campbell (2012), VanderWeele (2017a).
8 Nouwen (1972).
9 Hirschi (1969).
10 Emmons (2008).
11 Ng and Hou (2017).
12 Shanahan et al. (2019).
13 Jang, Johnson, Hallett, Duwe, and Hays (2018a, 2018b).
14 Jang et al. (2018a, 2018b).
15 Johnson (2011).
16 In order to protect the identity of mentors, volunteers, staff, or prisoners, pseudonyms are used.
17 In order to protect the identity of mentors, volunteers, staff, or prisoners, pseudonyms are used.
18 Maruna (2010).
19 Meninger (1996).
20 Meninger (1996).
21 Enright, Freedman, and Rique (1998).
22 Koenig, King, and Carson (2012).
23 Luskin (2003), Joseph (2012).
24 Toussaint, Worthington, and Williams (2015).
25 Lundberg (2010).
26 Worthington, and Wade (2019).
27 Johnson (2006).
28 Jang et al. (2017).
29 Kewley Larkin, Harkins, and Beech (2016).
30 Corcoran and Mears (2013), LeBel, Richie, and Maruna (2015).
31 Koenig, King, and Carson (2012), Koenig (2015), VanderWeele (2017a, 2017b).

32 Hallett et al. (2016), Rowatt and Kirkpatrick (2002).
33 Evans (2019).
34 Bradshaw and Ellison (2010), VanderWeele (2017c), VanderWeele, Jackson, and Li (2016), Vander-Weele, Li, Tsai, and Kawachi (2016).
35 Hirschi (1969).
36 Greenfield and Marks (2007), Lee et al. (2017).
37 Frink and Klimoski (1998), Hall and Ferris (2011), Stenning (1995).
38 Hall, Frink, and Buckley (2015).
39 Royle and Hall (2012), Stenning (1995).
40 Evans (2019).
41 Layman (2014), Lerner and Tetlock (1999), Tyler (1997).
42 Johnson (2006).
43 Royle and Hall (2012).
44 Lerner and Tetlock (1999), Royle and Hall (2012).
45 Evans (2019), Hall, Frink, and Buckley (2017), Lerner and Tetlock (1999).
46 Young, Gartner, O'Conner, Larson, and Wright (1995).
47 The InnerChange Freedom Initiative (IFI) is a reentry program for prisoners based on the life and teachings of Jesus Christ. Inmates begin the program 18–24 months before their release date and continue for an additional 12 months once they have returned to the community.
48 Johnson (2006, 2011).
49 Duwe and King (2013).
50 Duwe and King (2013).
51 Johnson (2011).
52 Johnson and Jang (2012), Koenig, King, and Carson (2012).
53 Johnson (2011).
54 Hallett et al. (2016, 2017).
55 Hallett et al. (2016).
56 Jang et al. (2018a).
57 Vanhooren, Leijssen, and Dezutter (2018).
58 Jang et al. (2018b).
59 Jang et al. (2018b).
60 Jang et al. (2019).
61 Johnson (2011).
62 Johnson et al. (2016).
63 Lee et al. (2014, 2016), Lee, Johnson, Pagano, Post, and Leibowitz (2017), Post et al. (2016).
64 Nouwen (1972).
65 Hallett et al. (2016).
66 Hallett et al. (2016, 2017), Hays et al. (2018), Jang et al. (2017, 2018).
67 Nouwen (1972).

References

Bradshaw, M., & Ellison, C. G. (2010). Financial hardship and psychological distress: Exploring the buffering effects of religion. *Social Science & Medicine, 71*(1), 196–204.

Cnaan, R. A., & Boddie, S. C. (2001). Philadelphia census of congregations and their involvement in social service delivery. *Social Service Review, 75*(4), 559–580.

Corcoran, J., & Mears, D. (2013). Social isolation and inmate behavior: A conceptual framework for theorizing prison visitation and guiding and assessing research. *Journal of Criminal Justice, 41*(4), 252–261.

Duwe, G., & King, M. (2013). Can faith-based correctional programs work? An outcome evaluation of the innerchange freedom initiative in Minnesota. *International Journal of Offender Therapy and Comparative Criminology, 57*(7), 813–841.

Emmons, R. A. (2008). *Thanks!: How practicing gratitude can make you happier*. Boston, MA: Mariner Books.

Enright, R. D., Freedman, S. R., & Rique, J. (1998). The psychology of interpersonal forgiveness. In R. D. Enright & J. North (Eds.), *Exploring forgiveness* (pp. 46–62). Madison, WI: University of Wisconsin Press.

Evans, C. S. (2019). *Kierkegaard and spirituality: Accountability as the meaning of human existence*. Grand Rapids, MI: Eerdmans.

Frink, D., & Klimoski, R. J. (1998). Toward a theory of accountability in organizations and human resources management. *Research in Personnel and Human Resources Management, 16*, 1–51.

Giordano, P. C., Cernkovich, S. A., & Rudolph, J. L. (2002). Gender, Crime, and Desistance: Toward a Theory of Cognitive Transformation. *American Journal of Sociology, 107*(4), 990–1064.

Giordano, P. C., Longmire, M. A., Schroeder, R. D., & Seffrin, P. M. (2008). A life-course perspective on spirituality and desistance from crime. *Criminology 46*(1), 99–132.

Greenfield, E., & Marks, N. F. (2007). Religious social identity as an explanatory factor for associations between more frequent formal religious participation and psychological well-being. *International Journal for the Psychology of Religion, 17*(3), 254–259.

Hall, A. T., & Ferris, G. R. (2011). Accountability and extra-role behavior. *Employee Responsibilities and Rights Journal, 23*(2), 131–144.

Hall, A. T., Frink, D. D., & Buckley, M. R. (2015). An accountability account: A review and synthesis of the theoretical and empirical research on felt accountability. *Journal of Organizational Behavior, 38*(2), 204–224.

Hallett, M. (2019). Confronting Christian penal charity: Neoliberalism and the rebirth of religious penitentiaries. In M. Hallett (Guest ed.), *Emancipatory justice: Confronting the Carceral state.* Berkeley, CA. Social Justice.

Hallett, M., Hays, J., Johnson, B. R., Jang, S. J., & Duwe, G. (2015). "First stop dying:" Angola's Christian seminary as positive criminology. *International Journal of Offender Therapy and Comparative Criminology, 61*, 445–463.

Hallett, M., Hays, J., Johnson, B. R., Jang, S. J., & Duwe, G. (2017). *The Angola prison seminary: Effects of faith-based ministry on identity transformation, desistance, and rehabilitation.* New York, NY: Routledge.

Hays, J., Hallett, M., Johnson, B. R., Jang, S. J., & Duwe, G. (2018). Inmate Ministry as Contextual Missiology: Best Practices for America's Emerging Prison Seminary Movement, *Perspectives in Religious Studies 45*(1), 69–79.

Hirschi, T. (1969). *Causes of delinquency.* Berkeley, CA: University of California Press.

Jang, S. J., Johnson, B. R., Hallett, M., Duwe, G., & Hays, J. (2017). Religion and misconduct in Angola prison: Conversion, congregational participation, religiosity, and self-identities. *Justice Quarterly, 35*(3), 412–442.

Jang, S. J., Johnson, B. R., Hays, J., Hallett, M., & Duwe, G. (2018). Existential and virtuous effects of religiosity on mental health and aggressiveness among offenders. *Religions, 9*, 182. doi:10.3390/rel9060182.

Jang, S. J., Johnson, B. R., Hays, J., Hallett, M., & Duwe, G. (2019). Prisoners helping prisoners change: A study of inmate field ministers within Texas prisons. *International Journal of Offender Therapy and Comparative Criminology.* doi:10.1177/0306624X19872966.

Johnson, B. R. (2004). Religious programs and recidivism among former inmates in prison fellowship programs: A long-term follow-up study. *Justice Quarterly, 21*(2), 329–354.

Johnson, B. R. (2008). The faith factor and prisoner reentry. *Interdisciplinary Journal of Research on Religion, 4*, 1–21.

Johnson, B. R. (2011). *More God, less crime: Why religion matters and how it could matter more.* Conshohocken, PA: Templeton Press.

Johnson, B. R. (2018). Why religious freedom is good for inmates, prisons, and society. In W. Jeynes (Ed.), *The Wiley handbook of christianity & education* (pp. 119–140). New York, NY: Wiley/Blackwell.

Johnson, B. R., & Jang, S. J. (2012). Religion and crime: Assessing the role of the faith factor, Contemporary Issues in Criminological Theory and Research: The Role of Social Institutions, pp. 117–150 (2012), in Richard Rosenfeld, Kenna Quinet, and Crystal Garcia (Eds.) *Contemporary Issues in Criminological Theory and Research: The Role of Social Institutions.* Collected Papers from the American Society of Criminology 2010 Conference.

Johnson, B. R., & Larson, D. B. (2006). *The inner change freedom initiative: A preliminary evaluation of a faith-based prison program.* Institute for Studies of Religion (ISR Research Report), Baylor University. Retrieved from http://www.BAYLORISR.org/publications/reports/.

Johnson, B. R., Larson, D. B., & Pitts, T. (1997). Religious programming, institutional adjustment and recidivism among former inmates in prison fellowship programs. *Justice Quarterly, 14*(1), 145–166.

Johnson, B. R., Lee, M. T., Pagano, M., & Post, S. G. (2016). Positive Criminology and Rethinking the Response to Adolescent Addiction: Evidence on the Role of Social Support, Religiosity, and Service to Others. *International Journal of Criminology and Sociology 5*, 75–85.

Joseph, S. (2012). *What doesn't kill us: A guide to overcoming adversity and moving forward.* London, UK: Platkus Books.

Kerley, K. R., Copes, H., & Tewksbury, R. (2011). Examining the relationship between religiosity and self-control as predictors of prison deviance. *International Journal of Offender Therapy and Comparative Criminology, 55*(8), 1251–1271.

Kewley, S., Larkin, M., Harkins, L., & Beech, A. (2016). Restoring identity: The use of religion as a mechanism to transition between an identity of sexual offending to a non-offending identity. *Criminology & Criminal Justice, 17*(1), 79–96.

Koenig, H. G. (2015). Religion, spirituality, and health: A review and update. *Advances in Mind-Body Medicine, 29*(3), 289.

Koenig, H. G., King, D. E., & Carson, V. B. (2012). *Handbook of religion and health.* 2nd ed. New York, NY: Oxford University Press.

Krause, N., & Hayward, R. D. (2013). Measuring communities of faith: A preliminary investigation. *Journal of Religion, Spirituality & Aging, 25*, 258–276.

Krause, N., & Hayward, R. D. (2014a). Religious involvement, practical wisdom, and self-rated health. *Journal of Aging and Health, 26*, 539–557.

Krause, N., & Hayward, R. D. (2014b). Work at church and church-based social support among older whites, black, and Mexican Americans. *Journal of Religion, Spirituality, and Aging, 26*, 22–40.

Krause, N., Hayward, R. D., Bruce, D., & Woolever, C. (2014). Gratitude to God, self-rated health, and depressive symptoms. *Journal for the Scientific Study of Religion, 53*, 341–355.

Layman, D. (2014). Accountability and parenthood in Locke's theological ethics. *History of Philosophy Quarterly, 31*, 101–118.

LeBel, T. P., Richie, M., & Maruna, S. (2015). Helping others as a response to reconcile a criminal past: The role of the wounded healer in prisoner reentry programs. *Criminal Justice and Behavior, 42*(1), 108–120. doi:10.1177/0093854814550029.

Lee, M. T., Pagano, M., Johnson, B. R., & Post, S. G. (2016). Love and Service in Adolescent Addiction Recovery, *Alcohol Treatment Quarterly 34* (2): 197–222.

Lee, M. T., Pagano, M., Johnson, B. R., & Veta, P. S. (2014). Daily Spiritual Experiences and Adolescent Treatment Response, *Alcohol Treatment Quarterly, 32* (2): 271–298.

Lee, M. T., Johnson, B. R., Pagano, M., Post, S., & Leibowitz, G. (2017). From defiance to reliance: Spiritual virtue as a pathway towards desistence, humility, and recovery among juvenile offenders. *Spirituality in Clinical Practice, 4*(3), 161–175.

Lerner, J. S., & Tetlock, P. E. (1999). Accounting for the effects of accountability. *Psychological Bulletin, 125*(2), 255–275. https://doi.org/10.1037/0033-2909.125.2.255.

Levin, J. (2020). *Religion and medicine: A history of the encounter between humanity's two greatest institutions.* New York, NY: Oxford University Press.

Lundberg, C. D. (2010). *Unifying truths of the world's religions.* New Fairfield, CT: Heavenlight Press.

Luskin, F. (2003). *Forgive for good: A proven prescription for health and happiness.* San Francisco, CA: HarperOne.

Makridis, C., Johnson, B. R., & Koenig, H. G. (2019). Does religious affiliation protect people's wellbeing? Evidence from the great recession after correcting for selection effects. Retrieved from *SSRN*: https://ssrn.com/abstract=3429422.

Maruna, S. (2010). *Making good: How ex-convicts reform and rebuild their lives.* New York, NY: American Psychological Association.

Meninger, W. A. (1996). *The process of forgiveness.* New York, NY: Continuum International Publishing Group.

Ng, S. M., & Hou, W. K. (2017). Contentment duration mediates the associations between anxious attachment style and psychological distress. *Frontiers in Psychology, 8*, 258. doi:10.3389/fpsyg.2017.00258.

Nouwen, H. J. M. (1972). The wounded healer: Ministry in contemporary society. New York, NY: Doubleday.

Post, S. G., Pagano, M., Lee, M. T., & Johnson, B. R. (2016). Humility and 12-Step Recovery: A Prolegomenon for the Empirical Investigation of a Cardinal Virtue," *Alcohol Treatment Quarterly 34* (2): 262–273.

Putnam, R. D., & Campbell, D. (2012). *American grace: How religion divides and unites us.* New York, NY: Simon & Schuster.

Putnam, R. D., & Feldstein, L. M. (2003). *Better together: Restoring the American community.* New York, NY: Simon & Schuster.

Rowatt, W., & Kirkpatrick, L. A. (2002). Two dimensions of attachment to God and their relation to affect, religiosity, and personality constructs. *Journal for the Scientific Study of Religion, 41*(4), 637–651.

Royle, M. T., & Hall, A. T. (2012). The relationship between McClelland's theory of needs, feeling individually accountable, and informal accountability for others. *International Journal of Management and Marketing Research, 5*(1), 21–42.

Shanahan, L., Hill, S. N., Gaydosh, L. M., Steinhoff, A., Costello, E. J., Dodge, K. A., Harris, K. M., & Copeland, W. E. (2019). Does despair really kill? A roadmap for an evidence-based answer. *American Journal of Public Health, 109*(6), 854–858.

Stenning, P. C. (1995). *Accountability for criminal justice: Selected essays.* Toronto, Canada: University of Toronto Press.

Toussaint, L. L., Worthington, E. L., & Williams, D. R. (eds.) (2015). *Forgiveness and health: Scientific evidence and theories relating forgiveness to better health.* New York, NY: Springer.

Tyler, T. R. (1997). The psychology of legitimacy: A relational perspective on voluntary deference to authorities. *Personality and Social Psychology Review, 1*(4), 323–345.

VanderWeele, T. J. (2017a). Religious communities and human flourishing. *Current Directions in Psychological Science, 26*, 476–481.

VanderWeele, T. J. (2017b). On the promotion of human flourishing. *Proceedings of the National Academy of Sciences, 31*, 8148–8156.

VanderWeele, T. J. (2017c). Religion and health: A synthesis. In M. J. Balboni, & J. R. Peteet (Eds.), *Spirituality and religion within the culture of medicine: From evidence to practice* (pp. 357–402). New York, NY: Oxford University Press.

VanderWeele, T. J., Jackson, J. W., & Li, S. (2016). Causal inference and longitudinal data: A case study of religion and mental health. *Social Psychiatry and Epidemiology, 51*, 1457–1466.

VanderWeele, T. J., Li, S., Tsai, A. C., & Kawachi, I. (2016). Association between religious service attendance and lower suicide rates among US women. *JAMA Psychiatry, 73*, 845–851.

Vanhooren, S., Leijssen, M., & Dezutter, J. (2018). Coping strategies and posttraumatic growth in prison. *The Prison Journal, 98*(2):123–142.

Worthington, E. L., & Wade, N. G. (2019). *Handbook on forgiveness.* 2nd ed. New York, NY: Routledge.

Young, M., Gartner, J., O'Conner, T., Larson, D. B., & Wright, K. (1995). Long-term recidivism among federal inmates trained as volunteer prison ministers. *Journal of Offender Rehabilitation, 22*, 97–118.

8

TOWARD RESTORATIVE CORRECTIONS

A Movement Well Underway

> Simply put, prisons do a poor job at reducing recidivism—regardless of whether one considers data on absolute levels of recidivism, or data on the relative levels of recidivism for those that receive custodial versus those receiving a non-custodial sanction....Thus, no systematic review of the research has shown imprisonment to have a specific deterrent effect. In fact, quite the opposite ...[1]

In an age of hyper-partisanship, it is increasingly rare to find any political issue where elected officials can find widespread consensus. And yet, concerned citizens and lawmakers alike have observed that current conditions in American correctional facilities routinely compromise the health, safety, and well-being of inmates. Indeed, the combination of current environmental factors—poor health care, unsanitary living conditions, high levels of violence, and an increased number of people with chronic diseases living in close proximity—can make a routine jail or prison sentence resemble that of a death sentence.[2]

The First Step Act (FSA), a bipartisan criminal justice bill passed by the 115th Congress in December 2018, focused on recidivism reduction through the development of a risk and needs assessment. The FSA is a positive development to be sure, but it only deals with federal prisons and federal prisoners. If one thinks of all correctional facilities in the United States, including jails, federal prisoners only make up a small percentage of the total prison and jail population. In addition, the FSA does not touch on many of the challenging issues currently facing the field of corrections. Stated differently, the FSA represents the tip of the iceberg when it comes to the changes that are needed for implementing major reform in all correctional facilities. It is a reminder that despite bipartisan support, meaningful prison reform, by and large, continues to elude policy-makers.

As mentioned earlier, older models of correctional practice incorporated less indiscriminately punitive sanctions and focused upon cultivating prosocial behaviors in offenders, particularly by incentivizing and meaningfully rewarding good behavior. Early American and Victorian-era prisons prioritized what Judith Rowbotham calls "desistance-focused" programming.[3] Desistance-focused programming utilizes a broader array of resources and partnerships than common in today's prisons. Specifically, Rowbotham reviews the collaborations anchored

DOI: 10.4324/9781003171744-8

within the London Police Court Missions program, documenting everything from apprentice-ships to early forms of probation sponsored by religiously motivated volunteers (2009). Interest-ingly, Rowbotham partially blames the still-emerging science of Criminology for the demise of a focus on desistance over the will of practitioners:

> Interestingly, the practical campaigns to promote desistance amongst recidivists were reaching their apogee at the same time as the development of that school of thought amongst early criminologists which used scientific determinism to encourage an increas-ing pessimism about the likelihood of effective reformation of persistent criminals in the late 19th century. In practice, there was a sustained and expanding will amongst many actually involved or practically interested in the criminal justice process to promote de-sistance. This expressed itself via the long-established informal efforts of magistrates and the strategies emanating from philanthropic societies.[4]

In a similar way, Shadd Maruna has suggested that contemporary utilization of desistance-focused programming is at a "turning point" in public policy—and that desistance itself is in danger of entering the "graveyard of former revolutionary ideas that deteriorated into careerist claptrap and academic jargon" unless its practical applications can be documented and gotten to scale.[5] If desistance-focused programming is to take hold in criminal justice, Maruna argues, "the 'real action' in desistance will move away from both the universities and the criminal jus-tice agencies and be centered around grassroots advocacy work."[6] The tendency for researchers to fetishize the prison, moreover, through granular research on the experience of incarceration must not be allowed to displace research highlighting the oppressive social relations at the heart of mass incarceration. The prison system as we know it must be dismantled. As Maruna puts it, "it's now or never" for desistance-focused programs to make their case (2016).

As we show here, a growing body of research documents the desistance-focused contribu-tions of religious programs in prisons. As we have extensively demonstrated here, in a number of recent studies, researchers have documented the salutary benefits of religious practice in prisons, particularly when offered by volunteers who come from outside of the traditional cor-rections environment.[7] This book documents the return and rapid spread of volunteer-based desistance focused programs in American maximum security prisons using religious volunteers and brought about by budget crises and program failure.

While criminologists have long sought to "reimagine the prison" in ways that might im-prove their performance,[8] sadly very little actual progress has been made. As we've described in this book, at this writing many state prison systems currently find themselves in prolonged crisis, with Alabama, Florida, Mississippi, Texas, and other states finding themselves in danger of federal intervention. At the conclusion of their important book *The American Prison: Imagining a Different Future*, Francis Cullen and colleagues conclude that new policies must be developed based on the following benchmarks—benchmarks that we believe are achieved by the programs we describe:

1 Prisons Must Improve, Not Harm Inmates
2 Prisons Must Be Just
3 Prisons Must Be Healthy and Safe
4 Prisons Must Be Accountable
5 Prisons Must Be Affordable and Reserved for Violent and Repeat Offenders
6 Prisons Must Be Developmental for Staff
7 The Humaneness Found in Prisons Must Provide Hope for a Better Future.

Seven years after the publication of Cullen and colleague's future looking book, with a few exceptions, it is clear that many of the ideas put forward in these chapters have not been attempted, much less realized. There is, however, one striking exception. Hidden in plain sight, a robust reform movement has been gaining momentum in many correctional facilities around the United States over the last several decades.[9] This movement, led by faith-motivated volunteers and prisoners themselves, advances a message of hope and forgiveness, reconciliation and mercy, gratitude and generosity. In spite of the litany of tragic problems found within so many correctional facilities, we have documented how faith-based prison programs, faith-based dorms, and most recently, prison-based seminaries, are showing there is a way to redeem and restore lives and even prisons.[10] Taken together, this research indicates these programs: can reduce recidivism, are protective against suicide and violence, encourage virtuous and prosocial behavior, and are cost-effective. This emerging body of evidence suggests religious partnerships are essential if we are to realize meaningful and scalable prison reform.

Paradigm Shift: Expanding Faith-Based Collaborations in Prisons

> To seriously shrink the prison population, however, conservatives will have to accept the construction of alternative government structures; liberals will have to accept that these will remain more paternalistic than they might like.[11]

American prisons today are in great crisis. The human beings serving time in American prisons frequently report what amounts to literal torture and dehumanization. Over the past many years, we have spent a significant amount of time inside some of America's largest and toughest prisons, in most cases having unrestricted access to the prisons. And we have learned that, in no small part due to budget constraints imposed by overuse of incarceration, prison officials find it increasingly impossible to adequately care for the citizens in their care—despite a deep and genuine desire to do so. In these understaffed and challenged environments, correctional authorities are now experimenting with creative new partnerships like that started by Warden Burl Cain at Angola described above. As noted throughout this book, these programs are the tip of the iceberg in terms of religious voluntarism in US prisons.

Unfortunately, academics are notoriously skeptical about religion, particularly when mixed with governmental functions like incarceration. Though religion has always been a feature of prisons, its precise role in prisons remains a contested topic.[12] When implemented properly, however, we believe programs run by religious volunteers and inmates themselves, like those we describe throughout this book, accomplish many of the goals highlighted by Cullen and colleagues above. Moreover, we believe that the evidence overwhelmingly shows that they do so. While some academics have argued that religion in prison works to obscure larger social disparities that work to drive mass incarceration,[13] we show how these programs actually work to confront them. More importantly, we show how these programs deliver immediate face-to-face resources for prisoners while rendering prisons themselves more transparent and "reinventive" and less punitive.

As this research documents, in response to what many believe to be the unacceptable condition of American prisons, religious volunteers all across the nation are mobilizing to devote private resources to assist men and women in some of the harshest prison environments. To put it directly, while in the past conservative religionists might have framed the problem of crime as one of individual sinfulness, the experience of many volunteers inside prisons has helped them conclude that prison environments are themselves part of the problem. For example, let's take a look at the issue of revenge.

Emile Durkheim famously argued the true social function of punishment is not crime control, but enhancing social solidarity. Vengeance, Durkheim suggested, plays a central role in punishment—particularly in satisfying the voyeuristic needs of onlookers to achieve revenge for crimes against society.[14] Revenge is a very real thing that affects many offenders currently housed within correctional institutions—but excessive punitiveness may not be the most effective response to offending. It has often been argued that prisons are breeding grounds for all manner of antisocial behavior, including destructive concepts such as revenge. The question is, is it possible to make prisons places that are less vengeful—and to question the role of punitivism in punishment? Moreover, is it possible to make prisons more forgiving places? If so, how would we accomplish such a task? Psychologists argue that we simply need to change the social environments that produce revenge.[15] Consequently, we need to make the social environments in which prisoners reside, less abundant in the factors that evoke the desire for revenge. Likewise, we need to make those same environments more abundant in the factors that evoke forgiveness.

As we have demonstrated throughout this book, prisons can actually work better when faith, hope, charity, and forgiveness prevail—instead of rejection, despair, retribution, or revenge. Increased knowledge, connectedness, and service to others foster new identities and positive meanings that anchor a sense of well-being and offer tangible pathways to a new start. We have demonstrated how these important faith-based networks, activities, and positive emotions have created an institutional climate that manages to push back against the dehumanizing conditions that characterize the typical prison environment, and help create prisons that are restorative. In our research at Angola, a place where most prisoners are serving life sentences with no hope of release, it is possible to gain wisdom, understanding, and even a bit of grace. The inmate ministers at Angola are a resource to inmates and correctional staff alike. The inmate ministers assist others in finding that meaning and purpose—and research—bear out the positive effects of cultivating a prosocial sense of self on lowering recidivism.

We have empirically documented inmates, many of whom are serving life sentences and living in the midst of deplorable conditions, are able to model prosocial behavior while having their environments made less oppressive through voluntary religious programming. This faith-based movement is advancing fundamental ideas proposed by most reform advocates—making prisons safer, more healthy, more virtuous, and ultimately, more restorative. In fact, we are beginning to see similar patterns emerge in prisons outside of the United States.[16]

Test the Efficacy of Partnering with Offender-Led Religious Movements

Our preliminary research into offender-led religious movements suggests that these movements may be a key factor in rethinking our approaches to correctional programs and rehabilitation. Obviously, we need more empirical research to confirm the nature, prevalence, and consequences of these movements. Are ORMs isolated or quite common? In comparison to other interventions, we need to know the effectiveness of these inmate-led programs. We need to understand how ORMs are replicated in different jurisdictions and correctional environments.

The question regarding potential replication of ORMs, however, presents policy-makers with a dilemma. ORMs, like those led by inmate pastors at Angola, pose a legal challenge to correctional agencies. The well-documented trusty system dating back to the early 1900s allowed inmates to wield authority over prisoners. Angola was one of many prisons where correctional staff designated select inmates to control and administer physical punishment to other inmates based on a hierarchy of power. The legal case of *Gates v. Collier*[17] ended the flagrant abuse of inmates under the trustee system at the Mississippi State Penitentiary (Parchman) that had existed for many decades. Other states using the trustee system were also forced to give it up under this ruling. Following the *Gates v. Collier* decision, states adopted policies preventing prisoners to hold positions of authority over other prisoners.

This legal decision, and subsequent policy change, has made it virtually impossible to or-ganize and establish formal inmate-led congregations. In spite of this, over 25 states now have fully launched prison seminaries, having graduates serve fellow inmates on an individualized basis and in congregate worship. Nonetheless, Louisiana remains the only state so far to allow inmates to form and lead their own religious congregations. Thus, Angola is the only prison we know of that allows formal inmate-led churches to exist, each having their own charters, polities, and doctrinal allegiances.

Interviewing volunteer inmate pastors at Angola, as well as correctional officers and other prison administrators, however, it is apparent that inmate ministers do not have—*nor do they seek*—"authority" over other inmates. A more accurate description is that ministers simply serve other prisoners—for no other reason than this is what serves them best. Indeed, the varied acts of service that our research uncovered at Angola suggest that inmate pastors represent anything but abusive authority. Trained in the methods of process counseling, Inmate Peer Ministers well know the futility of forcing change upon seekers. As inmates in prison, they also know fully well what overly aggressive and presumptuous proselytizing might get them: open conflict. As one Inmate Minister expressed to us, "[M]y status as Inmate Minister makes me even more of a servant to others, to give my time to the advancement of God's mission, which is the comfort-ing of his people: 'Feed my sheep.'"[18] In inmate-led churches, inmate ministers surely *lead* other inmates, but how and what they practice is actually "servant leadership," where the leader's main goal is to *serve*, not control, dominate, or lord authority of others. Finally, as we reported in Chapter 3, the prison seminary movement is spreading rapidly in prisons around the country.

In an age of evidenced-based government, empirical research can provide policy-makers and practitioners in government and the private sector with findings and data that can be used to produce better interventions and outcomes. The current push for criminal justice reform has brought together leaders from both sides of the political aisle. However, solutions to criminal justice reform often remain difficult to find because of budgetary constraints. Research in the sub-field of positive criminology suggests that positive and restorative approaches—including those that cultivate social connectedness and support, service to others, spiritual experience, personal integrity, and identity change—may be more effective than traditional approaches to punishment.[19] Consistent with restorative justice practices, these approaches seek to develop active responsibility on the part of individuals who have grown accustomed to a lifestyle of irresponsibility.[20] From this perspective, correctional practices should be devised to promote virtue. Consequently, the goal of justice or punishment should not be to inflict pain or exact revenge but rather to reconstruct and reform individuals.[21]

If offender-led religious movements are found to foster rehabilitation and identity trans-formation, and to be associated with recidivism reduction, one can argue for the potential of ORMs to make for safer prisons and communities, and to do so as a cost-effective alterna-tive. Thus, it would seem to make sense to pay more attention to these kinds of faith-based approaches and to promote them as potential aids to the common good. Policy-makers and practitioners should have access to rigorous research, which evaluates the value of ORMs in addressing topics like rehabilitation, drug treatment, educational and vocational programs, pris-oner reentry, and criminal justice reform more broadly.

Expand Public/Private Partnerships in Prisons

Faith-based activities in prisons and other correctional facilities are very popular. For example, beyond work, education, or vocational training, religious activities attract more participants than any other personal enhancement program offered inside a prison.[22] Community volun-teers are value added for correctional entities because they provide a host of services (e.g., mentoring, literacy, life-skills, etc.) and research has shown that these volunteers are helpful in reducing recidivism.[23] For example, groups like Kairos, Prison Entrepreneurship Program, Alpha, Salvation Army, Alcoholics Anonymous, Prison Fellowship, Delancey Street, and many others provide a no-cost, low-intensity pathway to such service (and other spiritual virtues) and could provide the institutional infrastructure that is needed to support a theoretically coherent set of evidence-based policies consistent with a positive criminology approach. It is important to note that faith-based communities already provide the bulk of community volunteers working with offenders within correctional facilities.[24]

The sheer pervasiveness of religious programs within correctional institutions provides an opportunity to better utilize these positive criminology approaches. In addition, programs like AA provide a platform and ready-made environment to make addiction treatment more accessible to offenders in various kinds of correctional facilities. Indeed, for those who are incarcerated, AA has been able to produce results at least as good as those in treatment.[25] Moreover, AA is already in existence in most prisons and other correctional institutions. Religious activities could easily be expanded to allow inmates time and instruction for completing the steps, which are designed to help an alcoholic gain access to a Higher Power. These programs foster increased spirituality that is linked to greater personal change when combined with service.

Faith-based dorms are increasingly common within prisons in many different states. For example, the Texas Department of Criminal Justice has 100 faith-based dorms operating within their 101 prisons.[26] The Chaplaincy Department coordinates the implementation of faith-based dorms. These dorms offer support and accountability, along with a faith-based curriculum and mentoring program. The programming is conducted by local faith-based community volunteers whose activities are directed by the unit chaplain and unit administration. Faith-based dorms are open to offenders of all faiths and generally include:

- Life skills classes.
- Spirituality classes emphasizing self-rebiographing and goal setting.
- Structured activities.
- Accountability/support groups.

Faith-based pre-release programs, like the Academy, operated by Prison Fellowship, "guides participants to identify the life-controlling issues that led to their incarceration and take responsibility for its impact on their community."[27] Drawing from a biblically based curriculum, the Academy specifically targets criminogenic needs by providing like skills, treatment for addictions, victim-offender reconciliation, and exposure to a prosocial environment. The Academy aims to assist prisoners become positive peer mentors and supporters of a positive culture.[28] In 2017, Prison Fellowship launched an ambitious ten-year mission to transform American correctional systems by having Academies in all 50 states by 2016. Moreover, PF's ten-year goals include producing more than 67,000 Academy graduates, with more than 50,000 graduates with a three-year recidivism rate less than 10%, and with approximately 17,000 graduates acting as positive peer models serving out their sentences.[29]

Conclusion

Citizens across the country are concerned because some 700,000 inmates are now returning to society each year. The prisoner reentry crisis is especially bad news for the disadvantaged communities to which most ex-prisoners will return. But the news is even worse for those inmates leaving prison. Most prisoners are unprepared to leave and are unrealistic about their chances to "make it" outside of prison in society. Generally, ex-prisoners do not have the education, skills, or positive social supports necessary to assist them in returning to society. As a result, many ex-prisoners commit new crimes in the first few weeks or months after release.

Research published in the *New England Journal of Medicine* found that during the period immediately following release from prison, deaths among former prisoners were more than 12 times the average for the general population.[30] Furthermore, the death rate for drug overdose among ex-prisoners was 129 times the death rate for comparable citizens.[31] This is why leading experts uniformly agree that the successful reintegration of former prisoners is one of the most formidable challenges facing society today. Indeed, prisoner reentry is a very dangerous time for ex-prisoners as well as society at large. And states do not have enough money to "fix the problem." We need a new series of public-private and secular-sacred partnerships that will enlist thousands of new volunteers to assist correctional authorities in the delivery of much needed educational and vocational programs, not only in prisons, but in the communities to which prisoners will be returning.[32]

Two realities point to a new window of opportunity to do something about the mass release of prisoners back into our communities. First, an established and mounting body of empirical evidence documents the significant role of the "faith factor" in crime reduction. Second, shrinking state budgets are making it necessary to consider new approaches that emphasize cooperation between secular and sacred entities in order to help former prisoners remain crime-free after leaving prison. Innovative approaches like many of those discussed in this chapter will only be successful if many new volunteers and groups are encouraged to partner with governmental agencies in confronting the prisoner reentry crisis. In sum, we are observing in real-time, an organic faith-based movement in American prisons (and beyond) that is creating the very environments that mitigate many of the problems currently facing the field of corrections. The theoretical and policy implications of these findings are profound.

Notes

1 Cullen, Jonson, and Stohr (2014, pp. 238–239).
2 Ross (2012).
3 Rowbotham (2009).
4 Rowbotham, Muravyeva, and Nash (2014, p. 108).
5 Maruna (2016, p. 289).
6 Maruna (2017).
7 Dubler (2013), Becci and Dubler (2017), Dubler and Lloyd (2019), Hallett, Hays, Johnson, Jang, and Duwe (2017), Jang et al. (2019a), Kewley, Larkin, Harkins, and Beech (2017).
8 Cullen et al. (2014).
9 Hallett, Hays, Johnson, Jang, and Duwe (2016), Hallett and Johnson (2014), Duwe, Johnson, Hallett, Hays, and Jang (2015), Hallett, Hays, Johnson, Jang, and Duwe (2015), Jang et al. (2018a), Hays et al. (2018), Jang et al. (2018b), Jang et al. (2018c), Jang, Johnson, Hays, Hallett, and Duwe (2019), Hallett, Hays, Johnson, Jang, and Duwe (2019).
10 Duwe and Johnson (2016), Duwe et al. (2015), Jang, Johnson, Hays, Hallett, and Duwe (2017), Jang et al. (2018), Johnson, Larson, and Pitts (1997), Johnson (2004), Johnson (2006), Johnson (2011).
11 Dagan and Telles (2014).
12 Sullivan (2009).
13 Griffith (2020), Erzen (2017).
14 Garland (1990).
15 McCullouch (2008).
16 Jang et al. (2019).
17 Gates v. Collier (1974).
18 Hays, Hallett, Johnson, Jang, and Duwe (2018).
19 Ronel and Elisha (2011).
20 Braithwaite (2005).
21 Johnson, Lee, Pagano, and Post (2016).

22 Beck (1993).
23 Bales and Mears (2008).
24 Duwe and Johnson (2016).
25 Forcehimes and Tonigan (2008), Tonigan (2008).
26 See www.TDCJ.texas.gov (2020).
27 See www.prisonfellowship.org (2020).
28 Participant complete a personal transition plan targeting skills needed for successful living, including financial responsibility, time management, healthy habits, legal issues, employment, and coping skills.
29 See https://www.prisonfellowship.org/about/academy/academy-case-statement/.
30 Binswanger et al. (2007).
31 Binswanger et al. (2007).
32 Johnson, Wubbenhorst, and Schroeder (2013).

References

Bales, W. D., & Mears, D. P. (2008). Inmate social ties and the transition to society: Does visitation reduce recidivism? *Journal of Research in Crime and Delinquency*, *45*(3): 287–321.

Becci, I., & Dubler, J. (2017). Religion and religions in prisons: Observations from the United States and Europe. *Journal for the Scientific Study of Religion*, *56*(2), 241–247.

Beck, A. (1993). *Survey of state prison inmates, 1991*. Washington, DC: U.S. Department of Justice, Office of Justice Programs, Bureau of Justice Statistics, NCJ-136949.

Binswanger, I. A., Stern, M. F., Deyo, R. A., Heagerty, P. J., Cheadle, A., Elmore, J. G., & Koepsell, T. D. (2007). Release from prison – A high risk of death for former inmates. *New England Journal of Medicine*, *365*, 157–165.

Braithwaite, J. (2005). Between proportionality & impunity: Confrontation, truth, prevention. *Criminology*, *43*, 283–305.

Cullen, F. T., Jonson, C. L., & Stohr, M. K. (eds.). (2014). *The American prison: Imagining a different future* (pp. 61–84). Thousand Oaks, CA: Sage.

Dagan, D., & Telles, S. (2014). Locked in? Conservative reform and the future of mass incarceration. *The ANNALS of the American Academy of Political and Social Science*, *651*, 266–276.

Dubler, J. (2013). *Down in the chapel: Religious life in an American prison*. New York, NY: Farrar, Straus and Giroux.

Dubler, J., & Lloyd, V. (2019). *Break every yoke: Religion, justice and the abolition of prisons*. New York, NY: Oxford University Press.

Duwe, G., & Johnson, B. R. (2016). The effects of prison visits from community volunteers on offender recidivism. *The Prison Journal*, *96*, 279–303.

Duwe, G., Johnson, B. R., Hallett, M., Hays, J., & Jang, S. J. (2015). Bible college participation and prison misconduct: A preliminary analysis. *Journal of Offender Rehabilitation*, *54*(5), 371–390.

Erzen, T. (2017). *God in captivity: Prison ministries in the age of mass incarceration*. Boston, MA: Beacon Press.

Forcehimes, A., & Tonigan, J. S. (2008). Self-efficacy as a factor in abstinence from alcohol/other drug abuse: A meta-analysis. *Alcoholism Treatment Quarterly*, *26*(4), 480–489.

Garland, D. (1990). *Punishment and modern society* (p. 66). Chicago, IL: University of Chicago Press.

Gates v. Collier, 501 F.2d 1291, was a landmark case decided in U.S. federal court (in 1974) that brought an end to the Trusty system and the flagrant inmate abuse that accompanied it at Mississippi State Penitentiary in Sunflower County, Mississippi.

Griffith, A. (2020). *God's law and order: The politics of punishment in Evangelical America*. Cambridge, MA: Harvard University Press.

Hallett, M., Hays, J., Johnson, B. R., Jang, S. J., & Duwe, G. (2015). First stop dying: Angola's Christian seminary as positive criminology. *International Journal of Offender Therapy and Comparative Criminology*, *61*, 445–463.

Hallett, M., Hays, J., Johnson, B. R., Jang, S. J., & Duwe, G. (2016). *The Angola prison seminary: Effects of faith-based ministry on identity transformation, desistance, and rehabilitation*. New York, NY: Routledge.

Hallett, M., Hays, J., Johnson, B. R., Jang, S. J., & Duwe, G. (2017). *The Angola prison seminary: Effects of faith-based ministry on identity transformation, desistance, and rehabilitation*. New York, NY: Routledge.

Hallett, M., & Johnson, B. R. (2014). The resurgence of religion in America's prisons. *Religions, 5*(3), 663–683.

Hallett, M., Johnson, B. R., Duwe, G., Hays, J., & Jang, S. J. (2019). U. S. prison seminaries: Structural charity, religious establishment, and neoliberal corrections. *The Prison Journal, 99*(2), 150–171.

Hays, J., Hallett, M., Johnson, B. R., Jang, S. J., & Duwe, G. (2018). Inmate ministry as contextual missiology: Best practices for America's emerging prison seminary movement. *Perspectives in Religious Studies, 45*(1), 69–79.

Jang, S. J., Johnson, B. R., Anderson, M., & Booyens, K. (2019a). The effect of religion on mental health among prison inmates in South Africa: Explanations and gender differences. *Justice Quarterly*. doi: 10.1080/07418825.2019.1689286.

Jang, S. J., Johnson, B. R., Hays, J., Hallett, M., & Duwe, G. (2017). Religion and misconduct in 'Angola' prison: Conversion, congregational participation, religiosity, and self-identities. *Justice Quarterly, 35*(3), 412–442.

Jang, S. J., Johnson, B. R., Hays, J., Hallett, M., & Duwe, G. (2018a). Existential and virtuous effects of religiosity on mental health and aggressiveness among offenders. *Religions, 9*, 182.

Jang, S. J., Johnson, B. R., Hays, J., Hallett, M., & Duwe, G. (2018b). Four Gods in a maximum-security prison: Images of God, religiousness, and worldviews among inmates. *Review of Religious Research, 60*(3), 331–365.

Jang, S. J., Johnson, B. R., Hays, J., Hallett, M., & Duwe, G. (2018c). Images of God, religious involvement, and prison misconduct among inmates. *Journal of Corrections Policy, Practice and Research, 3*(4), 288–308.

Jang, S. J., Johnson, B. R., Hays, J., Hallett, M., & Duwe, G., (2018d). Religion and misconduct in Angola prison: Conversion, congregational participation, religiosity, and self-identities. *Justice Quarterly, 35*(3), 412–442.

Jang, S. J., Johnson, B. R., Hays, J., Hallett, M., & Duwe, G. (2019b). Prisoners helping prisoners change: A study of inmate field ministers within Texas prisons. *International Journal of Offender Therapy and Comparative Criminology*. doi:10.1177/0306624X19872966.

Johnson, B. R. (2004). Religious programs and recidivism among former inmates in prison fellowship programs: A long-term follow-up study. *Justice Quarterly, 21*(2), 329–354.

Johnson, B. R. (2006). *The inner change freedom initiative: A preliminary evaluation of a faith-based prison program*. Institute for Studies of Religion (ISR Research Report), Baylor University. Retrieved from http://www.BAYLORISR.org/publications/reports/.

Johnson, B. R. (2011). *More God, less crime: Why faith matters and how it could matter more*. Conshohocken, PA: Templeton Press.

Johnson, B. R., Larson, D. B., & Pitts, T. G. (1997). Religious programming, institutional adjustment and recidivism among former inmates in prison fellowship programs. *Justice Quarterly, 14*(1), 145–166.

Johnson, B. R., Lee, M. T., Pagano, M. E., & Post, S. G. (2016). Positive criminology and rethinking the response to adolescent addiction: Evidence on the role of social support, religiosity, and service to others. *International Journal of Criminology and Sociology, 5*, 75–85.

Johnson, B. R., Wubbenhorst, W., & Schroeder, C. (2013). *Recidivism reduction and return on investment: An empirical assessment of the prison entrepreneurship program*. Institute for Studies of Religion, Special Report. Baylor University. Retrieved from http://www.BAYLORISR.org/publications/reports/.

Kewley, S., Larkin, M., Harkins, L., & Beech, A. (2017). Restoring identity: The use of religion as a mechanism to transition between an identity of sexual offending to a non-offending identity. *Criminology & Criminal Justice, 17*(1), 79–96.

Maruna, S. (2016). Desistance and restorative justice: It's now or never. *Restorative Justice: An International Journal, 4*(3), 289–301.

Maruna, S. (2017, October). Desistance as a social movement. *Irish Probation Journal, 14*, 5–20.

McCullouch, M. E. (2008). *Beyond revenge: The evolution of the forgiveness instinct*. San Francisco, CA: Jossey-Bass.

Prison Fellowship Ministries. (2020). Retrieved from https://www.prisonfellowship.org/about/academy/.

Ronel, N., & Elisha, E. (2011). A different perspective: Introducing positive criminology. *International Journal of Offender Therapy and Comparative Criminology, 55*(2), 305–325.

Ross, J. I. (2012). Why a jail or prison sentence is increasingly like a death sentence. *Contemporary Justice Review*, 1–13. http://dx.doi.org/10.1080/10282580.2012.707427.

Rowbotham, J. (2009). Turning away from criminal intent: Reflecting on the Victorian and Edwardian strategies for promoting desistance among petty offenders. *Theoretical Criminology*, *13*(1), 105.

Rowbotham, J., Muravyeva, M., & Nash, D. (eds.) (2014). *Shame, blame, and culpability: Crime and violence in the modern state.* Abingdon, UK: Routledge.

Sullivan, W. F. (2009). *Prison religion: Faith-based reform and the Constitution.* Princeton, NJ: Princeton University Press.

Texas Department of Criminal Justice. (2020). https://tdcj.texas.gov.

Tonigan, J. S. (2008). Alcoholics anonymous outcomes and benefits. In Galanter, M. & Kaskutas, L.A. (Eds.), *Recent developments in alcoholism: Volume 18. Research on alcoholics anonymous and spirituality in addiction recovery.* New York, NY: Springer.

9

EPILOGUE

Burl Cain

Commissioner, Mississippi Department of Corrections

As warden of Louisiana State Penitentiary at Angola, I had responsibility for the management and well-being of inmates and staff at America's largest maximum-security prison. An important feature of my tenure at Angola was the dramatic growth in the national incarceration rate during that same period, 1995–2015. Not only did the United States come to have the highest incarceration rate of any industrialized nation, but Louisiana outfitted the highest incarceration rate in the United States. Between 1995 and 2015, Louisiana's incarceration rate grew from an already-high 500 per 100,000 to over 800 per 100,000. The national average in 2014 reached only about 407 per 100,000—meaning Louisiana had roughly double the national average in rate of incarceration during my tenure as warden. But not only was Angola America's largest prison—during this period, Angola was arguably its toughest—wherein a sentence to Angola came to mean "natural life" for virtually all inmates arriving at the prison. Ninety percent of prisoners serving time at Angola died on site—many buried in the prison cemetery after serving decades with no family present at the internment. When I got to Angola the state was burying inmates in cardboard boxes, a policy I stopped.[1]

As a result of this growth in incarceration rate, we experienced dramatic overcrowding at Angola—and the continuous expectation that we do more with less. Meanwhile, most inmates arrived rightly believing they would never leave. Needless to say, this dramatically affected life inside. Louisiana requires prisoners to work and contribute to the life of the prison. In my experience, most prisoners appreciate the opportunity to work, preferring it to sitting idle in a cell. While Angola is many things, it is anything but a "warehouse" prison. As a plantation prison with a functioning farm, Angola grows enough food to serve the entire Louisiana prison system—creating inmate leadership positions in horticulture, machine mechanics, and animal husbandry with which we reward inmate trustees. These are earned and coveted positions—and there are many positive things to learn and do at Angola. Surplus potatoes and other goods are regularly sent from Angola to other prisons and shelters around the state. Inmates sell artwork and crafts to the public at the annual rodeo—which generates all funds used for inmate rehabilitation programs. There is a genuine sense of pride at Angola about this work. The prisoners make toys for homeless children and countless other acts of service.

DOI: 10.4324/9781003171744-9

But the longtime expectation that prison farms be self-sufficient has always challenged Angola for resources—and most of the time in American corrections prison administrators frankly struggle to staff their prisons. I told the Baylor team I'm not that great of a warden—I was forced to innovate in order to maintain safety of the prison. In the process, I came to view the prison differently.

When Congress revoked Pell Grant eligibility in 1994, it removed one of the key tools we had for rewarding good behavior. At a place like Angola, Pell Grants were especially prized resources. Suicide and violence become commonplace in prisons where inmates have no hope and no pathway for moving forward as human beings. As a religious man myself, I believe religion can help all of us to study and understand our lives—wherever we find ourselves. I have witnessed men in cells reexamine their life story through scripture only to "wake up" too late to save themselves. But when I say "wake up" I mean that they came to experience the power of putting God's love and acceptance first in their lives, which sadly would have dramatically changed their life course had they only experienced it sometime prior to prison. I am convinced that the experience of having too little love in offenders' lives is the key to understanding the puzzle of the American crime problem. The story I have heard most often from men in prison over my career is that inmates did not know their fathers or that their fathers/step-fathers were abusive to them. It literally makes me cry.

But I have also witnessed many of these same individuals—the absolute worst of the worst—become the best of the best. Life has often taught inmates to be takers. Gangs and prison rules only reinforce this selfishness, as does society. But many times over I have also seen these same men become energetic servants to those around them. But they achieve this change from their peers, not from the prison staff. I came to call this process "moral rehabilitation"—by which I mean that when people have a positive example and become part of something—inmates stop stealing from neighbors or harming those around them. They achieve a regard for others—like the Golden Rule. What's missing in prisons is basic morality and a means of teaching it. We have got to learn to allow peers who succeed to change the culture of the prison.

So we find ourselves at a turning point in American corrections. Are we going to continue with the failed policies of warehousing inmates or can we devise a means of being more truly correctional, less punitive, and more constructive? This book tells some of our story. The resources of our seminary offered Angola new life and a new focus—and a whole lot of good work to do in rehabilitation. These new resources from our outside partners helped tremendously and took the edge off for inmates. This did not solve all of our problems. But suddenly prisoners had a bit of a life again—but a life focused on the unique opportunity for starting over. That's what we need more of. I've spent my career lifting men up far more intently than pushing them down. I have come to oppose knee-jerk harshness for its own sake, mandatory sentencing without parole hearings, and warehouse prisons, for example, because these sap all hope from prisoners. People do often make mistakes—but they are also capable of change and personal growth. That's what "corrections" is all about—or at least it should be—and that's where we need to get back to as we move forward.

Note

1 As Warden I changed this practice, having inmates craft special coffins for deceased inmates and for seminary graduates to lead proper funerals. Family members were always welcome to attend if they chose to do so. https://www.theadvocate.com/baton_rouge/news/article_ad372de6-1ef9-11e8-b5bc-1fc0b4bcca77.html.

INDEX

Note: **Bold** page numbers refer to tables; *italic* page numbers refer to figures and page numbers followed by "n" denote endnotes.

States 21; organizational development 25; painful prison 21–23; rehabilitation programs 25; of religion 34–36, **36**; restorative rehabilitation 24; retributive approach 23; self-control theory 30–32; self-discipline 30; self-transcendent narrative 29; virtue begets virtue 25; "wounded healer" perspective 24

volunteerism, contemporary American society: Americans' Changing Lives study 46; CNCS 45; faith-infused networks 47; human services sector 44–45; social capital 47; US Congregational Life Survey 46

Walnut Street Jail 93
Ward, T. 6, 12
"warehouse" prison 133

Western culture, social norm 48
Will, Paul 64
Woodson, Robert L. Sr., 88
The Wounded Healer (Nouwen) 86–87
wounded healers 24, 51, 60, 72, 113; A-Team, real credentials 98; care culture 94; contemporary American corrections religious programs 99; "failed state" prisons 95–96, 100; forgiveness 102–103; inmate peer ministry 96–98; mass incarceration 93; models 117; offender-led programs 59–60; Parchman Farm 94–95; post-traumatic growth 101–102; redemption scripts 101; "reformation" process 100; restorative corrections 94; SCP Grant program 99; social acceptance 94; societal racial injustice 100; Walnut Street Jail 93

Made in the USA
Columbia, SC
10 September 2021